NEW SLEEVE AND PISTO

RESTORE POWER and COMPRESSION at these

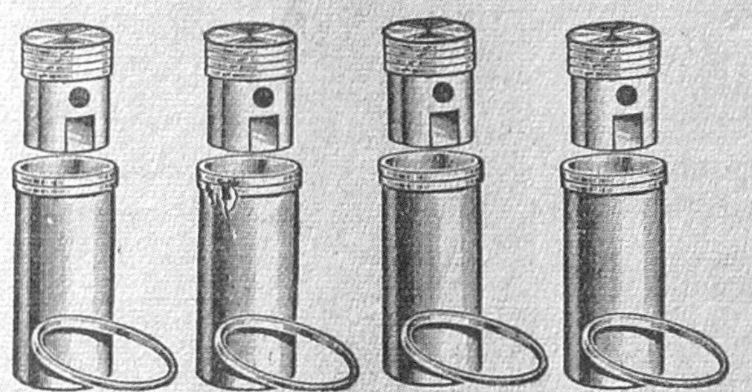

Precision Built for Long Life Assembled and Fitted at Factory

Sets consist of 4 NEW chrome nickel sleeves, each fitted with NEW piston, NEW pin, NEW improved rings, and rubber gasket where necessary. Sleeves and pistons are cast of best grade chrome nickel alloys, and are ground and honed for a precision fit. Clearance is set at the factory, to latest original equipment standards. Every part is built to the most exacting specifications, and these sleeve sets are the equal of any even though others ask more.

Choose the Type Which Suits YOUR Needs

Sleeve Sets are offered, wherever possible, in a choice of compression ratios to suit your individual requirements. Research has shown a big advantage in using high compression pistons and regular gasoline, and we offer these sets in our listing. It is not necessary to make any change in your engine to use high compression. The sleeves are installed in the regular manner, without altering the block, manifolds, etc. in any way. We do recommend a new set of "Cold" Spark Plugs, such as our AC2 or SP2. See page 3 for Plugs.

COMPARE ONLY YOUR DELIVERED COSTS—WE PAY THE FREIGHT ON $25.00 SHIPMENTS

For Allis Chalmers

Description	Price
For Model B, 3¼ inch pistons. Same Compression as original equipment, for use with all types of fuel. Stock Number S51. Weight 34 lbs. Complete Set for 4 cylinders........	$10.95
For WC, W, WF, Power Units. Set uses Regular Compression 4 inch pistons, same as originals, for tractor gas. Stock Number S55. Weight 50 lbs. Complete Set for 4 cylinders........	$16.95
For WC, W, WF. Power Units. Set uses High Compression 4 inch pistons, for greater power with gasoline fuel. Stock Number S57. Weight 51 lbs. Complete Set for 4 cylinders........	$20.75
For 20-35, 25-40, E, K. Set uses Regular Compression 4¾ inch pistons, same as original equipment, for all fuels. Stock Number S52. Weight 125 lbs. Complete Set for 4 cylinders.......	$28.95

For Case

Description	Price
For C, CC, and Combine P after No. 304364. Set uses Regular Compression 3⅞" Pistons, for distillate or tractor gas. Stock Number S12. Weight 49 lbs. Complete Set for 4 cylinders........	$18.45
For C, CC, and Combine P after No. 304364. Set uses High Compression 3⅞ inch Pistons for greater power with gasoline fuel. Stock Number S15. Weight 53 lbs. Complete Set for 4 cylinders........	$19.95
For A, 12-20, and Combines M, W, P (before 304364). Set uses Regular Compression 4⅛" pistons for all fuels. Stock Number S11. Weight 73 lbs. Complete Set for 4 cylinders........	$22.50
For L, LE, LI, LO, LJ, 26-40. Set uses Regular Compression 4⅝" Pistons for distillate and tractor gas. Same as originals. Stock Number S13. Weight 76 lbs. Complete Set for 4 cylinders........	$25.00
For L, LE, LI, LO, LJ, 26-40. Set uses High Compression 4⅝" Pistions for greater power with gasoline. Stock Number S16. Weight 80 lbs. Complete Set for 4 cylinders........	$27.25
For K, 15-27, 18-32. Set uses Regular Compression 4½ inch pistons, same as originals, for best performance on all fuels. Stock Number S14. Weight 83 lbs. Complete Set for 4 cylinders........	$25.50

For Twin City, Minneapolis Moline

Description	Price
For 12-20, 17-28, KT, TW, TY, MT. Regular Compression Type 4¼ inch pistons, for use with any grade of fuel. Stock Number S31. Weight 65 lbs. Complete Set for 4 cylinders........	$22.95
For Minneapolis Moline 17-30, type B. Regular Compression 4⅝" Pistons, same as originals, for use with any grade fuel. Stock Number S33. Weight 135 lbs. Complete Set for 4 cylinders........	$35.85

For Massey Harris and Wallis

Description	Price
For 20-30, Certified 20-30. Set uses Regular Compression 4⅜ inch Pistons, same as originals. Can also be used in J, K, OK, and Cub Jr. to increase bore and horsepower. Stock Number S41. Weight 60 lbs. Complete Set for 4 cylinders........	$24.50
For 12-20, Pacemaker, Challenger. Set uses Regular Compression 3⅞ inch Pistons, same as originals for any fuel. Stock Number S42. Weight 50 lbs. Complete Set for 4 cylinders........	$26.75
For J, K, K3, OK, OKO, Cub Jr., 15-27. Set uses 4¼ inch Regular Compression Pistons, same as originals for any grade fuel. Stock Number S43. Weight 75 lbs. Complete Set for 4 cylinders........	$31.75
For 25, 26-41, above Tractor No. 69000. Set uses Regular Compression 4⅜ inch Pistons, same as originals. Stock Number S44. Weight 60 lbs. Complete Set for 4 cylinders........	$29.85

For Oliver, Hart-Parr

Description	Price
For A, 28-44, 3-5 Plow. Set uses Regular Compression 4¾ inch Pistons, same as originals for any grade fuel. Stock Number S92. Weight 88 lbs. Complete Set for 4 cylinders........	$25.00
For Standard Row Crop, 2-3, 8-18, 18-28, 1930-37. Set uses Regular Compression 4⅛ inch Pistons for any grade fuel. Stock Number S93. Weight 76 lbs. Complete Set for 4 cylinders........	$26.25
For "70" Row Crop 70, 70HC, 70KD. Set uses Regular Compression 3⅛ inch Pistons same as original equipment. Stock Number S91. Weight 48 lbs. Complete Set for 6 cylinders........	$26.75

For IHC-McCormick Deering-Farmall

Description	Price
For Farmall F-12, F-14, W-12, etc. Set uses 3 inch regular compression pistons for ordinary fuels, same as originals. Stock Number S7. Weight 30 lbs. Complete Set for 4 cylinders........	$12.50
For Farmall F-12, F-14, W-12, etc. Set uses 3 inch High Compression pistons, for greater power with gasoline. Stock Number S8. Weight 35 lbs. Complete Set for 4 cylinders........	$13.95
For Farmall F-12, F-14, W-12, etc. Set uses Very High Compression 3 inch pistons for use only with 72 octane gasoline. Stock Number S9. Weight 38 lbs. Complete Set for 4 cylinders........	$15.75
For Regular FARMALL, F-20, T-20, and Combines. Set uses 3¾" regular pistons, same as originals for distillate or tractor gas. Stock Number S1. Weight 56 lbs. Complete Set for 4 cylinders........	$13.98
For Regular FARMALL, F-20, T-20, Combines. Set uses High Compression 3¾ inch pistons, for greater power with gasoline. Stock Number S2. Weight 60 lbs. Complete Set for 4 cylinders........	$15.95
For Regular FARMALL, F-20, T-20. Combines. Set uses very high compression 3¾ inch pistons, for use with 72 octane gasoline. Stock Number S3. Weight 64 lbs. Complete Set for 4 cylinders........	$17.95
For 10-20, Farmall F-30, W-30, all years. Set uses 4¼ inch regular compression pistons, same as original equipment, for tractor fuel. Stock Number S5. Weight 72 lbs. Complete Set for 4 cylinders........	$19.75
For 10-20, Farmall F-30, W-30, all years. Set uses high compression 4¼ inch pistons, for best performance with gasoline. Stock Number S6. Weight 76 lbs. Complete Set for 4 cylinders........	$20.75
For 10-20, Farmall F-30, W-30, late models. Set uses very high compression 4¼ inch pistons, for use with 72 octane gasoline. Stock Number S4. Weight 78 lbs. Complete Set for 4 cylinders........	$21.85
For 15-30, with 4½ inch block. All serial numbers below TG99925. Set uses 4¾ inch Pistons, sleeve walls being machined to fit right in without alterations. Increases power, uses no more fuel. For use with either tractor gas or distillate. Stock Number S22. Weight 75 lbs. Complete Set for 4 cylinders........	$22.95
For 15-30, with 4½ inch block. Set uses regular 4½ inch pistons, same as originals, for low grade fuel. Stock Number S20. Weight 78 lbs. Complete Set for 4 cylinders........	$23.45
For 15-30, with 4½ inch block. Set uses high compression pistons for best performance with high grade gas. Stock Number S21. Weight 85 lbs. Complete Set for 4 cylinders........	$24.50
For 22-36, 1929 and up, serial numbers above TG99926. Set uses regular 4¾ inch pistons, best for distillate or tractor gas. Stock Number S23. Weight 75 lbs. Complete Set for 4 cylinders........	$23.45
For 22-36, 1929 and up, serial numbers above TG99926. Set uses high compression 4¾ inch pistons, for best results with gasoline. Stock Number S24. Weight 78 lbs. Complete Set for 4 cylinders........	$24.50
For 22-36, 1929 and up, serial numbers above TG99926. Set uses very high compression 4¾ inch pistons, for gasoline of 72 octane. Stock Number S25. Weight 85 lbs. Complete Set for 4 cylinders........	$26.50

For Rumely

Description	Price
For "L", 15-25, 20-30. Set uses Regular Compression 5¹⁵⁄₁₆ inch Pistons, same as original equipment. Stock Number S53. Weight 109 lbs. Complete Set for 2 cylinders........	$31.75
For "M," 20-35; "X" 25-40, 1925-31. Set uses Regular Compression 6¹⁵⁄₁₆ inch Pistons, same as original equipment. Stock Number S58. Weight 150 lbs. Complete Set for 2 cylinders........	$69.50

REMEMBER: YOU SAVE WHEN YOU BUY FROM TRACTOR SUPPLY

WE PAY THE FREIGHT ON $25.00 SHIPMENTS •

See Page 2

WORK HARD HAVE FUN MAKE MONEY

WORK HARD
HAVE FUN
MAKE MONEY

THE TRACTOR SUPPLY STORY

BY NELSON EDDY

TSC TRACTOR SUPPLY Co.

BRENTWOOD, TENNESSEE

Publisher's Cataloging-in-Publication Data

Eddy, Nelson, 1958-
Work hard, have fun, make money : the Tractor Supply story / by Nelson Eddy. -- 1st ed.
p. cm.
Includes bibliographical references.
LCCN 2004096659
ISBN 0-9761066-0-4

1. Tractor Supply Company--History. 2. Hardware stores--United States--History. 3. Farm supply industries--United States--History. I. Title.

HD9745.U5T73 2004 381'.45683

Printed in the United States of America
Designed by Jeff Porter
Dye, Van Mol & Lawrence

Tractor Supply Co.
200 Powell Place
Brentwood, TN 37027
www.mytscstore.com

09 08 07 06 05 04 1 2 3 4 5

 DEDICATION 

To Tom Hennesy,
without whom, this book
would never have been
written because, more than likely,
Tractor Supply would have never survived.
Our beloved Giant Leprechaun,
you gave us far more than good luck.
You inspired us with your leadership
and honored us with your friendship.
You restored our faith
in our company and the future.

— Joe Scarlett

To Dorothy Scarlett
and your wonderful way
of recognizing possibilities
and seeing potential.
Your persistence and encouragement
are the reasons this book exists.
You thought enough
of Tractor Supply to suggest
its story be told.
And you thought enough of me
to make my story complete.
Thanks for 34 years.

— Joe Scarlett

CONTENTS

TSC TRACTOR SUPPLY CO

TSC
TRACTOR
SUPPLY CO

CHAPTER ★1★

HAVING FUN IS ITS OWN REWARD

AN INTRODUCTION

"EVEN IF A FARMER INTENDS TO LOAF,
HE GETS UP IN TIME
TO GET AN EARLY START."
- EDGAR WATSON HOWE

MOW JOE MOW. Working hard and having fun, Chairman Joe Scarlett is the embodiment of the Tractor Supply mission. Here, in the company's Gallatin, Tennessee, store, he sits astride one of Tractor Supply's success stories, a hot-selling riding lawnmower. Taken in July 2003, this photograph was a part of an Associated Press story that was whisked across the country.

AP/Wide World Photos

FUN IN THE NEW MILLENNIUM

Work hard, have fun, and make money.

Those seven words make up the heart of the Tractor Supply mission statement. It seems like a rather simplistic approach to business in this jaded age.

Maybe that's why it works.

Just ask Joe Scarlett. He's having fun.

You can see it in the wide-eyed way he lights up when he talks about his team. You can see it in the way he leans toward you in a conversation, like he's got the greatest secret in the world and he's only going to tell it to you. It's in the rapid-fire pace of his replies. The energy of his enunciation and emphasis. He can hardly wait for the question to give the answer.

Yes, Joe Scarlett is having fun.

IT'S JUST JOE

Joe Scarlett's official title is chairman of America's No. 1 Farm and Ranch Store, but he's more often described by those he works with as the coach, the cheerleader, the company's conscience, the chief missionary of the gospel of Tractor Supply. They're all references to his unbridled enthusiasm for the company and people he's worked with for more than twenty-five years.

The wave of enthusiasm that greets you when you meet Joe Scarlett for the first time is so surprising you immediately think it can't possibly be real. It's just for show, just his job. But the longer you know Joe, the more you know this isn't what he does – it's who he is. His wife of more than thirty-four years, Dorothy, will verify it with a knowing laugh.

"He's always been full of enthusiasm,"

Dorothy explains. "He's upbeat and passionate about everything he does. It's not just the company – though Tractor Supply is one of his great passions. It's his whole life."

Joe is passionate about everything. He doesn't simply take his son, Andrew, to a baseball game. Joe plots with him a visit to every major league ballpark. He pairs visits to his daughter, Tara, at college with store visits. It's a passion so consistent and so all encompassing that it has to be genuine. It's genuine and contagious.

You notice the same kind of enthusiasm in other folks who work for Tractor Supply and you wonder where it's all coming from. Then you meet Joe and you know. Call it Scarlett fever, this wonderfully infectious enthusiasm that runs rampant among the company's more than 7,000 team members. Just don't refer to him as Joseph Scarlett, chairman of Tractor Supply Company, unless you're standing behind a podium and introducing him to a bunch of suits. Even then…

"It's just Joe," he insists. "We don't have titles here. It's just Joe."

Don't believe him? Call his office when he's not there and listen to his voice-mail greeting. There's no telling what you might hear. Today it happens to be this: "Hi, this is Joe Scarlett at Tractor Supply Company and thanks for calling. We're on vacation in Mozambique, and you can reach us at the Ritz Carlton Maputo. I'll be back in the office midday on July 9. So leave a message and I'll get back to you.…And thanks for calling the No. 1 Farm and Ranch Retail Chain in the World!"

Just Joe having fun. And when Joe is having fun, he's liable to say anything, everything, exactly what he's thinking.

Joe holds to his beliefs and opinions pretty passionately. He's been known to whip off a letter to the local paper, sometimes to the chagrin of his communications folks, to add a little of his special brand of enthusiasm to whatever the hot topic of the moment may be – an editorial in the wake of the 9-11 attacks on America, an epistle on the state of American business ethics. Anything and everything is fair game. He writes a fan letter to the folks at Southwest, one of his favorite companies, and tells them of his unabashed admiration for what they're doing and how it's influenced what he's doing.

Even Southwest is stirred by Joe's enthusiasm. They call him back and ask if they can interview him for a feature in their magazine.

SMILEY FACE UNDERWEAR

Joe is having fun. And his fun has infused him with a powerful kind of confidence that people who don't have fun doing what they do can never possess. He encourages and inspires this same enthusiasm and confidence in the people around him.

Does everyone like it? No, but then, Joe is quick to say, "If you don't like it here, you need to go somewhere else. You can't do a good job if you're not enthusiastic about what you're doing." And he means it. He's having fun and wants you to have fun, too. If not at Tractor Supply, then somewhere else.

In many ways, a Tractor Supply Store is a pretty good reflection of Joe. A plain, straightforward exterior from which a ton of interesting things regularly flow onto the sidewalk for everyone to see, a ton of stuff but just a hint of all the wonderful things that wait inside.

The harder Joe works the more fun he seems to have.

Often you'll see him hop up from his desk to walk the halls, slapping high-fives with people he meets as he marches through the building. He starts staff meetings with a gong. He signs his message in the company newsletter with a smiley face. You know, THE smiley face – that little yellow ubiquitous

Chuck and Joe Charles Schmidt, the man who successfully launched Tractor Supply in 1938, and Joe Scarlett, the man who helped re-launch the company and return it to its former glory, have a fair amount in common. Neither Schmidt nor Scarlett grew up on a farm. Schmidt started out in Chicago and Scarlett grew up in New Jersey. Both enjoyed a unique sense of humor and had fun dressing up from time to time. And last but not least, each was encouraged to greatness by a wife named Dorothy.

survivor of '70s pop culture. It's something of a Scarlettian symbol. It's everywhere. His TSC teammates regularly amuse themselves with smiley face masks, smiley face frosted cakes and cookies, even smiley face underwear.

Some days you'll find him in the stores, meeting the employees where they work, talking to customers, checking displays. He does the same thing at competitors' stores. Sometimes he even calls them ahead of time and tells them when he's coming. He'll show up at their corporate headquarters, take them out for dinner. He shoplifts good ideas from anywhere he can find them and will even give the other guys credit.

"The Store Support Center? I got that from Hill's Discount Store. It was a great idea," Joe says. "We don't make any money here in these offices. What we do is support the people who make the money for this company – the people in the stores interacting with our customers every day. We do our job best when we're supporting the stores.

"It was a good idea. Unfortunately the guys who came up with it are now out of business."

Four times a year, Joe Scarlett and his team fly to a city in the corporate jet.

"Yes, we have a corporate jet. In fact, we have a whole fleet," boasts Joe, barely able to hide the hint of a smile before he can deliver the punch line.

"They're all 737s, and they all say Southwest on the tail."

Once a quarter, Joe and his top executives fly to a distant city and then take a road trip back home to Nashville, Tennessee, stopping along the way at every mom-and-pop farm and garden store, every TSC within sixty square miles of their circuitous route. They're brainstorming as they barnstorm across the country, talking strategy and product ideas and team member training needs and the best way to display birdfeeders and attract more women customers or differentiate their stores from the competition.

Joe is in charge of snapping the pictures on these road trips. He has a whole stack of photos from their last adventure of all the sites they came across along the highway – pictures of power tools and sump pumps and equine magazine racks. He flips through them now, still oooohhh-ing and aaaahhh-ing like a grandparent with a new baby picture.

These executive road trips sound like a lot of fun. Looking at the route stretching for many hundreds of miles on the map and all the winding back roads and all the motels, they also look like a lot of work.

KICKING BUTT

We know they're working hard and having fun. But are they making money?

Well, it took Tractor Supply sixty years to break the $500 million mark. But five years later, that sales number has more than doubled. Today, Tractor Supply Company is the No. 1 Farm and Ranch Retail Chain in the World – a billion-dollar company with more than 7,000 team members in more than 480 stores in thirty-one states across the country.

In 2002, at a time when key economic figures continued to wane in the wake of terrorist attacks, major corporate scandals and a sluggish American economy, Tractor Supply Company had its single best year in its sixty-five-year history. In a year when other retailers were cutting back or going bankrupt, Tractor Supply, an odd little niche retailer, was breaking the billion-dollar mark.

The company began 2002 by purchasing many of the assets of its closest competitor and successfully reopening eighty-seven of the former competitor's stores as Tractor Supply stores. It did all of this in four short months, during the company's busiest season of the year, and still managed to increase same-store sales. At a time when conventional retail wisdom would have had the company concentrating on sales and stock turns, Tractor Supply was focused on opening stores, trusting its current store teams to "do the right thing."

Tractors about only thing not sold at Tractor Supply

■ *Nashville-based company has 458 stores in 30 states and annual revenues of $1 billion.*

THE ASSOCIATED PRESS

COLUMBIA, Tenn. — The only tractors for sale at Tractor Supply Co. are the die-cast models being marked for clearance.

But hobby farmers, handy homeowners and animal lovers can get just about anything else they want at the store that have carved out a successful niche from big-box retailers such as Wal-Mart and Home Depot.

"Our customers are close to the earth, close to the ground. They're self-sufficient, and they need the tools and supplies to do the jobs themselves," said Tractor Supply's Chairman and CEO Joe Scarlett.

Founded in Chicago in 1938 as a mail-order tractor parts supplier, Nashville-based Tractor Supply now has 458 stores in 30 states — most in small towns and suburbs — annual revenues of more than $1 billion and a stock price over $50 a share.

"They're a textbook case for a good specialty retailer," said analyst Eric Marshall of First Dallas Securities. "They've identified their customers correctly and grown their business in a controlled yet effective way."

The typical customer?

"Somebody who maybe works in the city, lives a couple of miles out, has a couple of horses, two or three dogs, a bunch of cats and maybe some chickens," Marshall said.

Like Carol Anderson, a shelf stocker for Sears who keeps dogs and horses at her home in Columbia, a small town 40 miles south of Nashville best known for its Mule Day parade.

"My husband used to come here for everything," she said as she loaded automatic dog watering containers into her gold Chevy pickup. But he's no longer farming — the last two calves are headed to slaughter — so she shops Tractor Supply twice a month for dog food.

Animal products — ranging from squeaky toy cheeseburgers for dogs to horse vaccines — account for 30 percent of Tractor Supply's sales.

ASSOCIATED PRESS STORY ON JULY 21, 2003.

When 2002 came to a close, every one of the new stores was profitable. But perhaps even more amazing – given the focus on the Herculean effort to open so many new stores – existing stores didn't feel left out or neglected and contributed a same-store increase of 9.6 percent. Wall Street responded to the success with its own vote of confidence. The company's stock began 2002 at $34.12 per share, grew to $64.60, and then did a two-for-one split. Amid the rubble of over-leveraged dot com stocks, a good old ranch and farm supply store was making hay on Wall Street.

Or as Joe says with a smile, "Kicking butt and taking names."

The Tractor Supply team is making it all look easy. But it's never been that. You wouldn't know from Joe's upbeat banter, but Tractor Supply has had a tough row to hoe. His positive attitude isn't simply the result of a career fattened on a steady diet of success. He's seen his share of lean times and seen the dark underbelly of corporate America.

GETTING FIRED...UP

Before showing up at the door of Tractor Supply, Joe was part of an early regional discount chain called Two Guys. The company eventually closed its doors. Joe wound up at Tractor Supply partly because there weren't a whole lot of career options for a refugee from a failed retailer with a questionable reputation.

"Oh, it was a wonderful learning experience," Joe maintains. "A fantastic lesson in what not to do."

Things weren't much better when he arrived at Tractor Supply. The company had already suffered more than a decade of confusion and misdirection as a small cog in a much larger corporate machine. Tractor Supply had been operated by two successive conglomerate owners – first Stanley Yarmuth's famed National Industries of

Louisville and then J. B. Fuqua's equally well known, Atlanta-based Fuqua Industries. It was a sad state of affairs for a proud organization that until the 1970s had enjoyed an undaunted history of success and prosperity.

Tractor Supply's beginnings are one of those classic American stories of how hard work, a good idea and good people can prosper.

The company was founded in 1938 at the dining room table of a twenty-six-year-old Chicago brokerage house worker who had never spent a day on a farm. Charlie Schmidt saw an opportunity for a mail-order business to supply fairly priced tractor replacement parts to frugal farmers whose only other option was to pay a premium to the dealer or manufacturer of their equipment.

It was a natural. Schmidt's company made $50,000 with that first catalog and didn't look back for the next thirty years. In 1939, the company added retail operations to give employees something to do when they were filling catalog orders. Twenty-seven years later, Tractor Supply had expanded to 141 stores and $46 million in business.

It was a lot of hard work, but Charles Schmidt had a knack for drawing some pretty amazing folks into his business and creating a great deal of positive energy and loyalty. A lawyer, a big city banker and a former employee with the legendary mail-order business Montgomery Ward – they all followed Schmidt and jumped into a business many of them were seemingly unsuited for. Nearly all of those early employees, when asked why they did it and why they stayed, point to the fledgling company's "family feel." There's nothing like hard work and fun to forge a strong bond.

The company chugged along pretty steadily for its first thirty years, thriving and expanding, going public and turning some heads with some amazing numbers for a meat-and-potatoes sort of business in the age of the emerging and sexier electronics industry. The only major challenge that loomed on the horizon seemed to be keeping up with the customers as they underwent a dramatic change. Or, maybe, disappeared.

The American farming landscape was changing. When Tractor Supply first opened its doors in 1938, 90 percent of its customers were farmers.

A YOUNG CHARLES SCHMIDT STANDS OUTSIDE THE HOME OFFICE.

CHARLES SCHMIDT IN 1942 WITH ONE OF TRACTOR SUPPLY'S FIRST INVESTORS, HIS WIFE DOROTHY

Thirty years later, the post-World War II manufacturing boom and the consolidation of family farms and rise of corporate farms meant Tractor Supply's traditional customer base was vanishing. The farm store chain was forced to go to town in order to keep up with its customers, who were leaving the farms for city work.

And so Tractor Supply dropped the folksy reference to "tractor" and called itself simply

TSC. The new name stood for Town, Suburb, and Country. Along with broadening its customer base, TSC broadened its wares, carrying everything from home appliances to women's hosiery. It bolstered its corporate holdings by adding a chain of Chicago discount stores and sporting goods stores to its mix. The company continued to grow as it walked farther from its traditional niche.

Tractor Supply becomes TSC Stores. Wichita Falls, Texas, 1967.

Finally, in 1969, fearful of what an increasingly complex future held for the once-thriving farm store chain, the founding father of Tractor Supply, Charles E. Schmidt, sold the budding retail conglomerate to an even bigger conglomerate. At a time when folks were fleeing the farm, Schmidt left the farm supply business to begin a banking venture.

TSC Industries was acquired by National Industries, which, in turn, was acquired by Fuqua Industries as part of the buy-and-sell corporate climate of the '70s. Without a clear vision, TSC would flounder, finding itself in a marketing "no man's land" between home improvement and farm store, confusing its employees, disappointing its customers and dragging down its sales.

In 1980, a year after Joe came to the company, Tractor Supply lost nearly $13 million. It was a staggering loss for a business that was doing less than $100 million at the time. As head of personnel, Joe witnessed firsthand the distasteful task of helping downsize a company that had never seen a layoff in its history. It must have seemed like he'd signed on for the last gasps of a once-great farm store chain now gone fallow, the fertile soil of its historic success left untended by the colossal conglomerate that had plowed it under. Tractor Supply seemed doomed to wind up a classic case study of how conglomerates pillaged the marketplace in their heydays during the late '60s and '70s.

One of Joe's Tractor Supply contemporaries during those dark days recalls that the employment section of a *Wall Street Journal* left in the executive washroom looked like a chain-link fence – the pages were tattered and full of holes from fleeing executives cutting out prospective job information. Joe himself was looking and was certain he was about to get fired when the "undertaker" who had been called in to salvage or scuttle the company asked Joe to come by his office.

So what happened? Well, you'll just have to read the rest of the book to find out. But, need-

How Old Is Tractor Supply Really? The year 1938 is typically pointed to as the beginning date of Tractor Supply. And it's true Charles Schmidt incorporated his business that year. However, the mail order business didn't start shipping out orders until 1939. It's often reported the first store opened that same year. Yet, Gard Abbott, who joined the company in 1939 and went to open the Minot store, claimed it didn't really open its doors until January of 1940. So as a retail business, Tractor Supply is two years younger than its 1938 start date.

less to say, Joe wasn't fired. He did get fired up. The undertaker turned out to be the world's largest leprechaun.

THE LUCK OF THE IRISH

Ironically – or perhaps not so ironic if you believe, as do Joe and company, that real opportunity often goes masquerading as an obstacle – the poor performance of Tractor Supply under Fuqua may have been one of the most fortunate things to happen to the newly hired Joe Scarlett and the company. The negative $13 million just may have been Joe's and Tractor Supply's lucky number. By bleeding a river of red ink, Tractor Supply might have unwittingly ushered in what would be the beginnings of the most profitable period of its history. The losses may have been the much-needed manure that fed new growth.

In 1980, J. B. Fuqua, one of the undisputed captains of the corporate buy-and-sell approach to wealth-building, responded to Tractor Supply's huge losses in characteristic fashion, sending in one of his most trusted lieutenants to fix the company or put it on the chopping block. Fuqua dispatched the shrewd and savvy Tom Hennesy, a.k.a. the "Undertaker," a man he'd trusted with similar situations.

An imposing figure at six-foot-four-inches tall and 300 pounds, Hennesy complemented his calculating business acumen with the heart of a giant. He also complemented the Irishman's gift of gab with the rare ability to listen to those close to where the money was made and to quickly size up a business's potential.

He was the right man at the right time. Only one of Fuqua's closest protégés could convince him Tractor Supply was worth saving and to later lead the leveraged buyout that would wrest the company from the conglomerate's grasp. He was even able to wrest a little bit of Fuqua's money away to finance the eventual deal.

Tom Hennesy would return Tractor Supply to basic operating principles and to profitability. He would return the company to its traditional customer with a simple and straightforward way of doing business and working with others that would ultimately become the basis for the company's mission and values. He would return a personal touch to the company, and he would teach Joe Scarlett the simple joys of working hard, having fun and making money.

Tom Hennesy, Joe and their team would return Tractor Supply to its historic roots.

RE-PLOWING A FAMILIAR FIELD

Tractor Supply returned to its roots in the early 1980s. Not just in terms of serving people who worked the land but in the simple philosophy that shaped the early success of the company. Once again, clear vision and a dedicated team's efforts reawakened the long-overlooked core brand, reinvigorated the workers, renewed customer confidence, returned the company to profitability, and restored the company's good name.

TOM HENNESY AND JOE SCARLETT HAVING FUN.

Literally. Tractor Supply became Tractor Supply again. Even during the time it advertised to the world that it was TSC, customers just kept calling the stores and asking for "Tractor Supply."

The story of Tractor Supply's return home is an amazing one. On the surface, its return to the farm store niche defied convention. The traditional farm customer who had first given rise to Tractor Supply was disappearing from the American landscape. In fact, what once represented 90 percent of the business now only accounted for less than 9 percent of it. The demise of the American family farm was an undisputed and well documented fact. But a powerful new customer base was emerging.

THE LURE OF THE LAND

Americans have always had a special affinity for the land. Land and its promise lured the first settlers to this place. It's no accident that they called this country "The New Land." They came to America to escape the "Old Country" and land controlled for centuries by the gentry, the privileged, and titled. They came to a new land looking for wide open spaces.

Our forefathers and first presidents drew their livelihood from the land. And when the land stretching along our Eastern Seaboard was populated and claimed, the promise of land, and more freedom and more opportunity just beyond the Appalachian mountain chain called to the early pioneers to venture out.

"Go West, young man," Horace Greeley urged. And they did.

Then in the 1900s, big cities, new industries and the need to make a living drew them from the land. One by one, the children of the farmers and hunters and pioneers, who first populated this country, were lured to the city. Americans left

the land but didn't forget their roots. They left the land physically but never shook it completely from their hearts and imaginations.

A century later, the crowds and challenges of city life, coupled with the resources amassed by those who work in the city, allowed many Americans to walk away from the city and turn their sights back to the land. To look back to the rural places, the small towns, and the independent way of life their families had enjoyed generations ago. And so the trends that had marked American migration for centuries reversed itself, and Americans found themselves returning to the land.

During the '90's, rural route addresses grew at a rate 25 percent more than during the previous decade. People whose families had left the land generations ago were still touched by its lure – the promise of freedom, of being your own boss, your own person, working your own land. And so, some opted to divide their time between the city and the country, in essence working two jobs: complementing their paychecks from downtown employment with the fulfillment found only through working with your hands. Others chose to move out of the city and suburbs to live in adjoining rural counties and invest their hard-earned resources in a little land. Marketing folks tagged this growing consumer segment "part-time farmers" and "hobby farmers."

Of course, as most marketing tags go, these two labels are not very satisfactory. As any "part-time farmer" will tell you, there's no such thing. Show me a man who's a part-time farmer and I'll show you a man with two full-time jobs. Then

NORTH DAKOTA WHEAT FIELD NEAR WILLISTON, NORTH DAKOTA, 1941

AP/Wide World Photos

there's this business of "hobby" farmer. It sounds a little too casual, like some distant collector who keeps porcelain barns and barnyard animals and replica cast-iron tractors in a curio cabinet. Nothing could be farther from the truth. Hobby farmers spend time in the field, work up a sweat, dig their own fence post holes, and fight many of the same battles "real" farmers do.

Regardless of labels, there are plenty of hobby and part-time farmers to keep TSC busy. The reborn Tractor Supply tapped into them, and, once again, the company began growing like a weed.

Along with these two emerging segments, Tractor Supply moved its historic dependence on grain and fiber growers, an industry dominated by corporate farmers, to ranchers and smaller farmers, folks with a few head of cattle or chickens or what-have-you, businesses where smaller interests could still thrive.

Library of Congress

TRACTOR SUPPLY WAS BORN OUT OF NECESSITY.

LIGHTNING STRIKES TWICE

Tractor Supply returned to its roots, but it's not the same company. The Tractor Supply of today is a very different animal than the mail-order company that Charles Schmidt first founded at the end of the Great Depression.

Today's Tractor Supply relies on new technology, new retail philosophies, new distribution systems and merchandising techniques, and a new breed of executive. It's interesting to note that many of these elements were missing when the company floundered during the '70s. They're the basic elements. If they're missing, it doesn't matter how good your product or your pricing, your business just won't work.

At Tractor Supply these elements come together in the first seven words of the company's mission – Work hard, have fun, and make money. The power of that simple statement works itself out in a thousand other truths, logically flowing from this source. It means knowing what you stand for and what you won't stand for. It means treating people right, those you work with and the customers you work for. It means doing whatever it takes, being ready to run headfirst into a wall, spending less time worried about why a thing can't be done and more time figuring out how it can be done. It means being fair and honest and always striving to do the right thing. It means always thinking, dreaming, learning, and being ready and willing to admit your mistakes. It means surrounding yourself with good people, developing and valuing them. It means knowing how to have fun, putting yourself into what you do, and drawing your enjoyment out of the company instead of just your livelihood.

This, then, is what makes Tractor Supply so successful, now and when it first started. Simple, common sense stuff. But there's nothing so uncommon as common sense and nothing so complex as sticking to the simple stuff.

When it was founded, Tractor Supply was a business with a family feel. It still is today.

FROM LITTLE MORE THAN A TINY STOREFRONT WITH A COUNTERTOP FOR CATALOG ORDERS, TRACTOR SUPPLY HAS GROWN TO BECOME AMERICA'S NO. 1 FARM AND RANCH STORE.

Founder Charles Schmidt quickly surrounded himself with good people who attacked what they did with passion in their eyes rather than an eye on the time clock. The new Tractor Supply has followed the same formula. Both Schmidt and Scarlett believe in getting good people and then getting out of the way so they can get the job done. Having fun was part of Tractor Supply's early company culture. It still is. Listening to the customer and doing whatever it took to make it right was a core edict in Schmidt's day just as it is today.

Charles Schmidt liked to say, "Good is never good enough." Joe Scarlett is fond of saying, "If it ain't broke, let's break it…and make it better."

But what perhaps is most remarkable is the fact that these practices and principles, the key ingredients of Tractor Supply's success then and now, were not carefully preserved in any management manual or painstakingly handed down from founder to current management through the generations. The chain was broken. The history and culture were forgotten during a decade spent inside the belly of a huge corporate conglomerate whose principles and directives were, in many respects, counter to the Tractor Supply culture. Given this, it's amazing how similar the key elements of Tractor Supply's earliest and current success have remained.

It's as if lightning struck twice at Tractor Supply. It's a rare and defining moment in American business for a company to make its way to Wall Street. Tractor Supply has done it twice.

If the Tractor Supply culture and principles have been so successful, have worked so well twice in two very different eras and business environments, maybe the Tractor Supply story is one worth telling, a history worth repeating and preserving.

That's what Joe thought. He thought it might be fun to record the story.

And so this book.

TRACTOR SUPPLY TEAM MEMBERS IN NEW YORK FOR THE BELL RINGING ON FEBRUARY 18, 2004

We Can D

27 Washington Blvd.

Phone: Haymarket 1523

Prairie Farmer

The Freshman Football Team

Wm. C. Cle

Guaranteed

CHAPTER ★2★

FROM THE BROKERAGE HOUSE TO THE BARNYARD

THE BEGINNINGS OF TRACTOR SUPPLY

"WHILE THE STORM CLOUDS GATHER FAR ACROSS THE SEA,
LET US SWEAR ALLEGIANCE TO A LAND THAT'S FREE.
LET US ALL BE GRATEFUL FOR A LAND SO FAIR,
AS WE RAISE OUR VOICES IN A SOLEMN PRAYER:

GOD BLESS AMERICA, LAND THAT I LOVE,
STAND BESIDE HER AND GUIDE HER
THROUGH THE NIGHT WITH A LIGHT FROM ABOVE.
FROM THE MOUNTAINS, TO THE PRAIRIES,
TO THE OCEANS WHITE WITH FOAM,
GOD BLESS AMERICA, MY HOME SWEET HOME."

- IRVING BERLIN, "GOD BLESS AMERICA," WRITTEN IN 1938
TO ALLAY AMERICA'S FEARS IN THE FACE OF A WORLD AT WAR.

STRIKING A BLOW FOR LIBERTY

Not only did the demands of World War II change the face of the American workforce, it changed the face of a fledgling company called Tractor Supply. Tractor Supply would give its best and brightest to support the war effort on two separate fronts – key company executives Gard Abbott and Bill Cleary joined the army while Charles Schmidt served on the home front making sure America's farmers had the tools to feed the boys abroad.

Library of Congress

ALIENS ATTACK UNCERTAIN AMERICA

America was shrouded in uncertainty in 1938. The memory of the Great Depression still lingered, and many were out of work. In Japan, Italy, and Germany, the rumblings of World War II were just beginning, and the people of the United States were torn over the prospects of fighting again overseas. Labor unions were flexing their muscles, and the conflict between companies and their workers often led to open violence.

Fearing outside influences and attacks on the "American Way of Life" on its own shores, the House Committee on Un-American Activities was formed.

America's paranoia was so palatable that it didn't take much to stir up panic among the people. As incomprehensible as it may seem today, a live Halloween radio broadcast of a radio drama based on H.G. Wells' *War of the Worlds* inspired hundreds of thousands of listeners to panic, some even to the point of packing their most cherished belongings and fleeing their homes in fear of an invasion of attacking aliens from outer space.

Today, it seems fantastic that a simple radio broadcast could fuel such rampant fear. But America was still getting used to the immediacy of radio news. Gone were the days when it took weeks for news to travel from the source of a conflict or violence and the time it took to arrive helped temper people's reaction to it.

Now, live broadcasts from the immediate scene of a terrible tragedy served to magnify its effect.

Defense of the Land
Tractor Supply was born at a time when America's love of the land was perhaps never greater. A 1942 poster urges Americans to "Buy War Bonds" to aid their countrymen in defense of the land and freedom around the world.

CITY SLICKER

The world and America were filled with uncertainty. This was an unlikely time to venture out with a new business. But a twenty-six-year-old from Chicago's Southside named Charles E. Schmidt had meticulously studied the lay of the land and was absolutely certain his fledgling farm supply business would succeed. Given the uncertainty of the age and the fact that Schmidt had a family, a wife and a year-old son, it may not have seemed like a good time to take risks. Especially in a field in which he had absolutely no firsthand knowledge.

"The ironic thing is that for a guy who amassed a fortune in the farm business, I don't think he ever set foot on a farm in his life," said Schmidt's youngest son, Richard Schmidt, with a shake of his head and a smile.

Schmidt was a big city boy. He'd lived his whole life in Chicago's Southside. But what he may have lacked in firsthand knowledge of the farm and rural life, he more than

CHARLES SCHMIDT DURING HIS FOOTBALL-PLAYING DAYS AT THE UNIVERSITY OF CHICAGO, 1929

made up for with a powerful sense of confidence and drive that were beyond his years.

His confidence was apparently the product of a difficult childhood. Schmidt was born on June 5, 1912, the son of a strict Irish mother and Prussian father. A physician who went into the drugstore business, his father, Florian Schmidt, was an overbearing and intimidating man.

Wresting himself from his father's control proved a principal goal of Schmidt's young life. Later, after he had succeeded beyond anyone's wildest reckoning, he would remember with a special pride the day he freed himself from his father's authority. In describing the moment, Schmidt used a powerful, emotionally charged word. He said he had been "emancipated."

"My father once described to me the day he felt he truly emancipated himself," recalled Richard Schmidt. "He was just starting high school and he came home at six, just barely in time for dinner. His parents were angry because they didn't know where he was.

"He remembered the sense of freedom that he felt when he stood up and said, 'You know, I got up this morning, all by myself. I got dressed, all by myself. I got down and found the right trolley to get to school, all by myself. I registered for my classes, all by myself. After school, I went out and signed up for football, all by myself. And I found my way home for dinner, all by myself.

"'I feel it's time I make my own decisions.' "

Schmidt's fierce sense of independence and determination to make his own way and take charge of his life in many ways mirror the passion and strength of character that characterize his customers who worked the land. People who work the land, whether it's four acres or a back forty, discover in their connection with the land a sense of freedom and independence in doing it themselves. Schmidt may have not empathized with his customers when he began serving them with his early mail-order business, but he certainly shared their desire for independence.

GOOD PASTURE AND THE PITFALLS OF GENIUS

Complementing Schmidt's inner strength was a commanding physical presence. Six feet tall and blessed with an athletic build, Schmidt had a striking bearing. He played football in high school and later at the University of Chicago. His personal presence, however, exceeded his physical stature. His receding hairline gave him an air of maturity that many expected in a business leader, and he'd inherited a very erect carriage from his mother.

"I'm told that whenever she sat down at the table," said Richard Schmidt, "his mother never leaned against the back of the chair. She sat completely upright."

Many who knew Charles Schmidt are quick to describe his warmth, giving nature, and sense of humor. They also describe a certain quiet distance, a tension that a few saw as aloofness, the sense they couldn't ever really know him. That may have been an extension of the tension Schmidt experienced early in his life, the tension between his father and him, which was compounded by an ongoing feud among the extended members of the Schmidt family. The family was at odds over money, battling for control of the estate left by Charles Schmidt's grandfather, a gifted inventor, lawyer, and successful Chicago real estate magnate.

Before his death, Charles Schmidt's grandfather had amassed a fortune in real estate. Trained as a lawyer, he decided to write his own will. Apparently, there were limits to the elder Schmidt's genius, because the will didn't stand up in court, leaving the family embroiled in a legal battle that ultimately dissipated the fortune and severed many family ties.

While he never inherited any of his grandfather's money, Charles Schmidt was blessed with his own measure of brilliance and ingenuity and, perhaps, because of the grandfather's will that divided his family, he was painstaking in preparing the foundations of a financial undertaking before venturing out.

Charles Schmidt was not your classic risk-taking entrepreneur. Though he decided to launch his business in an uncertain time, he did it with the highest degree of certainty.

"He was very bright and he was very thorough," said Richard Schmidt. "He would think about a problem and think about it and think about it and he wouldn't take any action until he really understood all facets of the problem.

"He never did anything that he wasn't pretty sure what the outcome was going to be."

An early childhood friend and later Tractor Supply co-worker, Bill Cleary, remembered it this way: "He was really one of a kind. If he set his mind that he was going to accomplish something, he could study the fundamentals and absorb enough of them to get started doing it himself. Then his adaptability just carried him through until he became an expert."

BUSINESS BY ACCIDENT

But for all his personal drive and his strong desire to be independent, Schmidt didn't set out to be an entrepreneur. His first love was sports, particularly football. And he was good at it. His Mt. Carmel High School team won an impressive citywide championship. He went on to play football for the University of Chicago. Schmidt's attention stayed focused on sports until he suffered a serious injury during football practice. He broke his neck and, for a time, physicians feared he would be paralyzed.

"I think it was the third week of the season," recalled Gard Abbott, one of Schmidt's close college friends and another early Tractor Supply co-worker and eventual president of the company. "Very serious injury. Didn't think he would survive for a few hours. Then they thought he would be paralyzed, but he recovered and they told him he would never play football again.

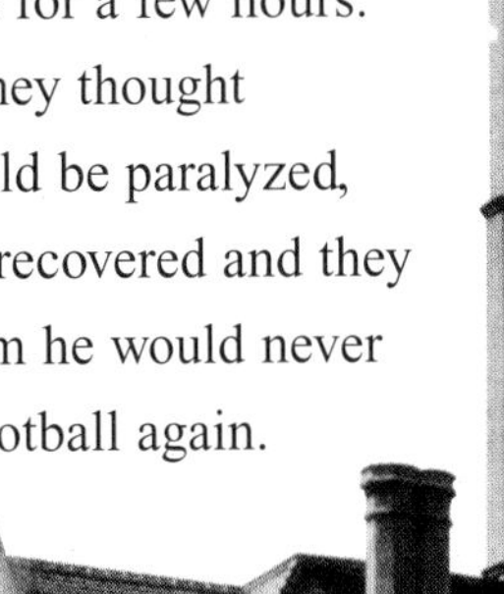

MITCHELL TOWER ON THE CAMPUS OF SCHMIDT'S ALMA MATER, THE UNIVERSITY OF CHICAGO

University of Chicago Football Team, 1929
Charles Schmidt seated in front row, the fourth from right

"I think this changed his life a good deal. Up until that point he had been more oriented to football than perhaps he was to scholastics. From that point on, he was a better student and became involved in a lot of other activities that perhaps wouldn't have been important to him."

Schmidt refocused his energies, studying business, although he didn't receive his diploma because of an unpaid library fine. An odd, overlooked detail in the life of a man who would prove so meticulous. Ironically, Schmidt would later more than repay the library fine that kept him from graduating by giving the University of Chicago millions of dollars. And the University that withheld his diploma would confer on him an honorary degree.

CHARLES SCHMIDT AS HE APPEARED IN HIS COLLEGE YEARBOOK, 1932

LATER IN THE EARLY 1960s WITH HIS WIFE DOROTHY

After college, Schmidt, who was married to Dorothy Faris, tried for a brief time to make a living selling insurance.

"Dad first tried to work in the insurance business, selling insurance, during the Depression," Richard Schmidt explained. "That wasn't very successful and he told my mother, 'This is not the way to make money in this world.'

"That's when he decided to start his own business."

But before he could launch his own business, he needed to figure out just what kind of business he wanted to start. He needed more experience, and he needed financial backing. So Schmidt turned to a Chicago brokerage house for work, landing a job at the firm of Shields & Company. In the days before ticker tapes and computer screens, Schmidt's job was to hand post the latest financial information on marker boards for the brokers.

IT BEGINS WITH A BROOM

"He basically got the job," said Richard Schmidt, "because not only would he post the transactions, but he also agreed to sweep the floor at the end of the day."

Charles Schmidt was never afraid of hard work. He embraced it. The Great Depression may have made starting a new business during the '30s a risky venture, but his work ethic and his fiercely independent spirit got him the job that ultimately introduced him to the idea for Tractor Supply.

It's interesting to note that "work hard" is the first part of Tractor Supply's modern mission statement. It all begins with hard work. It's as true today at Tractor Supply as it was then of Charles Schmidt.

Schmidt's work ethic earned him the respect of two customers of Shields & Co – Ben Ettlestone and Leonard Leterman. The two businessmen were partners in a wholesale automobile supply company whose name pragmatically combined their two last names – Leterstone.

"Ben and Leonard had their eye on Chuck [Schmidt] when he was a board marker at Shields," said Bill Cleary. "Businessmen are always looking for comers apparently, and they had Chuck up as 'There's one we want.'

"Lo and behold, he wasn't a board marker too long, a year or two, when they propositioned him and, I would say…they made him an offer and his eyes probably popped out of his head."

Leterstone sold wholesale automotive parts to car owners who were looking for cheap, reliable parts. The company also had a business that sold replacement parts for farm tractors, called Tractor Replacement Parts Company. So the idea for a company outside the tractor and farm equipment industry selling replacement parts wasn't a new one. But then, the genius of retailing has always been adapting what works and making it better. Schmidt knew a good idea when he saw one and he would make it better. He would focus his business entirely on the tractor replacement parts market.

THE SEARS OF FARM SUPPLY

Schmidt only worked with Leterstone for a short time before he ventured out on his own. So why did he decide to go into farm supply rather than capitalize on the American craze for the automobile? There were more than 30 million automobiles on the road in America at the time, and the economic straits of auto owners during the Depression demanded that many motorists do their own maintenance and repair. Why did Schmidt instead veer off into tractor supply? Perhaps it was partly out of loyalty to Leterstone, partly because tractor supply was a relatively untapped niche, but mostly because the young Schmidt was starting with very meager financial resources. He'd determined that supplying tractor parts could be forecast more precisely.

Buying a tractor in 1941 was as easy as ordering it from the Sears, Roebuck and Co.

"Dad told me once, 'I tried to figure out what business could I go in where I could have some control over the outcome, where everything wasn't a gamble on the front end,'" recounted Richard Schmidt.

"He actually analyzed it, sat down, and tried to figure it out. And from what he knew about the commodities exchange in Chicago and from his brokerage background, he realized, 'You know, farmers know whether they're having a good year or bad year long before the product goes to market. Wouldn't it be nice to be able to sell a product to a customer and to establish inventories

Moline tractor factory in Minneapolis proudly displays its product in 1939.

Library of Congress

and distribution to the customer and know where the money was coming from?'

"So he decided that he was going to supply farmers with implements, equipment, replacement parts – become the Sears of farm supply. During tough years, he'd sell patch-up parts. You know, power blocks for John Deere tractors and things to overhaul an engine to squeeze one more year out of it. In good years, he'd offer air-conditioned cabs for their tractors and all of the luxury stuff they wouldn't buy otherwise."

And he did it all at a price that was so attractive to the customer that they'd take a chance and do business with a new company. He sold replacement parts direct to a customer who would otherwise be forced to go to the dealers and equipment manufacturers like John Deere and International Harvester for parts and repairs. It was a monopoly primed for exploitation and competition.

"When farmers wanted to buy a new piece of equipment," explained Cleary, "they went to the dealer. Most farmers in those days did their own repair work. They did it during the winter when they had no crops in the ground."

Schmidt saw the vacuum in the marketplace, the niche created by the dealers and manufacturers. He saw a frugal customer made more frugal by the Great Depression. There was a need for an inexpensive parts supplier.

Charles and Dorothy Schmidt on the University of Chicago campus

Bearings, one of the early products that put Tractor Supply in business

DO YOU BELIEVE IN TSC?

Apparently, Schmidt's idea was sound enough that Ben Ettlestone and Leonard Leterman joined him as silent partners. In exchange, they agreed to arrange credit for Schmidt with the suppliers of bearings and other parts they already kept in stock. In essence, Leterstone fronted Schmidt with his initial inventory. He also scraped what little he could from his household budget and a meager amount of start-up money from a bank and his wife, Dorothy. Schmidt set out to start a business with just a few thousand dollars.

America's largest farm and ranch store chain would have humble beginnings. Today, the little bit of household savings Schmidt invested in his business has become more than a billion-dollar business.

Like the customers Tractor Supply serves, the size of the initial investment was miniscule compared to the sweat equity required for the company to thrive. It took more than an idea and money. It took hard work. And Charles Schmidt had great confidence in his ability to think and his willingness to work hard.

"My father said, 'There are a lot of guys out there who are smarter than I am, but they're only giving it 70 percent and I'm giving it 100 percent. There's nobody whose 70 percent is as good as my 100 percent,' " explained Richard Schmidt.

"You can come out on top of people who are a lot shrewder and smarter than you as long as you're giving it everything you've got."

Schmidt worked on his idea for years. So thorough were his plan and his thinking that he was able to lure people away from good-paying jobs to work right alongside him and realize his dream. Bankers, lawyers, it didn't matter. They came to work for Schmidt and his tractor supply notion.

Tractor and Tractor Supply – Both Born in Chicago It was long thought the word "tractor" originated in 1906 when W. H. Williams, sales manager for the Hart-Parr Company, wanted to replace the words "gasoline traction engine" in an ad with something snappier. But the very first record of the word goes back to 1890 and a patent issued for a "tractor" designed by George H. Edwards of Chicago.

Think about it for a moment. America wouldn't fully loose itself from the grip of the Great Depression until the boom that followed World War II. Giving up a job to go into an unproven venture would not be a matter to be taken lightly in 1938.

But that's exactly what people did.

People with good, secure jobs left them to work with Charles Schmidt and his idea to make money moving tractor parts. People like Bill Cleary and later Gardner Abbott.

"Chuck approached me and asked if I would be interested [in working for his company]," said Cleary. "I worked for a bank at the time, First National of Chicago. The bank was a good, safe place, but by 1936 or 1937, Chuck had done a whale of a lot of studying and thinking, and that was the nucleus for something that became Tractor Supply.

"He asked me if I would quit the bank and if I would be able to finance myself until I got into the business. I said, 'Yes.'"

Gard Abbott came to work with Charles Schmidt and Tractor Supply in October 1939. This amazing power to lure good people is a recurring theme in the life of Charles Schmidt. It's also a recurring theme in the life of Tractor Supply. Good people have been central to the company's two most successful periods in its history.

"Don't be misled," said Joe Scarlett, Tractor Supply Company's current chairman. "The Tractor Supply story isn't really about catalogs or stores. It's a people story. It's a story about the power of vision and enthusiasm and hard work and people."

Charles Schmidt had very little to offer those first few employees except a clear-cut, well-thought-out idea; a passion and enthusiasm for what he was doing; and the hard work he invested in his idea. Effort and enthusiasm. Working hard and having fun.

That was the magic that brought a banker and lawyer to work for Tractor Supply. The money would soon follow. Money would be the measure of hard work and having fun, and it would also serve as a great prime for the business pump, the thing needed to keep the hard work and fun coming.

INSIDE TRACTOR SUPPLY'S STERLING, ILLINOIS, BRANCH, 1949

HUNTING TRACTORS WITH A RIFLE

So Charles Schmidt brought Bill Cleary into the business before he could even pay him. He needed Cleary's accounting skills to help him with the statistical information necessary to get his first catalog into the hands of the right people.

"He approached me to work in the company," said Cleary, "because my background was in accounting, and he asked me if I would do all of the statistical work."

1941 CATALOG

Schmidt's selection of Cleary as one of his first employees demonstrates two more key strengths that have since become part of the company's culture and values. One is the confidence and lack of ego required to admit you need the help of someone who surpasses you in a particular area, someone who brings a strength to the team that you may not possess.

"Some people manage by trying to control and hold down the people below them," observed Richard Schmidt. "He wanted people to rise up. He loved to be challenged for his job because as soon as he found someone who could challenge him – who could do what he was doing as well as he could – he could move on. He could step back and broaden the perspective.

"He didn't feel he had to know more than the people working for him in order to be their boss. That was very key to the way he thought."

The other insight Cleary's selection illustrates is Schmidt's approach to marketing. He knew that taking advantage of the niche he was focused on would require an equally focused approach to marketing and sales. He would have to gather statistical information about his customers in order to successfully operate his mail-order business on the shoestring budget. Where was the highest concentration of people with tractors? What was the most efficient way to deliver a catalog to them and the cheapest way to deliver the parts they ordered?

"Shotgunning a market wasn't the way he wanted to do business," said Richard Schmidt. "He wanted the sniper's rifle. If he could get a list of people who had tractors and already needed the parts he was trying to sell, that to him was the rifle shot. He could hone in on a market and spend as little money as possible sending free catalogs."

And so Schmidt recognized the need for Cleary's statistical talents. Of course, he also needed a catalog.

TSC'S FIRST CATALOG

It didn't look like much, that very first Tractor Supply catalog. Just twenty-four pages of thin newsprint. One color. Simple line drawings to give the customer some general sense of the stuff the company was selling but leaving more up to the imagination than the artwork could really communicate. Any question of quality was handled with the blunt assurance – "Satisfaction or Your Money Back." With so little space, that very first catalog didn't offer much variety. It focused mainly on the essentials, on the parts a customer would most likely need to keep his tractor going. Nothing exotic. Bearings and gaskets.

This was the tail end of the Great Depression and squeezing another season out of a tractor was

BUY TRACTOR PARTS BY MAIL...

TIME Not Distance COUNTS

(IN LIGHT AREA) **48** HOURS, OR LESS, FROM CHICAGO

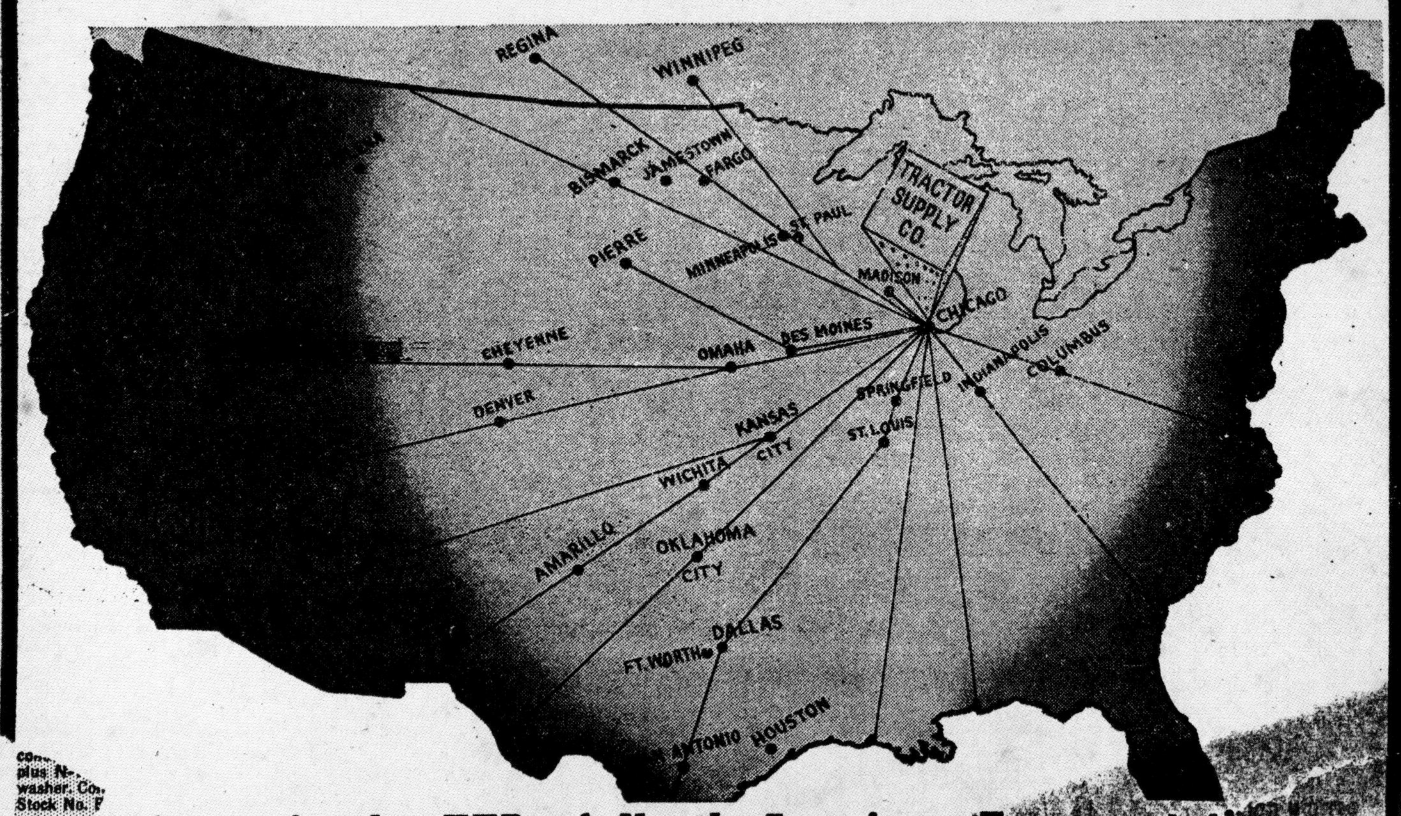

"Chicago is the HUB of North American Transportation"

Stock on Hand to Fill Your Order in 6 Hours or Less

Catalog No. 139
1939

If You Own A

We Pay Freight On $25 Shipments

Tractor Supply Co.

1217 Washington Blvd. Chicago, Illinois

NEW
Stock Only
No Used
Goods

FRONT COVER OF TRACTOR SUPPLY'S FIRST CATALOG.

critical, as was fixing a tractor that went down in the middle of planting or harvest.

The 1938 Tractor Supply catalog is a far cry from today's massive Blue Book with tens of thousands of items, with everything from paddleboats for ponds to solar-panel-powered gate openers. What the customer found inside that first catalog was important, but even more important to the success of the company was the degree of thinking that was poured into it.

"Before we were even in business, somebody had to prepare the catalog," said Bill Cleary. "There was the first taste of real genius! A young man [Charles Schmidt]...with absolutely no direct experience in ever setting up what turned out to be a twenty-four-page catalog, and very, very little honest-to-God experience in [the field] he was entering.

"Did it all from scratch."

The challenge was to pack as much into every page as possible, to keep down the number of pages and the cost of mailing but still have enough there for the customer to buy in order to justify the cost of the catalog in the first place. Schmidt slaved over the catalog at the dining room table in his little Chicago apartment. He worked line by line, cutting a word here, a word there, so he could include another product. It was all about economy. Not a word wasted. Not even on the name of the company.

"Our first name was Tractor Owners Supply Company," said Bill Cleary. "That was too cumbersome, so we changed it to Tractor Supply Company."

Aren't we all glad it's not TOSC?

Schmidt also worked painstakingly to set up suppliers for everything that he'd include in the catalog, relying on Leterstone and its suppliers for most of what he would sell.

"I can't begin to convey to anybody, in my honest opinion, the total genius it took for somebody to think all of this up and be able to do it out of his own head, with his own hands, with his own fingers, with his own typing, measuring every little inch of that catalog to crowd as much stuff as we could into twenty-four pages," said Bill Cleary. "He had that all figured out so that even if the catalog paper...wasn't cut to the last splinter, the catalog might be overweight, then you were going to have to pay for two instead of one. All of this, to me, living through it and seeing what I saw, is the sheer genius of one human being.

"It still amazes me."

ADDRESSING THE FARMER

With that first catalog, Schmidt managed to wedge in 2,000 items, according to Cleary. And mail the whole thing for a penny.

But mail to whom? Schmidt may have believed in the targeted approach to marketing, but this was 1938, and list-building was not the sophisticated science that it has since become. It wasn't as easy as buying a list from a direct-mail source. But Schmidt had that figured out, too.

"I didn't know what a farm tractor was in those days," Bill Cleary remembered with a smile. "But he knew the government had publica-

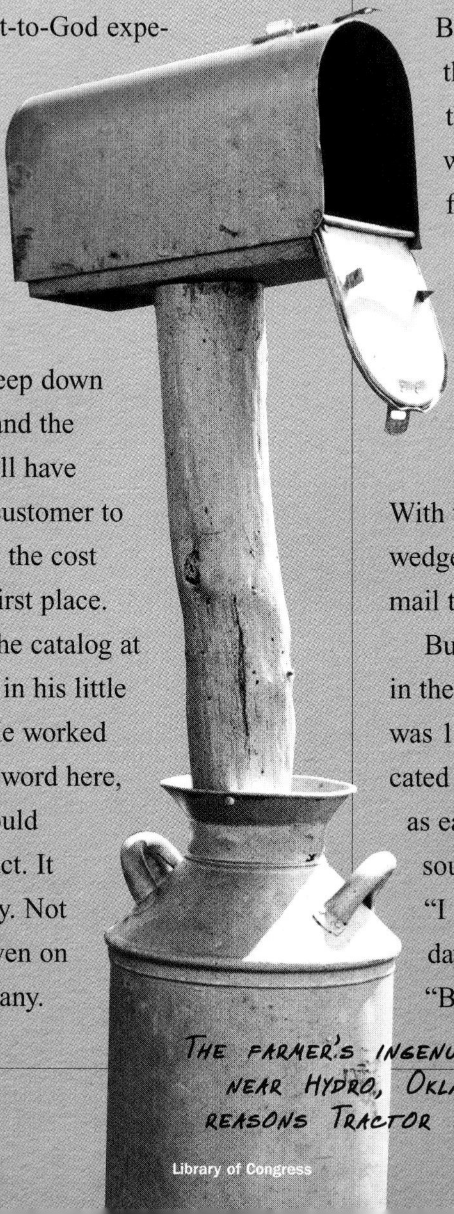

THE FARMER'S INGENUITY AS ILLUSTRATED BY THIS MAILBOX NEAR HYDRO, OKLAHOMA, IN 1939 WAS ONE OF THE REASONS TRACTOR SUPPLY'S PARTS FOUND A READY BUYER.

Library of Congress

tions that told you how many tractors there were in the United States by counties in each state. The government post office put out, and probably still does, a booklet that showed every post office in the country and how many RFD [Rural Farm Delivery] boxes they had."

Though it was time consuming and tedious, Schmidt could better afford the expenditure of his own personal energy to target customers than he could the cost of blanketing rural America. He had to make sure he made every precious catalog count. There were no cash reserves. And there would be no second chances. But Schmidt was confident. He had worked it all out.

He'd cross-index which counties in which states had the most tractors with the list of post office boxes for those counties. He would only mail to the counties with the greatest number of tractors. Of course, there were thousands of rural counties in America in 1938. He would have to go through them. State by state. County by county.

This is where Bill Cleary's statistical expertise proved invaluable.

"My original job was to chart every county and every state we were interested in: how many tractors there were in the county, how many people were there, how many rural [post] boxes there were," Cleary said.

"To show you how crude it was, so far as our approach, but how cheap it was, we finally decided – Chuck decided – that we're going to shoot the wad on catalogs, make or break almost.... He was not afraid to gamble where he felt he could do something about the odds."

"Most of them [the catalogs] the first time around were going to go in the garbage because most of these people didn't have any tractors. But if they didn't have any tractors, that meant somebody else got one who had two or more tractors."

GOOD. BUT NOT GOOD ENOUGH

Apparently a good number of those first catalogs found their way into the hands of tractor owners in need of tractor supplies. The company sold $50,000 worth, all of it by mail. This was at a time when the minimum hourly wage was a quarter. In today's dollars, the company's first year's sales would amount to more than $640,000. In its very first year, Tractor Supply had done incredibly well.

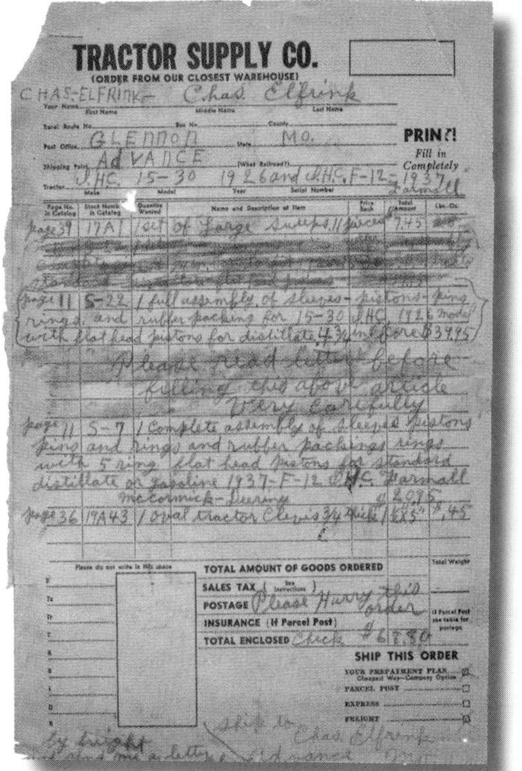
TRACTOR SUPPLY CO.
(ORDER FROM OUR CLOSEST WAREHOUSE)
Your Name: CHAS-ELFRINK Chas. Elfrink
Post Office: GLENNON State: MO.
Shipping Point: Ad VANCE
Tractor: I.H.C. 15-30 1926 and I.H.C. F-12 1937
PRINT! Fill in Completely

TOTAL AMOUNT OF GOODS ORDERED
SALES TAX (See Instructions)
POSTAGE Please Hurry this order
INSURANCE (If Parcel Post)
TOTAL ENCLOSED Check
SHIP THIS ORDER
YOUR PREPAYMENT PLAN Cheapest Way—Company Option
PARCEL POST
EXPRESS
FREIGHT

A 1948 Tractor Supply catalog order

"But good was never good enough for Charles Schmidt," Richard Schmidt said.

Rather than being reassured by the success of his approach to targeting customers, Schmidt was concerned about the number of customers his catalog mailing may have missed. How could he target his approach even more? How could he deal with the customer directly, one on one?

What if he opened a store? And where would be the right place to open it?

N.E. N.W. 13
CITY LIMITS
MAP OF
OFFICE OF CITY ENGINE
CITY ENGINEER
SCALE • 1 • INCH • 300 •
S.E. N.W 13
After 10 days
Motor Route No. 1,
NUNN, Weld Co., COLO.
Tractor
4615

CHAPTER

★3★

MINOT, WILLISTON, OMAHA AND BEYOND

THE ROOTS OF AMERICA'S NO.1 FARM AND RANCH STORE

"IN THE UNITED STATES THERE IS MORE SPACE WHERE NOBODY IS THAN WHERE ANYBODY IS. THIS IS WHAT MAKES AMERICA WHAT IT IS."

- GERTRUDE STEIN

MINOT FOR MILES

Far from the Chicago cityscape and the place of its birth, Tractor Supply moved closer to its customer in 1939 when it chose to open its first catalog store in Minot, North Dakota. Six decades and several generations later, agriculture continues to be one of the leading sources of income for the good people who populate America's border with Canada, and Tractor Supply continues to serve them with a Minot location.

Library of Congress

WHY NOT, MINOT? It's pronounced MYNOT and it rhymes with "Why not?" says a quick-witted local. They have a dry sense of humor in North Dakota. Probably some sort of personal defense against the steady wind and harsh winter weather that blow across the prairie here. These are a hardy people with a pleasant lilt in their voices, a legacy of their Norwegian ancestors, who came here to homestead, earn a piece of land and an opportunity.

★

They came here to farm and ranch. And that, mostly, is what they still do here. Farming and ranching are still the number one industry in Minot. A small community in a state that ranks forty-seventh out of fifty when it comes to population. The official state beverage is milk. The state dance is the square dance.

So if Charles Schmidt was looking for a rural area to open his first store, Minot was a good one. But it wasn't the only candidate.

Thorough thinker that he was, why did Charles Schmidt choose a town nearly a thousand miles away from the company's headquarters in Chicago as the logical location for the first Tractor Supply Store?

For Schmidt, the secret may have been where Minot is located, just fifty-five miles from the U.S. border with Canada. In their time-consuming, county-by-county analysis of tractor ownership for the first catalog mailing, Schmidt and Cleary had figured out that Texas and Saskatchewan, Canada, represented the two biggest potential targets for Tractor Supply.

"They were going to put out another catalog and put up a place in Minot, North Dakota, because they were going to pre-pay shipments to Canada and that was close to the Canadian border," said Gard Abbott, manager of the first Tractor Supply Store and later the president of the company.

FARMING FERTILE LEGAL FIELDS

"I met Chuck one night in Chicago, and he said, 'We're going to open a branch in Minot, North Dakota,'" Abbott explained. "I'd never heard of it and had to get out an atlas to see where it was. He said, 'Why don't you go up there and you can be manager.'"

Abbott objected on two pretty logical grounds. He didn't know anything about Minot and he knew even less about running a farm supply store. He could have also added the fact that he was working as a lawyer.

Schmidt's reply was simply, "It doesn't make any difference." And it didn't to him. Schmidt always relied on what he knew. And he knew that Gard Abbott was a good man. The two had first met in 1929 at the University of Chicago where they roomed together. After he completed his undergraduate work, Abbott went on to law school and then to work in a Chicago law firm. It didn't matter that he had no background in agriculture or retail. Neither did Charles Schmidt. What mattered most to Schmidt was Abbott was a good man. He'd figure it out.

As surprising and illogical as Schmidt's offer to his former roommate may seem, Gard Abbott's reaction is even more stunning.

He went.

"Nobody left where they were working to go to work for Chuck Schmidt because he was going to pay them so much more money," said Richard Schmidt. "He went and got people to work for him because he wanted them. Feeling wanted was what attracted them to him.

"He said, 'I want your brain working alongside my brain. We're gonna figure out how to make this work. I didn't know how to start the first one but I figured it out. You go up there. You'll figure it out.'"

The selection of the first manager of that very first store is a testament to not only the strength of Charles Schmidt's confidence and commitment but also the confidence and commitment it inspired in others. Gard Abbott went to Minot.

The soft spoken, unassuming big city lawyer packed up for North Dakota to open a new store for a business that was barely a year old. The people who didn't know anything about direct mail were now expanding their ignorance into the farm supply retail industry. They didn't know what they couldn't do.

And so they did it.

NOT MUCH TO LOOK AT

The old wooden frame building at 509 Third Street, N.E., in downtown Minot still stands today. It's off the beaten path but in sight of an old grain elevator and within earshot of the railroad tracks.

THE FIRST TRACTOR SUPPLY STORE, MINOT, NORTH DAKOTA

Tractor Supply vacated that building back in 1966 and moved to a larger space on 20th Avenue. Today, Tractor Supply is currently in its third Minot location, an attractive building on a more heavily traveled street on the outskirts of town.

Even in this small community, the locations of those two stores, the first Minot store and the current one, are evidence of the shift in Tractor Supply customers. The first store served the farmers who frequented the grain elevator and sent their produce by rail to market. Today, the company serves the broader needs of the rural community and part-time farmers and ranchers who divide time between their land and their downtown jobs, so its location along a major thoroughfare on the way out of the city makes more sense.

The size of the stores speaks volumes, too. The small clapboard building that housed the first store had a small storefront with plenty of room in back to stock parts for the catalog orders. It was more of an outpost for the mail order than a retail center. Today's store is larger and its stock is kept out front, literally out front, more and more of it ready to greet the customers as soon as they step out of their cars or trucks.

"It really wasn't too much to look at from the outside," the seventy-two-year-old Delmar Nelson recalled, talking about the first time his dad took him to the Minot store when he was growing up in

Minot. "Of course, it's what was on the inside of the store that we were coming for. Farmers aren't too much into what's on the outside anyway.

"Back then, we only got into town three or four times a year. It was a big deal. You thought you were going to take a fly across the ocean almost, you know. We'd take lunch along and go out to the park and have dinner. You might buy clothes and take care of things at the courthouse. And then maybe go to Tractor Supply."

It was a simpler time. Appearances didn't account for much, but how far you could stretch a dollar did. And Charles Schmidt sure knew how to stretch his customers' dollars.

"It was a small frame building, I suppose about fifty-by-one hundred," recounted G.G. Henny, another Minot-area native whose dad took him to that very first Tractor Supply Store. "The supplies weren't displayed very fancy at that stage. They were pretty much displayed how they came, in the boxes that they came in.

"But it was the original thing, and we all liked it as farmers."

The farmers of Minot did like that first store. They were so eager to take advantage of the low prices the company's catalog promised, they couldn't wait. Literally.

"…I understand it [the Minot store's first shipment of merchandise] arrived about the same time that the catalogs were being delivered to the customers," recounted Wes Walker, another early Schmidt hire who would become president of the company. "The shipment was packed in wooden boxes that were later used as stock bins in the store.

"The farmers were in such a hurry to get their repairs at these new low prices that they helped unpack many of the boxes, hoping to find the parts they had come for."

These were exciting times, fast and furious, fly-by-the-seat-of-your-pants, jump-in-with-both-feet-and-grab-something-to-do kind of times. In addition to serving the Minot community as a retail store, Branch No. 2, as it was called, also fulfilled catalog orders to North Dakota, Montana, and Canada. Branch No. 1, the home office in Chicago at 1217-1227 West Washington Boulevard, served the rest of the country.

CATALOG ILLUSTRATION OF THE FIRST HOME OFFICE AT 1217 WEST WASHINGTON BOULEVARD

NO, WLS IS ACROSS THE STREET FROM US

In the early years of the company, everything was make-do, including the home office in Chicago. Although Tractor Supply was born at Charles and Dorothy Schmidt's kitchen table, it quickly outgrew the Schmidt apartment. Mailing catalogs, receiving orders, shipping and receiving, and warehousing inventory for some 2,000 parts required more space.

Schmidt found that "space," and it was little more than that, at 1217 West Washington Boulevard. There, with his meager budget, before the first orders rolled in, he rented part of a vacant floor in an old brick warehouse. It was little more than a 35,000-square-foot loft at an address that probably wouldn't have inspired much confidence in prospective employees, let alone the business community and suppliers.

"It was very dismal," Kay Gorecki Walker described it. Other than Dorothy Schmidt, Walker was the first woman to work for Schmidt, and she

THE SMILE-A-WHILE GANG HITS THE EARLY MORNING AIRWAVES TO CHEERFULLY BEGIN THE DAY FOR WLS's RURAL LISTENERS. FROM THE PRAIRIE FARMER WLS FAMILY ALBUM, 1940.

paid more attention to the surroundings than the young entrepreneur did. "If you knew Chicago, 1217 West Washington was just one block off of Madison, which was strictly derelicts. Washington wasn't much better.

"There were only two places to eat. One was across the street. We were kind and just called it the 'greasy spoon.' Or you could walk down the street to the drugstore, but you always had to be careful because of the drunks. Our office wasn't very fancy at all. I'm sure it was what they could afford and nothing more."

The home office did have one respectable neighbor. A Chicago landmark and rural favorite, the WLS radio station was directly across the street from it. Originally owned by Sears, Roebuck & Co., the WLS call letters stood for World's Largest Store. The retail giant had begun the station in the heyday of radio to produce farm programs.

Besides sharing Tractor Supply's rural farm customer as an audience, the company's neighbor also had Nashville ties. The Solemn Old Judge, George D. Hay, was announcer there before he moved to Nashville as the first program director of WSM radio and, later, the founder of the Grand Ole Opry radio show.

In 1928, Sears decided to sell the station to *Prairie Farmer Magazine* rather than International Harvester Company, which was among the companies interesting in buying it. With the purchase, the radio station moved to Washington Boulevard and continued to build its national reputation, broadcasting such perennial small town favorites as the *National Barn Dance*.

Perhaps knowing that the health of a business is mainly in people's perception and wanting to start off on the best footing, although not the best business address, Schmidt tried to put a little bit of a positive spin on Tractor Supply Company's location. Although guided most of the time by the risk-averse, analytical side of his personality, Schmidt also was blessed with a good bit of creative talent and a rich sense of humor. With his tongue firmly embedded in his cheek, Schmidt unfurled a banner across the front of the building where the home office of his new company was located. On it were emblazoned the words, "Tractor Supply Company. WLS Is Directly Across The Street From Us."

Schmidt's ingenuity surfaced in other ways. He called on his customers to help him better target his catalog mailing, offering them a free screwdriver set for sending in the names and addresses of five friends who owned tractors.

LETTERS FROM THE HEARTLAND

The orders came pouring in to Minot and Chicago, sometimes written on the order blanks printed in the catalog. Just as often, the orders came as personal letters scrawled out on penny postcards and small scraps of paper or whatever happened to be handy. They were written in painfully executed chicken scratches and pencil hieroglyphs that tested the limits of legibility. Some were obviously written by a hand more comfortable digging a posthole than posting a letter. The letters came from all over, from exotic places like Hanks, North Dakota; Haxtun, Colorado; Stuttgart, Arkansas; Belgrade, Missouri; Manhattan, Kansas; and "The Pheasant Mecca of America," Alpena, South Dakota, not to be confused with the neighboring "Pheasant Paradise" of DeSmet, South Dakota, a.k.a. "City of Good, Pure Water" and the "Shortest Hard-Surfaced Route."

RETURN IN 5 DAYS TO
BARUTH BROS.
ALPENA, S. DAK.
The Pheasant Mecca of America
Tractor Supply Co.
4615 So. 26th Street
Omaha,
Neb.
ALPENA: The Liveliest, Busiest Town of Its Size in S. Dak. - Pop. 500.
GOOD ROADS: 4 m. to Fed. 281; 8m. State 37; 13 m. Fed. 14; 9 m. State 34.
ON THE MILWAUKEE ROAD — ALPENA WELCOMES VISITORS AND HUNTERS

CUSTOMER LETTER, 1941

Sometimes the writer didn't have a checking account and sent postage stamps as legal tender. Sometimes they asked for a part and carefully listed it by catalog number. Other times, the writer, unsure of precisely which number should be given or, perhaps, urgently needing a part to finish the season's harvest, copied down every part number he could find on his tractor.

Along with ordering parts and merchandise from the catalog, the correspondence was often filled with questions, advice, comments on the quality of a particular part or purchase, recommendations to send a catalog to a friend, or requests for another catalog for themselves because a guest had spirited theirs away.

To look through the pages and pages of correspondence is to thumb through the lives of people working hard to make some kind of living from the land. Because they believed they were getting a break from this company called Tractor Supply – getting a break when they really needed one, a few cents off of a part here and there that might make the difference between breaking even or going broke – a deep emotional connection was being forged between company and customer. And so they began including bits of personal news and information among the litany of numbers for tractor parts.

It's almost as if the tractor were a part of their family; and, since they were already telling you the vital stats surrounding their most constant companion in the field, they might as well let you in on how they were doing or the health of a child or chicken or the particular habits of their women.

RED HEADED WOMAN

Along with his $8.78 order for a gasket set and three oil filters and booster cables, Bert Wilson acknowledges in his letter that his "red headed woman is a honey, 267 lbs. of human flesh, the most even tempered woman I ever saw, stays mad all the time" and then goes on to discuss a replacement he needs for a tractor piston. In another letter, the same Bert Wilson mingled questions about oil seals and requests for a brake pedal shaft with the admission that:

"I got a bulldog, seven horses, three tractors and a red headed woman. The red headed woman says if I am going to keep her I will have to tie a tin can on the bulldog's tail, shoot the horses and run the tractors into the river.

"I have a rather hard decision to make.... In the meantime, I got to have some repairs."

There are the touching notes, as well. One fall day, an order came in to Chicago for corn picker parts. The check that accompanied the order was unsigned and, therefore, no good. Instead of delaying the shipment and sending the check back to be signed, Tractor Supply sent the corn picker parts anyway, realizing the parts would be needed for the harvest. Three days later, a letter came back from the customer with a signed check.

"Dear Sir," the letter began, "We are very grateful to you for making an exception and sending the merchandise as there was a time element involved at this time of year, and we still have 100 acres to pick. Thanks again, Mrs. Milo Butler."

A postscript at the end of the letter offered an explanation for the mistake that could have cost the writer's family part of their crop – "P.S. Milo's mother, 90-years-age, broke her leg three weeks ago and is in the hospital but doing very well. Too many things on my mind, it was my mistake in failing to sign the check."

Of course, there was the occasional criticism, but many times it was offered in the spirit of a friend offering a hand rather than the cold hard tone of what others have called "customer complaints."

"Woops! Pop, have you got a new stock boy or sumpin'?" wrote N. C. Larahee. "I ordered wrenches, grain saver guards, a pin punch, etc., and all I received was a starter for a John Deere Tractor. I have got it repackaged and will send it on its way. As soon as it is rec'd please look up my original order and ship pronto please. Your suffering customer."

The honesty and integrity of Tractor Supply's customers also shows through in their correspondence with the company. A sum as little as 70¢

Max's Good Turn Back in the late '50s, one of Max DeForest's jobs was turning away the constant crush of people wanting a Tractor Supply franchise. At that time, Charles Schmidt didn't plan to sell franchises. But one day two brothers showed up at the office all the way from Springfield, Missouri. Max felt sorry for them and wanted Charles Schmidt to just give them a few minutes. He ended up giving them the first Tractor Supply franchise. Thirteen years later Max DeForest's favor was finally returned. The Race Brothers sold their retail business to Max in 1971 after he left Tractor Supply.

Bert Wilson Grand Tower Ill
Sept 22 1961

Dear Sirs:

I got a bull dog 7 horses 3 tractors and a redheaded woman the red headed woman says if I am going to keep her I will have to tie a tin can on the bulldogs tail, shoot the horses and run the tractors into the river. I have a rather hard decision to make and in the meantime I got to have some repairs. I got the old case up on her feet so I am starting on one of the H's dont know what model but I bought it for a 49. I think it is nearer a 39. any way I am going to start on a couple of oil seals

brake pedal shaft (2 used) #0-17944

F-1713 Shipnut 6 oz - each 79 (2) 12 oz 1½# 2½ 1.58

Steering improvement plate 8a7K 3/4 1.29

too much returned to the customer warrants a letter of thanks. An extra part that was received by a customer in a mail order is promptly returned.

These customer letters, some as many as sixty years old, exist today because they were passed around the office and saved by employees. Chief among those who kept customer letters was Wes Walker. He understood the value of connecting with the customer, the value of relationship.

Today, Tractor Supply continues to share success stories and customer letters, humorous and touching, as well as the occasional critique. They are shared by e-mail and fax and distributed across the country, reprinted regularly in the Tractor Supply newsletter, *The Voice*, for everyone to see and note. It is a culture of communication as comfortable and natural as a bunch of cowboys swapping stores around the glow of a campfire. Only the fire here are the words of the Tractor Supply customer, the small glowing embers able to ignite change, spark improvements, and feed the company desire to do better by its customers.

MINOT MAKES HAY

It must have been a difficult transition for Schmidt, who was so hands-on in the development and creation of the company's catalog, to stay put in the company's Chicago office, far away from what was going on at his very first store in Minot. When Schmidt did go to Minot to give Gard Abbott a hand for what he said would only be a couple of weeks, he stayed a couple of months.

Curious about her husband's extended absence after about a month and a half, Dorothy Schmidt followed him to Minot. When she arrived, according to Wes Walker, she was quickly put to work in the makeshift, whatever-it-takes style that characterized the early days of this fledgling business.

"They gave her an orange crate for a chair," wrote Walker, "rigged up an old typewriter and put her to work answering catalog requests, customer letters and invoicing."

Wes Walker, 1942

In its first year of operation, the Minot Tractor Supply Company Store did $125,000 in business. And taking a page out of Charles Schmidt's guide to hiring good people, Gard Abbott hired the local banker's son, Russ Zehringer.

Of the success of the early days, Schmidt said with classic understatement that "the only problem was filling the orders and taking the checks to the bank."

That first store. It was housed in a simple, makeshift building. Run by a Chicago lawyer who didn't know retail or farming. But for all of that, it sure struck a powerful chord with the farmers. Tractor Supply was off to a good start.

The key was finding more talent. Schmidt's Leterstone connection proved invaluable again with the hiring of Wes Walker.

HIRING THE CUSTOMER

Charles Schmidt first met Wes Walker back in 1932 while Schmidt was working for the Leterstone Company. Walker was the buyer in the venerable Montgomery Ward's automotive department and Schmidt sold him door handles for old cars.

"I knew Charlie in Chicago for about four years," said Wes Walker in an interview for an unpublished account of Charles Schmidt's life. "I left Montgomery Ward and went to Decatur,

Illinois, as general manager of an automotive chain. I was about twenty-seven. I was there about six months and he came down one day and said, 'I didn't come down to sell you anything. I came down to offer you a job.'

"That evening we went out with my wife and we had dinner, and he said, 'I'm going to open a store in Omaha and I would like you to be the manager.'"

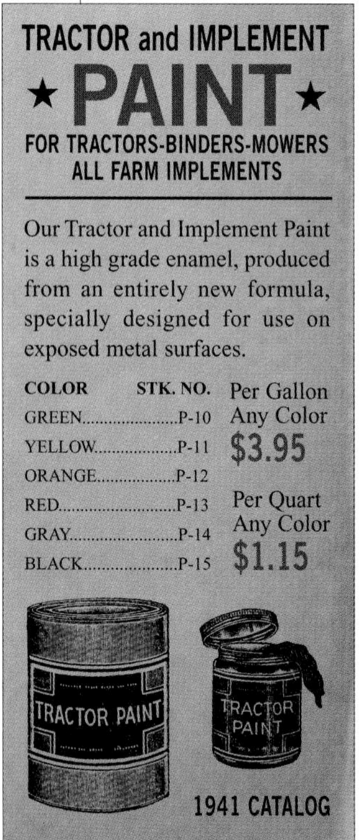

Schmidt must have been used to the scenario by now. Walker gave essentially the same excuse that Cleary and Abbott had earlier. He didn't know anything about tractors. Which was only partly true. Walker had grown up on a farm and went to Iowa State, an agricultural school.

Of course, Schmidt's answer to Walker was the same: "You'll learn."

That was in the summer of 1940. By November of that year, Walker was in Omaha to open Branch No. 4. Once again, Schmidt had successfully lured a man away from a good-paying job. In fact, Schmidt paid Walker $100 less a month than he was making at his previous job.

Walker wasn't the first person with farm experience that Tractor Supply hired to run one of its stores. That distinction goes to Carl Pietsch, who joined the company eight months prior to Walker's arrival. Pietsch went to Williston, North Dakota, to open Branch No. 3. Both the Williston and Omaha stores opened in the spring of 1941.

In a little more than a single year, the number of Tractor Supply stores had tripled, from one to three.

The company that was started on a dining room table now had a life of its own. It was thriving. Customers flocked to the store, sometimes even before the merchandise was unpacked. They really liked it, and they wanted more of it. And that's a retailer's biggest thrill.

The customers weren't the only ones to believe. The people who stood right beside you and worked hard believed as well.

This wasn't the last time that a leader with vision would rally a team to work harder than any of them had ever worked before in their lives. This wasn't the last time uncertainty would be replaced by amazing success. Remember this moment at Tractor Supply. History would repeat itself. Lightning would strike twice.

QUITE A COMPLEMENT

Schmidt had found a wonderful complement to himself. Where he was a big city boy, Walker had been raised on the farm. Where he was sometimes quiet and, perhaps, struck people as a little stiff, Walker was gregarious and easygoing. Where Charles Schmidt was controlled, Wes Walker was spontaneous.

"Walker was great. He was always very much a people person," said Max DeForest, who was mentored by Walker and eventually became a company executive. "Later, when we started having conventions and would bring together all of the store managers, Walker would be up half the night playing poker with the guys and they all loved him for it.

"Abbot didn't do that. He was a super guy – a gentleman's gentleman. And Charlie didn't do it. But Walker would."

What Schmidt and Walker shared was a passion for what they were doing, a great capacity for working hard and loving it.

"He [Walker] struck me as someone who was always as serious as a heart attack but with these periodic bursts of humor," remembered Richard Schmidt. "He had a tremendous laugh that came out of nowhere. He was the kind of person who would look at you with a completely straight face and then just burst out laughing."

Recalled DeForest, "He would pull things with his customers someone else might get in trouble for. Maybe he'd put an extra zero on a check and let them sign it. Then he'd tell them what they'd done. Instead of being shocked, they'd laugh.

"Everybody liked him. They trusted him."

Trust is an important commodity among small town people and folks who work the land. They have to trust you if they're going to trade with you. A broken combine during harvest time, a bearing that goes bad and leaves a tractor standing still in the field during spring planting, a part you've ordered from far off Chicago that comes back wrong – these are devastating for people trying to coax a living out of the land. Trust was not something to be taken lightly.

Another thing that inspired everyone's trust in Walker was the way he talked. He was pretty straightforward. He didn't pull any punches or, for that matter, throw any that didn't need throwing.

"I remember when I started there [at Tractor Supply]," said DeForest. "He kind of let it be known that nobody was going to tell you what to do. 'If you don't find something to do around here,' he said, 'we probably don't need you.' And he fired some people.

"It was kind of like he didn't want to look back and see you standing there waiting. You had to be out in front all the time.

"But he was good. And he was fun to work for."

He worked hard. Had fun. And he knew how to make money. Schmidt predicted Walker's Omaha store would do $100,000 that first year. It wound up doing $105,000. Chalk it up to Schmidt's eye for sizing up an opportunity and being right on the money. The extra $5,000 was Walker's way of doing more than what he was asked. Like Schmidt, Walker was driven.

CHARLES SCHMIDT RELAXES ON VACATION IN FLORIDA.

"Wes was always in a hurry," said DeForest. "I can still picture him with one leg curled down under him and his other foot flat on the floor – that was the way he drove. We'd go out across Nebraska to visit a store. In the winter, it was cold, and you'd freeze to death because his car had a gas heater that starved when you were driving down the road and only put out heat when you slowed down for a town. But, even so, Wes never stopped. He just kept going.

A VISIT TO PIONEER PRESS, THE PRINTERS OF THE TRACTOR SUPPLY CATALOG. IN THE FRONT ROW ARE JOHN PUGSLEY, GARD ABBOTT, LEON HANDKIN, AND WES WALKER.

"He covered a lot of territory."

To Charlie Schmidt it must have all been too good to be true – the people he'd assembled and the success of their hard work. But it was short-lived. A world war would put a stop to a lot of things.

A DREAM DEFERRED

The Japanese attack on Pearl Harbor, December 7, 1941, sent a shudder through America, a shudder that would resonate through every chamber of the heart and every facet of life.

The attack on Pearl Harbor galvanized the American people and solidified their resolve. Young men immediately swarmed recruiting offices around the country. Women, too shy to even mention their undergarments in public, were suddenly donating their rubber girdles to the war effort or painting seam lines down the backs of their legs since silk for stockings was needed for parachutes. Children canvassed their neighborhoods and collected scrap to be recycled and fashioned into war implements. Car plants rolled out tanks. Typewriter factories replaced the tapping of keys with the rat-a-tat-tat of machine guns in production. People rushed to buy war bonds. The men went to war and the women went to work.

SAVE ON SLEEVE SETS

RESTORE COMPRESSION AND POWER
STOP WASTING FUEL AND OIL

Matched Cylinder Sleeve Sets, assembled at the factory. All NEW Parts, made exactly to original specifications of improved materials as described on page 4. Assembly consists of 4 new cylinder sleeves with pistons matched, and complete with pins and rings, fitted, ready for installation.

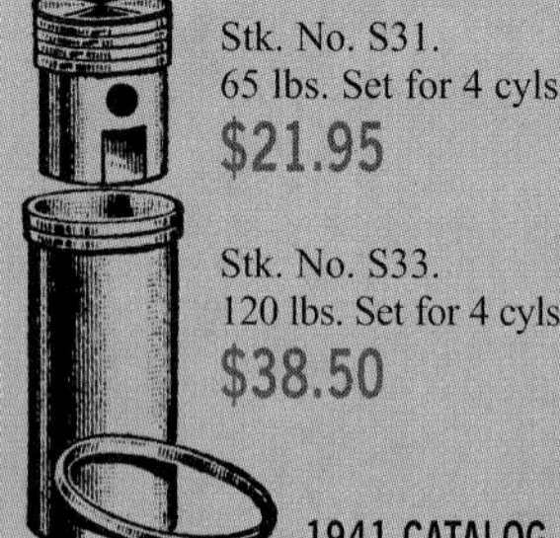

Stk. No. S31.
65 lbs. Set for 4 cyls
$21.95

Stk. No. S33.
120 lbs. Set for 4 cyls
$38.50

1941 CATALOG

In a three-year period, 12 million Americans left their homes to go to war while another 15.3 million Americans moved, many looking for jobs in a defense factory. Every citizen became part of a massive war effort. People put their plans on hold.

Nowhere was this truer than at Tractor Supply. The company that had grown so fast was now forced to put its plans for future growth and expansion on hold because of the war effort. Some of the company's employees left for the armed forces or war plant work. Gard Abbott enlisted in the army. He wouldn't return to Tractor Supply until 1946. Even more devastating was the loss of Bill Cleary, Schmidt's oldest and closest friend. Cleary left on December 31, 1941, and joined the army, too. But it may have been a conflict closer to home that caused him to leave. In a letter to Wes Walker just three days before Cleary's departure, Schmidt explained the reasons were "basically personal and, I fear, not entirely clear to each of us."

Schmidt clearly struggled with the loss, writing to Walker, "Coming as it does on top of the countless other hardships which confront us and everyone else trying to do business in today's hectic world, Bill's absence will create many problems. No one knows better than I how great has been his contribution to the success we have enjoyed in the past three years. To replace his efforts will be almost impossible but it will be necessary to try."

Two days later, another letter made its way to Walker. This time it was Cleary trying to explain the situation.

"It is with sincere regret that I find it necessary to resign from my position with the company," wrote Cleary. "I reached this decision after due deliberation over a sufficient period of time. I had hoped up to the last minute that the necessity of such a move could be averted. However when a stalemate is reached there are but two things one can do – either withdraw his opinion or his person.

"I have chosen the latter."

Cleary continued, "No useful objective would be obtained in attempting to set forth chronologically the events leading up to this point. For my part I am satisfied that the records show the existence of conflicting interests and opinions among the stockholders. Being in the minority I am left with but one honorable alternative."

PEARL HARBOR, HAWAII. A small boat rescues a seaman from the 31,800 ton USS West Virginia burning in the foreground. Smoke rolling out amidships shows where the most extensive damage occurred. Note the two men in the superstructure.

Library of Congress

The reasons for Cleary's resignation are unclear. Obviously, he and Schmidt had come to some serious disagreement, one that Bill Cleary, to his credit, never discussed outside his letter to Walker. It was a situation that, perhaps out of respect, people who were around then are still reluctant to discuss.

Cleary would leave the company and never come back to it. In his best friend's absence and the labor drain of a world at war, Schmidt would pick up the pieces as well as pick up the slack and just work that much harder.

"The war came, and it was rather drastic," Kay Walker said. "All our young people that were there [Tractor Supply] left.... We got a couple of men from I don't know where to work the shipping room. And Mr. Schmidt worked the shipping room. I know many a time he sat and put labels on. He'd pack the orders and haul them over to the post office.

"He worked very, very hard."

There were those who were critical of Schmidt, because he was still relatively young and didn't serve in the armed forces during World War II. The old neck injury that kept him from continuing his college football career probably kept him out of the action overseas, too. Had Schmidt never sustained his football injury would there have ever been a Tractor Supply? Perhaps not. According to Cleary, the football injury caused Schmidt to study business more seriously. It was also the football injury that kept him out of World War II. It's unlikely that Tractor Supply could have survived Schmidt's being called to war.

"He didn't serve in the military, and he was criticized by his friends," Richard Schmidt remembered.

"I know that he and Gard Abbott had words about his not being involved. But he had just gotten the company started and it was in its very critical early years. If he had not been there, the company would not have survived.

"He felt that it was very important the company survive and, as a farm supply store, that it continue to help the nation's farmers in their work to make material for the war effort."

The 1942 wartime catalog explains the company's policies and philosophies during the growing conflict overseas, reminding its customers that "Farmers everywhere are being urged to cooperate with the National Defense Program in repairing and using old equipment where possible to conserve materials urgently needed for emergency defense. We urge you to repair while adequate repair parts stocks are available."

It appears Schmidt was not above using the added "encouragement" of limited availability of parts to nudge his customers a bit and help bolster advance sales.

"All of our warehouses have been filled to capacity with Guaranteed New Repair Parts," the 1942 catalog copy continued, "to take care of the

We Never Stop Loving Our Toys The first toy farm equipment shows up in the Tractor Supply Blue Book in 1961. It was a clever way to plant a passion for the land in children, and besides that, it was a great seller. The toys have been back for some time, now. Of course, Tractor Supply has always had its share of nifty toys for adults, too. You're never too old or too young to have fun.

unprecedented demands the existing emergency will impose.

"It will pay you to think months ahead in planning repairs and buying needed repair parts now."

During World War II, Tractor Supply catalogs reflected what was going on in the country. The 1943 catalogs depict scenes from the home front. The spring catalog's cover art that year showed a man riding a tractor. He's waving to Army planes flying overhead in formation. In a nod to the women who filled the wartime workforce, the fall 1943 catalog showed a woman driving a tractor in the field.

Despite much of the original management team leaving the company during the war and despite the uncertainty of the times, Tractor Supply Company continued to grow. Merchandise was difficult to get. But the company proved that even in tough times – especially in tough times – Tractor Supply could maintain its strong performance.

This same dynamic holds true today.

"We look at difficult times as an opportunity," remarked Joe Scarlett. "So much of our merchandise is to help with repairs and fixes. People who work the land often need us more during difficult times to extend the life of a piece of equipment than they do when times are good."

A GOOD FEELING

Business success is rare. The bulk of new businesses fail. The U.S. Small Business Administration reports that only half of new businesses survive four years. Whether for lack of a good idea, good people, a good business model, a good business environment, or ample resources, most new ventures fail.

So when a business succeeds so completely and immediately as Tractor Supply succeeded in those early years, something remarkable has happened. In turn, something special imprints itself on the hearts and minds of the people who are a part of that singular success. There is a natural exhilaration, a sense that something wonderful is taking shape that makes all of the inherent hard work of launching a business more than worth it. There is the sense of commitment to something bigger than yourself and the reward of seeing that commitment pay off in terms of customer acceptance and financial reward. All of the hard work, the feeling of being part of a bunch of people thrown together to sink or swim, and the long hours working together create not only a successful business, but also happy and fulfilled people who will apply this energy to the next task at hand. Under trying and difficult circumstances, a special bond is formed. The people who started Tractor Supply simply describe it as "family."

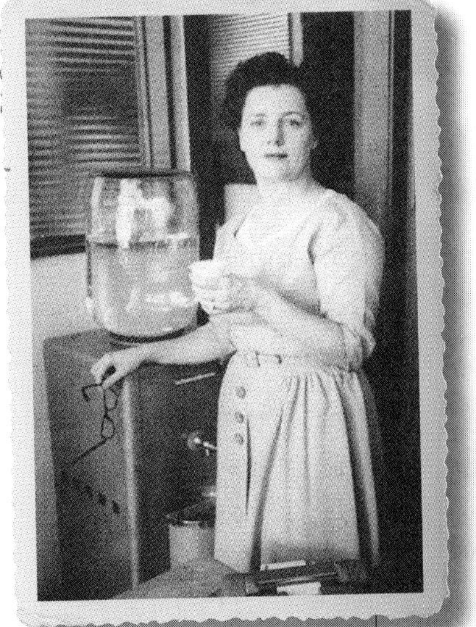

KAY GORECKI WALKER AT THE TRACTOR SUPPLY WATER COOLER. SHE WOULD STAND BESIDE THE COMPANY THROUGH GOOD AND BAD FOR FORTY YEARS.

"Even though it wasn't a great-paying job, it was a good feeling," Kay Gorecki Walker, Tractor Supply's first executive secretary, wistfully recalled as she thought back on the early days of the company when it was just a handful of people rattling around the Chicago offices and warehouse and just a few simple stores.

Kay Walker, then Kay Tracy, began working for Tractor Supply in 1941. Charles Schmidt was out of the office, and she was hired by Bill

Cleary at the company's first home at 1217 West Washington Boulevard. Walker's hire was one of those chance happenings that seem to determine the entire course of a life.

"I was downtown with my girlfriend and she applied for a job at an agency," said Walker. "I applied, too, and they gave me this slip of paper and I thought to myself, 'I'm not going there.'" But despite the dreary address scribbled on the piece of paper handed to Walker, she decided to apply.

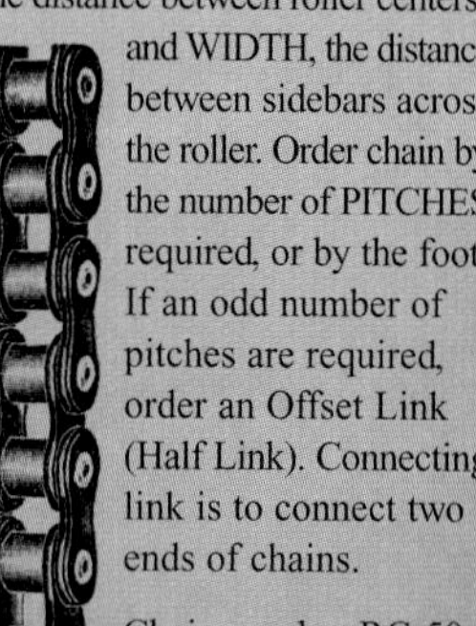

"I went in and I met Mr. Cleary. He didn't hire me right away, but he called me before I got home and said that I was hired," Walker said, shaking her head and amazed at the small turns of events that brought her to the company where she spent most of her life and made her dearest friends.

"I was hired at the huge salary of fifteen dollars a week plus fifteen cents for Social Security. And they didn't have a desk for me. We had a table and since I was short, I sat on telephone books to reach the table.

"So that was my beginning, and I thought it was only temporary because two weeks later I was in the hospital with an appendectomy. I thought surely I've lost the job, because at that time jobs were scarce. You didn't get a job like that," Walker said.

"But Mr. Cleary kept it open for me."

It was a simple kindness extended to a new employee that caught her attention and ultimately captured her heart. Sure, it was a small group of people, a shabby place, and lots of hard work. But there was a good-natured feeling of fun to the fledgling business, the people and the place that drew you in. Even though, like most offices of the day, business was conducted in a suit and tie, it was a place that had its playful moments and a group of people who knew how to have fun.

SHARING EVERYTHING

Kay Walker had worked at Tractor Supply three months before she met Charles Schmidt. When she did, his entry and manner were a little less grand than she might have expected.

"He came bustling in wearing a raccoon fur coat and looked just like he was out of college," said Walker, shaking her head still in disbelief more than half a century later.

"Well, he was very jubilant and happy to see everybody, grinning from ear to ear. His hat was on the back of his head and he had this fur coat on. And so I immediately stopped him and asked who he wanted to see.

"He looked at me and said, 'Young lady, I'm your boss!'

"So that was that. That was my first meeting with Mr. Schmidt."

It was a warm introduction to a man and company that Walker could only describe as family. In fact, Walker would later marry into the Tractor Supply family. But that's a story for much later.

"There're no other words to express what I felt for those people – just family," said Walker. "Mr. Schmidt sat across from Mr. Cleary and there was just one other girl and myself in the office. Naturally, we had coffee, and we would post your name on the calendar and you had to bring the sweet rolls that day. Neither Mr. Cleary nor Mr.

Schmidt was ever excused from bringing their share. And, well, it was a good feeling.

"If you had something happy in your life, it was happy in their lives. And if you had a problem, it was everybody's problem."

Walker had more than one occasion to see this unwritten company policy of caring for the individual exhibited in her own life. She only worked at Tractor Supply a short time before her husband enlisted in the service. She moved south with him but kept in contact with the company and even did some work for Mr. Schmidt, helping him in his ongoing refinement of the company's mailing list. While she was in Texas with her family, Walker looked up the names of farmers who owned tractors and lived in the surrounding counties and then sent the lists to Schmidt. He paid her for her work.

"It was more than I earned, I'm sure," said Walker.

In 1943, Walker's husband was killed in the war. Schmidt asked her to return to Chicago and work as his executive secretary. To prepare for the job, she went to secretarial school only to discover someone had already paid for her tuition.

The company's kindness wasn't limited to Kay Walker. Schmidt shared Tractor Supply's good fortunes with those who worked to make it possible. He set up a pension plan and profit-sharing and health care benefits for all of the employees.

"The profit-sharing was wonderful," said Kay Walker. "We didn't get it till the end of each year, but as long as I can remember, he gave us 10 percent of our annual salary. It was written so that he could give us as little as three percent and not more than 10 percent. But he always gave us 10 percent.

"So that was a big plus and those who left, left with money."

Calling every employee by name, whether they worked on the loading docks or in the front office, sharing the company's profits with everyone, taking an interest in the individual circumstances of individual's lives – all of these efforts contributed to the positive environment that, along with a good idea and good people, propelled Tractor Supply in its early years. They were part of the million and one things that contributed to what's been described by everyone from the president of the company to a warehouse worker as the company's "family feel."

JOHN SCHACK – WILLISTON MANAGER IN 1944

"His company back in the early years had a family-type environment," Richard Schmidt explained. "Not that there wasn't a very structured hierarchy of positions and an organizational chart as to who reported to whom. All those lines of communications were very clear. But everybody was part of the same family. When the company was doing well, everybody felt good about it and they felt like they contributed. When the company was having troubles, everybody felt that they could put in a little extra to try and each do his share to move the company along.

INTERIOR SHOT OF STORE RUN BY MAX DEFOREST IN 1949

"I think he [Charles Schmidt] had the ability to communicate to people that they weren't just employees, that they were part of a bigger company family and that their individual efforts were recognized and appreciated."

HANDWRITTEN NOTES

To show his appreciation to Wes Walker, whom he hired away from an automotive chain for $100 less a month, Schmidt made up the money with a bonus check at the end of the year. Over the years, others received personal notes with promotions and bonuses for a job well done. The money was quickly spent, but many of the employees kept those personal notes for the rest of their lives.

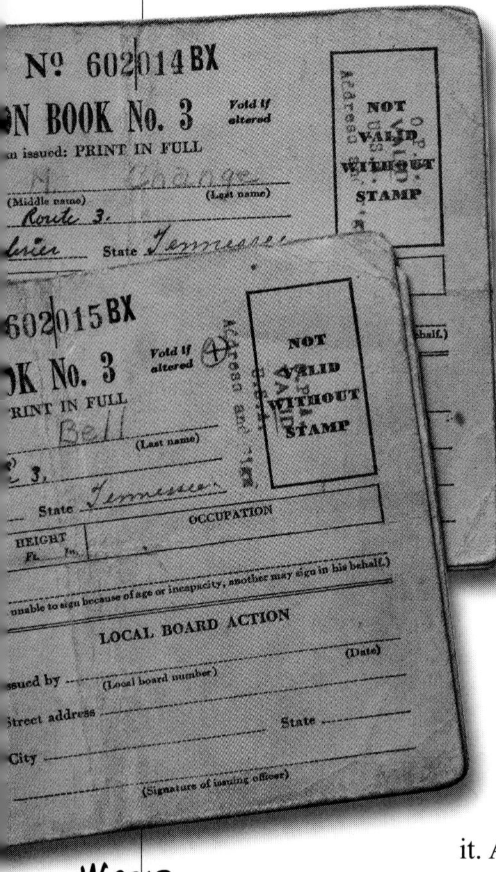

Max DeForest, a World War II hero who fought in the Battle of the Bulge and then came to work for Tractor Supply when he returned home, kept a letter from Schmidt more than fifty years after he first received it. And fifty years later, when he reads the yellowed and tattered letter out loud, he can't help but fight back tears.

WORLD WAR II RATION BOOKS

"Dear Max," the letter from Schmidt began. "As our fiscal year draws to a close it is apparent that the hard work of all of us and good luck combined to make this one of the best years ever experienced. We won't know the final outcome until our accountants have pored over the figures for many weeks, but the results cannot be anything other than good.

"You probably noted the check enclosed which I hasten to say is a special goodwill offering on the part of your company, tendered as an expression of appreciation of hard work and skillful planning which you contributed to make 1953 so good.

"In determining the amount of your check, I figured roughly that it represented something like $25 a month extra for each of the 12 months just passed, plus an advance payment of $25 a month for each of the coming 12 months. Sort of retroactive pay raise, in effect, plus a paid-in-advance raise for the coming year.

"Good luck with it, and nurse it along."

Schmidt used money to motivate. But he never viewed money as the goal of business, it was the tool to reaching the goal. He used the money as a tool to motivate and reward the hard-working people who were so critical to making his kitchen table reverie a reality. Bonuses, profit sharing, setting aside pension funds were all important elements in keeping the company's drive going, its employees motivated – the third ingredient of the unspoken recipe of working hard, having fun, and making money. But as important as spreading the wealth was, we cannot overlook the significance of the personal gestures, letters, and notes that accompanied the checks. There was a bond here beyond money – a family tie.

"During the war when so many things were rationed, Mr. Schmidt always made sure I had gas in my car," Kay Walker remembered. "And I had plenty of shoes, so I gave him my ration book for shoes. He had two young, growing boys, and I imagined he and Mrs. Schmidt had a hard time keeping them in shoes."

Simple gestures of caring made a business feel like a family.

Growing up, the natural bonds of Schmidt's biological family had been severed over financial disputes surrounding his grandfather's will. Perhaps in reaction to this, Schmidt created a company family and worked hard to make sure that the resources united rather than divided.

"In every sense of the word, it was a family company," said Richard Schmidt. "My father recognized the difficulty he experienced as a child growing up in a family feuding over his grandfather's assets and, in the end, losing everything. This was something that motivated him. He never made a decision that put a son at odds with a son or any family member. He said you always have to take everything and everyone into consideration, think through a problem.

"I think that's also how he approached his business. His management style was one of the things that really separated him from the rest. He didn't just make a decision and say we're going to do A versus B. He would think in terms of what decision A would mean to the next series of decisions. Sometimes you end up getting surprised when you're making a decision and don't think all the way through the problem to determine the effect, how one decision changes the whole environment you're working in, and how that affects the next decision you have to make.

"He kept thinking you can always make it better. In a business family sense, he was always concerned that everything he did would not put people in a stressful position."

TRICKLE DOWN TRUST

Schmidt's management style would create amazing loyalty. Along with sharing the company's successes, Schmidt encouraged individual initiative. Once he had good people in place, he let them work and make their own decisions without second-guessing them. He trusted them. Trust is not just a founding principle at Tractor Supply, it's a foundation principle – a principle that's trickled down from the top and taken hold at every level. It was nurtured among customers who saw the folks in the store doing whatever it took to serve them. And it still crops up as an important draw for the company today. An attitudinal survey done by Tractor Supply in 2002 showed customers responding in overwhelming numbers that "Tractor Supply is a store we can trust."

Trust was earned because trust was given, beginning with the man who began the company.

"If he hired someone and they made a decision, he would stand behind it and back them up," Richard Schmidt said. "He was fiercely loyal to his people. He always felt that if there was a problem with the actual decision someone else made, he would deal with that person one-on-one later. In public, he would stand behind the person.

"This gave the people who worked with him tremendous courage to make bold decisions when they needed to, because they knew they weren't gonna be Monday morning quarterbacked or criticized for the decisions after-the-fact by their boss."

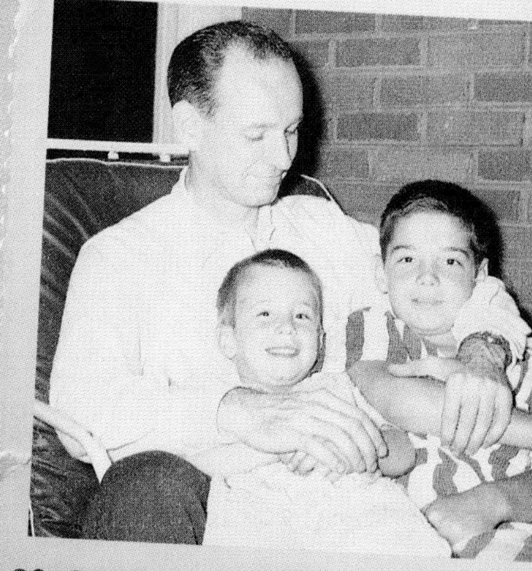

CHARLES SCHMIDT WITH HIS TWO BOYS, RICHARD AND CHUCK JR., 1945

It was the perfect management style to lure the independent-minded people who'd left the farm to go to war and would soon return home at the close of the conflict. They'd seen a lot overseas: friends dying on a foreign battlefield, Hitler's unspeakable brutality, the frightening intensity of the Japanese soldiers in the South Pacific. After all they'd been through, after all they'd done, after all they'd witnessed in defending the cause of democracy, they would look for a place where they were empowered and trusted to dedicate themselves with the same sense of urgency and sacrifice.

And Tractor Supply Company was ready for them.

"LET'S TAKE ALL THE FARM BOYS"

Although it only added one new store during the war years, and despite the rationing of critical materials such as metal and rubber and the lack of a readily available labor force, Tractor Supply continued to prosper during World War II. In fact, the austerity of farmers and folks on the home front may have solidified the company's early development.

Equipment manufacturers who were too busy fulfilling defense contracts were limited in what they could produce and sell to the agricultural market. Any new model changes to tractors were minimal. There wasn't a big market for new equipment anyway, since many of the country's farmers were content to patch up existing equipment and make do until the war was over. Obviously, repair and replacement parts would be in demand and the already frugal farmer would be even more price-conscious given the international state of affairs. Tractor Supply was perfectly poised to take advantage of the opportunity.

First Minot store front

In a Chicago newspaper interview with Charles Schmidt in 1964, he described business during the war years as so good that "nothing we could do could hurt us."

After the war, Charles Schmidt greeted the returning farm boys with a job. It didn't matter that they didn't know a thing about running a retail operation. They understood the merchandise and they knew the customer and they'd managed to get home safely.

According to Wes Walker, "After World War II, Charlie said, 'Let's take all of the farm boys.' I was in Omaha, Nebraska, after I opened up the store and always had three or four extra [farm boys] working there, running the business. When we opened a store, I sent one out."

The returning farm boys proved good hires and one, Max DeForest, proved exemplary.

HE DIDN'T KNOW WHAT HE COULDN'T DO

Max DeForest was born and raised on the farm not far from Omaha in southwestern Iowa. He had a deferment because he lived and worked on a farm and the food and fiber farming produced were critical to the country's war effort, but DeForest opted to enlist.

"When I was finishing high school, World War II come on and I was very determined to be a part of that," explained DeForest. "I didn't have to, of course. I had an automatic deferment because of the farm. I had a brother younger than myself, and I took the deferment until he was about ready to graduate. I went to the Draft Board and said, 'I'm ready to go.' I ended up in Europe. Landed over there during the Battle of the Bulge and had a lot of experiences. I come out of it well.

Max DeForest (right) is decorated for valor April 1945. A year and a half later DeForest would embark on a career that would make him a hero at Tractor Supply.

“I did get hit a couple times. The last time took me out for about five weeks. Who knows – it may have saved my life.

“Everything in life can wind up a blessing.”

DeForest, like Schmidt, was blessed. He was blessed with a marvelous ignorance – he didn’t know what he couldn’t do.

“I can’t believe how young I was when I did different things,” DeForest said. “I think all my life I thought I could do anything. My dad thought I could, too, because he just let me go.”

FARM AIR COMPRESSOR

DRIVES FROM ANY 1/4 H.P. ELECTRIC MOTOR

This is not a toy but a small, dependable compressor for intermittent farm use where a reliable power air supply is needed. The unit is light and portable, yet ruggedly built for trouble free service and will operate for hundreds of hours without upkeep expense.

SHIPPED IMMEDIATELY FROM STOCK IN ALL BRANCHES

1946 CATALOG

DeForest talks around it. What he isn’t telling you is that he became a hero during World War II. For that story, you have to look in a regimental newspaper written during the time.

“Nobody likes combat, least of all the men who do the fighting and dying. Bravery and unconquerable spirit add a certain nobility to an otherwise terrible business,” the military reporter recorded.

“Take the case of Max DeForest of Company F. Moving across an open field, the first scout, he spotted a tank and a machine gun nest. DeForest fired a grenade from his M1, which burst directly over the nest and silenced the crew. Despite the fact he had been wounded, he refused to be evacuated and joined the company in the attack on Hill 305. When the battalion pulled back that night to reorganize, he went to the aid station only after direct order from his company commander.”

When asked about it, DeForest tried to explain in his understated way, saying he just did what he had to do.

“I spotted the tank and the tank spotted me,” DeForest simply said. “I didn’t give up. I wasn’t hurt bad.”

Tractor Supply’s formative years as a company, the early ’40s, were an extraordinary time in our country’s history. America’s “Greatest Generation” made the supreme sacrifice to free a world threatened by dictators and despots. It was a generation that did whatever it took, both on the war front and on the home front. America’s personal sacrifice, hard work, and undying determination made the difference. And American ingenuity overcame insurmountable enemies. It was an experience that contributed to the culture of a country and a company called Tractor Supply. This was a generation that didn’t know what it couldn’t do. And there’s nothing more empowering.

When the farm boys who were soldiers came home, they came back to work instilled with a sense that anything was possible. Presented with the right vision, they would do whatever it took to see it succeed. As long as they were given a fair shot at getting ahead, they’d work hard and find a special joy in the doing.

Many exemplified this spirit, perhaps none better than Max DeForest.

“I came back home in December of ’45,” said DeForest. “At that time the Omaha stockyards were king of that area. The commission men who worked there seemed to do very well…so I went to work for a livestock commission firm. It wasn’t too long before I told my wife that the only way you get ahead in these outfits is you’ve got to marry the right guy’s daughter. And I’m already married. So, I’d just as well leave.”

"WE'RE NOT NEAR AS SMART AS YOU THINK"

Near the Omaha stockyards where DeForest worked was Tractor Supply Branch No. 4, the store that Wes Walker had opened for Charles Schmidt in 1941.Catalogs weren't the only thing Tractor Supply targeted to the customers. Charles Schmidt also used his "rifle" approach to locate his stores near where his customers congregated. Places like the stockyards.

DeForest left the stockyards and came to work at Tractor Supply. Wes Walker hired him. DeForest was just twenty-three years old and he appreciated the trust the company showed in him.

"I don't think I'd worked there more than a few months and I was carrying a key to the store. Something you wouldn't think about doing today," said DeForest. "There were several of us working there that seemed to have a lot of old-fashioned ambition. Maybe a truckload of merchandise would hit the dock late in the day and two or three of us would get together and say, 'What are you doing tonight after supper' and then 'Let's go down and put that stuff away.'

"We'd go back down to the store, and the boss would come in the next day and it was gone." DeForest worked at the Omaha store for two years.

"During that two years, I did a lot of things," DeForest remembered, shaking his head with a smile. "I was a jack-of-all-trades. In fact, I've looked back and I'm amazed at some of the things they expected me to do or trusted me to do. Twenty-three is pretty young.

"We sold over-the-counter merchandise, but we did a lot of mail-order work in between customers. Whatever work there was to be done, that's what you did."

It was hard work and it wasn't for everyone.

"I remember one time I overheard Wes Walker talking to some guy that was a little disenchanted and he said, 'Hey, nobody around here calls you dear.'

"He was blunt like that, but he was also very fair."

The hard work wasn't for everyone, but for those who enjoyed hard work, Tractor Supply proved a whole lot of fun and profit. DeForest's hard work and initiative were rewarded. Two years later, in 1948, he was asked to open the store in

OUTSIDE THE STERLING, ILLINOIS, BRANCH IN JANUARY 1949

MAX DEFOREST OPENS THE OMAHA BRANCH IN 1965 WITH A WHITE HAT AND A RADIO BROADCAST.

Sterling, Illinois. Again, DeForest was impressed by the company's trust and inspired by it.

"Went there in December of '48 and got the store opened in January of 1949," explained DeForest.

"What I can't believe, when they sent me in there, they just turned me loose."

Nearly sixty years have passed, and this man who would later be a beloved TSC vice president of operations still shakes his head in disbelief and wonders what it was that inspired the company's trust. Much the same way that he describes his

MAX DEFOREST (LEFT) AT A STORE OPENING IN 1965

heroic act in World War II as "I spotted the tank and the tank spotted me." The hard work and initiative that DeForest took for granted, Tractor Supply didn't.

"I only had a high school education," explained DeForest. "A country boy that went into war and came back.

"After I got into Chicago, finally, I was in the home office. I was very much aware that I was the only one at that level who was not educated. There were all types of degrees there. It bothered me.

"So one day, Charlie had me in his office," Max recalled, "kind of quizzing me and feeling me out about my goals. I was making pretty conservative comments when he leans over the desk and looks me in the eye.

"'Max,' he said, 'Why don't you reach for the top? It's not crowded up here and we're not near as smart as you think we are.'

"I thought, what a classic statement. And, well, I did finally wind up an executive."

DeForest didn't just "wind up" an executive. He worked his way up.

Richard Schmidt would have the same high opinion of DeForest's work ethic, from the opposite end of the food chain. The younger Schmidt worked for him in the Chicago warehouse.

"Max was just down to earth," said Richard Schmidt. "He wouldn't fit the corporate mold that you'd think of today of a senior corporate officer. Max used to roll up his sleeves and do the work. In fact, I used to joke with Max as he was showing me how to build some shelving for the warehouse that required using some relatively heavy iron cutters and things like that. He'd roll up his sleeves and kind of do a bit of the work himself as he showed you what to do. And you'd say, 'Well, I'm not really sure how you bent that corner piece there. Could you show me again?'

"If you baited him long enough, he'd have half of your job for the day done before he turned it over to you."

"I LIKED TO SELL"

DeForest's work ethic was complemented by a good dose of ingenuity.

"Before Sterling was opened, Tractor Supply rented little buildings, very inexpensive, but they had a brand new building built there," said DeForest. "It was the first. Looking back, it was so small – 50-by-54.

"I set identification letting people know what everything was and I did some things to merchandise. For example, I would never throw a box away if I could save it, because it made it look like I had more merchandise. If I had one of something, I'd put it out, but I'd keep the box sitting up there to try and impress people with inventory that I didn't really have," DeForest said with a chuckle. "Little things like that.

"If I had a good volume item, if I had a stack of them, maybe I'd move half of it to the back room one day and let it go for awhile like I'd sold them down. Then I'd move it back to show activity. I liked to sell. I got along good with customers. I remembered their names well and had a lot of fun with them. It was a lot of fun."

Making his store look full. Moving inventory. Keeping things fresh and alive. The buzz of activity in the small store. Remembering customers' names. What DeForest called "the little things" and innately seemed to understand, although not revolutionary concepts, required work, attention to detail, diligence, and care to execute properly.

Again, after so many years, more than anything else – even though he would receive financial incentives and promotions and greater responsibility – it is the personal gesture, a simple appreciative note that DeForest fondly points to as the response to his work.

"I got a copy of a letter – I wasn't supposed to get it, but they sneaked a copy to me," said DeForest. "It was a letter from Charlie written to my former boss, a guy by the name of Bill Beal. He'd written to him about how beautiful my store was. He said it was the prettiest thing he'd ever seen, even better than the new International Harvester dealers.

"I've still got that letter."

Did Schmidt just happen to let DeForest see this letter? Maybe. But this wasn't the first time a letter had found its way into the "wrong" hands to be used as a powerful means of motivation.

"We had a store manager who felt overlooked and was always asking for help," recalled DeForest with a chuckle. "I was sort of at the opposite end of things. They'd tell me, 'Max, you've gotta get some more help. You can't keep up with that.' We'd send in weekly reports. Well, one time I'd had a heck of a good week and Wes Walker supposedly sent my weekly report back to me with a note telling me I was doing great with only the small staff I had and I needed to add somebody.

"Well, it was mistakenly mailed to this store manager who was always complaining and it kind of embarrassed the guy."

How did Max manage to motivate his staff even though he was always short a person?

"I don't know," DeForest said with wide-eyed frankness. "I've talked to some of the old timers. There was a magic there. We would just do anything. When I was getting the Sterling store ready to open, I was there over Christmas. Whatever it took to get it done, you did it.

"I can't really think of anything that was outstanding. I got a lot of production out of people because it was fun. I'd tell 'em, 'Yeah, when the customer's all through buying something, then go ahead and sell them something else,'" DeForest chuckled.

GARD ABBOTT AND MAX DEFOREST

THIS CERTIFICATE IS TRANS
GOODBODY & CO
FIFTEEN
SUPPLY
SSABLE CLASS
BLUE
VALUE

CHAPTER ★4★

HONEST MERCHANDISE

STOREFRONTS —WITHOUT FACADES— GENUINE PARTS —WITHOUT THE— BALLYHOO

"FARMING LOOKS MIGHTY EASY
WHEN YOUR PLOW IS A PENCIL,
AND YOU'RE A THOUSAND MILES
FROM THE CORNFIELD."

- PRESIDENT DWIGHT D. EISENHOWER

THE FARMER'S FRIEND

On workbenches and farmhouse tables, Tractor Supply Co. catalogs and Blue Books sat patiently, waiting to help a customer with a project that needed doing or a tractor that needed fixing. Speedy service and a ready inventory during times of crisis helped build Tractor Supply's reputation among its many loyal customers.

MISSING FROM THE LIBRARY OF CONGRESS Tractor Supply's early stores were small, one-story, already existing structures. They weren't very sophisticated retail operations, even by the standards of the day. After all, the company was founded as a mail-order business by a man who never set foot on a farm and never ran a retail business. The stores weren't run by retailers. After the war, they were run by customers who had been hired.

A company could do far worse than have its customers run it. In fact the only true retailer in the original bunch of Tractor Supply executives was Wes Walker. And he understood the importance of the customer. Walker grew up in the Montgomery Ward way of doing business and the old retail adage that the customer is always right.

"We treated our customers right, too," said Walker. "If they had a complaint, we fixed it. Didn't argue with them. It's the Ward philosophy. That's probably where we got most of it."

In the company's second catalog, the 1940 edition, the small print on the first page states plainly "Any unsatisfactory item will be exchanged promptly." By 1941, this plainspoken promise was expanded into a full-fledge guarantee deserving a full paragraph of copy on page 3 of the catalog:

"We guarantee every item we sell. Any part, which does not pass your most critical inspection, may be returned for a full cash refund.... We are proud that many thousands of tractor owners favor us with the opportunity of serving them, not just once, but many times, as their needs arise. This repeat business is adequate proof of our slogan, 'You Save When You Buy From Tractor Supply,' not only on the initial cost but in the steady, trouble-free service which our merchandise gives.

Satisfaction Guaranteed
Two promises have always been a part of Tractor Supply – value and satisfaction. The 1940 catalog is a perfect illustration of this. The cover proclaims – "You Save When You Buy from Tractor Supply" while on the very first page, it plainly states "Any unsatisfactory item will be exchanged promptly."

"Check among your neighbors – You will undoubtedly find many who deal with us. They'll gladly tell you how reliable they have found us."

To prove the point, this third edition of the Tractor Supply catalog was laced with customer photographs and testimonials. The salt-of-the-earth accolades run the gamut from "well satisfied" to "very satisfactory" and came from impressive agricultural hot spots such as Gordon, Nebraska, and Velva, North Dakota.

"I am glad to tell you," Mr. Warren R. Donner, farmer, is recorded in the 1941 catalog as saying, "that your reputation for fair dealing is well known to every farmer in this part of the country."

By 1942, the catalog christened itself "The Home of Friendly Service" and by 1949 it noted

"Our Famous Service" and "Our Reputation For Fair Dealing" and proclaimed "Over 100,000 Repeat Customers."

The early catalogs are a fascinating testament to the company's fortunes and business philosophy. For the "Sears of farm supply," a million insights into the company's development can be harvested from the now tattered and yellowing pages of the Tractor Supply catalog.

First, not many copies of the earliest Tractor Supply catalogs exist. There weren't many copies of this slender little volume printed. The Library of Congress – the great repository of every published item ever produced in the United States – does not have a copy of a Tractor Supply catalog. But early customers do. They held on to them. Originally, for purely practical reasons – they wanted a Tractor Supply catalog on hand should a piece of equipment break down.

Mac McKittrick and Charles Schmidt outside the company's offices.

Second, we see the emergence of the company color scheme. As early as 1940, the catalog was printed in two colors – black and red. The red was a bright and brilliant barn red used as an accent color in the catalogs. It's appropriate that the company's current red comes from its catalog beginnings.

The company's early attempts at marketing slogans are recorded in the catalog. The 1940 catalog cover shows a farmer on a tractor, proclaiming to the world that, "You Save When You Buy from Tractor Supply!" This is the first record of this concise catch phrase that the company would rely on as the finest distillation of its retail message for the first thirty years. The 1941 catalog would repeat this slogan ten times within its forty pages, including emblazoning it in bold type on both the front and back covers.

Other slogans would crop up from time to time – "The Best Costs You Less at Tractor Supply" poetically stated the company's stance and fed the farmers' very real fear that perhaps they were just paying for a brand name when they returned to the original manufacturer for replacement parts. The slogan "The Symbol of Savings to Modern Farmers Across the Nation" first showed up in the 1960 Blue Book alongside the words Tractor Supply Co. reversed out of the company's trademark four-sided shape.

For the most part, the catalogs are all about selling and not about marketing. There is a very practical and utilitarian feel to the early two-color communications, illustrated with their crisp, antiquated line engravings of bearings and pistons and gaskets. There seems to be no consistent logo for the company. Not even a consistent logo type, just type. Mostly a heavy almost athletic block type, but not always. It's not until the 1953 Blue Book that the words Tractor Supply Co. appear reversed out of the now familiar four-sided company mark printed in red. That figure is called a trapezium and was created for the company by Tractor Supply engineer Mac McKittrick.

TRACTOR SUPPLY CO.

The use of the company's complete name reversed out of the trapezium appears fairly consistently on the front page of catalogs and Blue Books until 1967. In 1967, the name Tractor Supply is dropped from the trapezium and is replaced with "TSC Stores," reflecting the corporation's attempt to distance itself from its farm equipment roots.

YOU SAVE WHEN YOU BUY FROM TRACTOR SUPPLY!

YOUR ORDER SHIPPED THE SAME DAY RECEIVED

or Your Money Refunded by Return Mail!

WE PAY THE FREIGHT

ON $25.00 SHIPMENTS. SEE PAGE 2

TRACTOR SUPPLY CO.

1217-27 WASHINGTON BLVD.
CHICAGO, ILL.

509 3rd STREET N. E.
MINOT, N. DAK.

$6.95
COMPLETE
With 3 Foot Stack
Stk. No. AC19 28lbs.

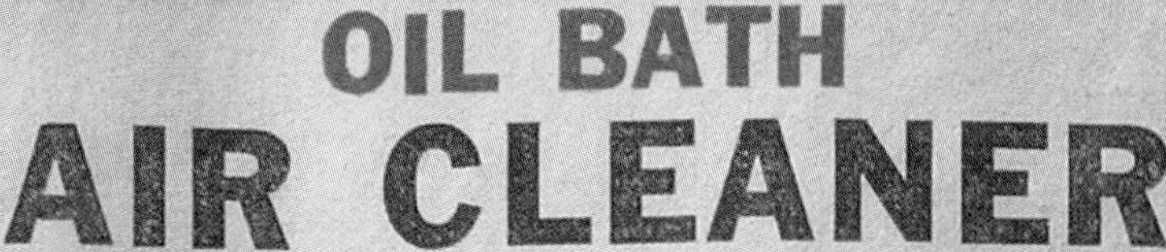

OIL BATH AIR CLEANER

FOR CARS . . . TRACTORS . . . TRUCKS COMBINES . . . POWER UNITS, ETC.

Don't Miss This Opportunity to Protect All Your Engines Against Dust and Dirt!

HUNDREDS ALREADY IN USE:

On Popular Tractors such as Deere "D" and "GP," Hart-Parr, McCormick-Deering 10-20, 15-30, and Farmall, Twin City, Allis Chalmers, Case, Wallis, Fordson and others.

Ideal for Installation on Combines, Threshers, Trucks and Cars

The many advantages of an OIL BATH Air Cleaner are apparent to All. Almost without exception, new farm machinery is equipped at the factory with this equipment since the money saving feature of removing dust, dirt, straw and other impurities from the internal engine parts have been proven conclusively. Take advantage of this lucky purchase to modernize and protect all older engines.

UNCONDITIONALLY GUARANTEED!

This late type air cleaner, the same as used on original equipment by a leading tractor and truck manufacturer, strains the air through a maze of copper screening and forces it through the oil reservoir where all dust and dirt particles are trapped and settle to the bottom. It is unconditionally guaranteed to remove all harmful abrasives from the air intake on any motor on which it is installed. There are no moving parts, nothing to wear or get out of order. Install one now—Check the oil reservoir after a week or two and see how much damaging material has been kept from your engine. IF YOU ARE NOT SATISFIED WITH YOUR PURCHASE, YOU MAY RETURN IT FOR A FULL CASH REFUND.

INSTALLATION AND SPECIFICATIONS

We have equipped these cleaners with universal mounting brackets, easily attached to the block, cowl, fender, or any flat surface. Side bracket has holes adjustable from 4 to 6½ inches apart. Air outlet is 2 inches in diameter. Mount the cleaner in any convenient place on your tractor, connect the air outlet to the carburetor air intake with 2" flexible tubing, such as ordinary radiator hose. Cleaner with brackets is 17¾" high overall, 8½" maximum width. The stack on number AC19 is 3 feet high.

Stock Number AC19
Cleaner with stack and brackets as shown at left. 28 lbs. **$6.95**

Stock Number AC20
Stack only, for use only with AC18 cleaner. 8 lbs. **$2.45**

Stock Number AC18
Cleaner without stack as shown at right. 20 lbs. **$4.95**

$4.95
COMPLETE
Without Stack
Stk. No. AC18 20 lbs.

OIL FILTER

Replaceable Cartridge Type . . . Keeps Oil Pure and Bright

$4.85
Complete

One of the greatest abuses of a motor is dirty oil. Oil, if cleaned and kept free of particles of dirt, carbon, and metal, which accumulate in the crankcase would remain useful for many times its ordinary life.

This filter has the new "Magic Stone" filtering element which removes all foreign matter down to 4/10,000ths of an inch. Every minute microscopic particle of abrasive material is removed and kept from the engine. The oil is also clarified and kept free of discoloration, so that it remains bright and clean. While we do not believe that any filter will keep oil in proper lubricating condition indefinitely, we know that this filter will prolong the useful life of your oil from two to four times. This means that you have to drain and refill your crankcase only one-half to one-fourth as often. The cartridges are inexpensive, and should be renewed periodically. It is impossible to state how frequently replacement should be made since operating conditions vary so greatly; we have found 100 to 200 hours to be the best average. Replacement is recommended when the oil begins to darken in color.

For real economy of operation and much better lubrication with resultant longer engine life, we recommend that you install one of these filters on your engine and use our "Lucky Penn" motor oil shown on page 13 opposite. Your lubrication costs will be cut to an unbelievably small fraction of what you pay now.

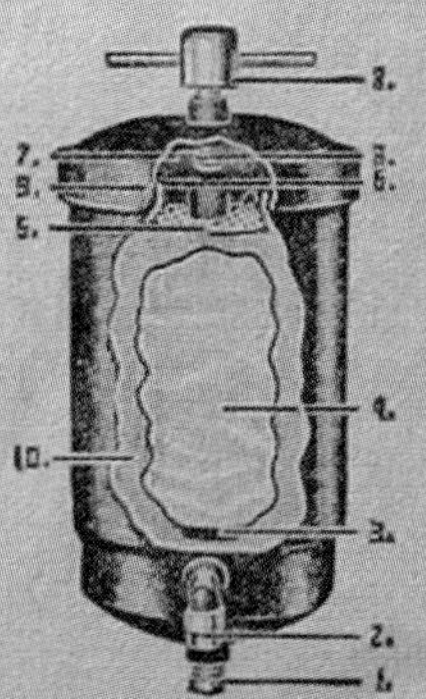

1—Drain
2—Inlet
3—Stone
4—Clarifier
5—Outlet
6—Seal Plate
7—Air Chamber
8—Set Screw
9—Seal Lugs
10—Cartridge

Filters are supplied with all necessary fittings, but are less copper tubing. Specify make and model of tractor, car, truck or machine when ordering.

Stk. No. 19B28—Filter for Tractors, Cars and Trucks with crankcase capacity 5 to 8 quarts. Will operate satisfactorily on larger motors, but cartridge must be changed more frequently. 9 lbs. EACH **$4.85**

Stk. No. 19B48—Filter for engines with crankcase capacity over 7 quarts. 11 lbs. EACH **$5.95**

Stk. No. 19B29—Extra Cartridge for 19B28 filter. 2 lbs. **59c**

Stk. No. 19B49—Extra Cartridge for 19B48 filter. 2½ lbs. **75c**

Stk. No. 19B30—¼" Copper Tubing for installing Filter. Sold by the foot. Specify length 4 oz. PER FOOT **4½c**

SPARK PLUG TIRE PUMP

CLEAN, FRESH AIR HIGH PRESSURE

Fits Any Spark Plug on Tractor—Car—Truck

Saves Hours of Back-Breaking Hand Pumping—

LET YOUR MOTOR DO THE WORK.

Complete Outfit, as pictured at right. Consists of pump unit, heavy rubber hose, complete set of adaptors for 14 MM, 18 MM, ½" and ⅞" spark plug holes so that you can use your pump on your tractor, truck or car. Packed in durable case, everything complete. De Luxe type has 16 ft. hose and accurate pressure gauge. Standard type has 12 ft. hose and is without gauge.

If you have ever pumped up by hand a tractor or truck tire you can appreciate the big saving in time and hard work this pump offers. Simply remove any spark plug, insert the pump bushing, connect the hose to the tire, and run the motor at a medium idling speed. The pump does the rest. A fast flow of clean, fresh air is forced into the tire, building up to the desired pressure in a very few minutes. The air pumped in contains no gas or fumes and is guaranteed not to injure the tube.

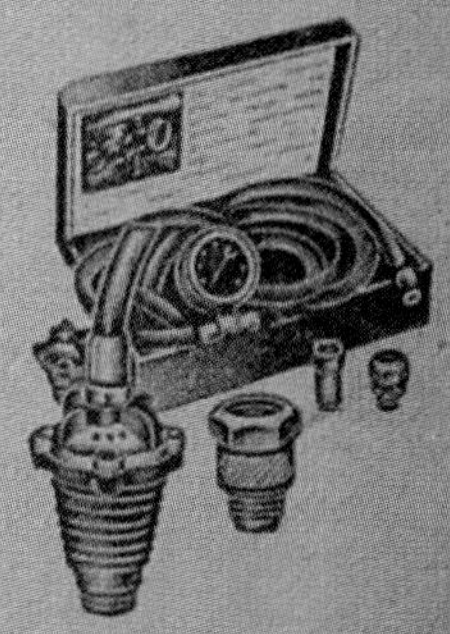

Stk. No. 19B14—DeLuxe Pump Kit, pump unit, all adaptors for any size plug, 16 ft. hose and Calibrated Pressure Gauge. Shipping weight 3½ lbs. **$3.25**

Stk. No. 19B15—Standard Pump Kit, pump unit, all adaptors but no gauge. Shipping weight 3 lbs. **$2.19**

Save on MOTOR OIL

BUY BETTER LUBRICATION FOR LESS MONEY

LUCKY PENN

100% PURE PENNSYLVANIA

The Finest Premium Oil in the World
Every Can Bears This Emblem:

63c gallon
in 15 gal. lots
4c Fed. Tax Included

2 Gallon Sealed Tin.
Stk. No. PO2. 17 lbs. . . . **$1.49**

5 Gallons, in Heavy Kerosene Can pictured at right.
Stk. No. PO5 47 lbs. **$3.79**

15 Gallons, in Steel Drum.
Stk. No. PO15. 135 lbs. . . . **$9.45**

($1.50 deposit required on drum)

Specify whether S.A.E. 30, 40 or 50 wanted

For Your Protection, Buy Oil in Refinery Sealed Cans

Be sure you get the quality and grade you pay for. Our oils are sold only in sealed containers, sealed at the refinery immediately after filling to protect you against dust or dirt entering the cans. Also, only in refinery sealed cans are you sure you get your money's worth, without substitution, adulteration, or mixing.

The cheapest way to buy oil is to take the 15 gallon drum size, on our exchange plan. With your initial purchase you pay $1.50 deposit on the drum. When the drum is returned your deposit will be refunded in full, or it may be applied against the purchase of a second drum. Your oil costs you much less, and shipping charges are small. If you drop in to our warehouses, in Chicago or Minot, take a drum home with you. Buy your oil this clean, easy, way, in reasonable quantities, as you need it. All prices include Federal Tax of 4c, a gallon, state sales tax extra.
We carry a full stock at all times of S.A.E. weights 30, 40, and 50.

FREE KEROSENE CAN

All 5 gallon oil shipments are packed in this extra heavy pour can, invaluable around a farm. Unusually heavy construction, reinforced at edges and seams. Easily worth $1 at any store.

EXCELOYL

From Fine Mid-Continent Crudes—The Equal of 20c-25c Quart Oils.

45c GALLON
In 15 gal. lots.
4c Fed. Tax Inc.

2 Gallon Sealed Tin.
Stk. No. EO22. 17 lbs. **98c**

5 Gallons, in Heavy Kerosene Can pictured at left.
Stk. No. EO55. 47 lbs. **$2.75**

15 Gallons, in Steel Drum.
Stk. No. EO155. 135 lbs. . . **$6.75**

($1.50 deposit required on drum).

WE CANNOT PAY FREIGHT ON OIL SHIPMENTS

We are sorry that we cannot include oil in our freight prepayment plan. However, shipping charges via freight are quite low. For example, 100 lbs. of oil can be shipped via freight about 200 miles for as low as 60c.

GREASE

Guaranteed Finest Quality, Heavy Bodied Grease, free of impurities "All Purpose"

Heavy bodied, for grease cup or guns, on tractors, cars, or trucks. 5 lb. steel pail. **Stk. No. GP5.** 5½ lbs.

59c

"High Pressure Gun Grease"

Waterproof lubricant for tractor, car, or truck. Recommended for use with pressure guns.
Stk. No. GG5. 5 lb. steel pail. **69c**

Wheel Bearing Special

An extremely heavy grease, especially adapted for front and rear wheel bearings on tractors.
Stk. No. GW5. 5 lb. steel pail. **75c**

600W Transmission Lubricant

In five gallon heavy pour pail, with lid. The pail alone is worth $1.25. The grease is the accepted standard for use in transmissions of tractors and heavy trucks. Full bodied, it stands up longer.
Stk. No. GT5.
Shipping weight 50 lbs. 5 Gals. **$2.95**

BARREL PUMP

Fits any 15, 30 or 55 gallon drum or barrel.
Pumps any lubricant, kerosene, alcohol, galsoline, etc.
Stk. No. L38.
6 lbs. **$2.95**

FITTINGS

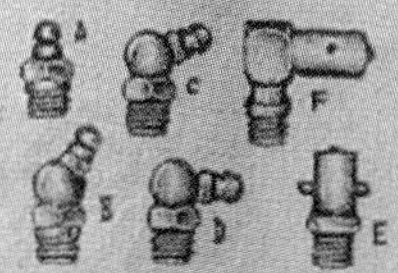

3c each

Same high quality you'd pay twice as much for elsewhere.

Same as original equipment used by leading tractor and automotive manufacturers. Hydraulic type, for all push or Zerk fittings. Pin type for Alemite equipment.

Description	Stk. No.	Each
a) Straight, Hydraulic, ⅛" thread.	L10	3c
b) 30° angle, Hydraulic, ⅛" thread.	L11	7c
c) 67° angle, Hydraulic, ⅛" thread.	L12	7c
d) 90° angle, Hydraulic, ⅛" thread.	L13	7c
a) Straight, Hydraulic, ¼" thread.	L16	9c
b) 67° angle, Hydraulic, ¼" thread.	L17	13c
e) Straight, Pin Type, ⅛" thread.	L14	4c
f) 90° angle, Pin type, ⅛" thread.	L15	10c
e) Straight, Pin type, ¼" thread.	L18	8c
f) 90° angle, Pin type, ¼" thread. . . .	L19	13c

⅛" thr. meas. 13/32" actual diam. ¼" thr. meas. 17/32".

FITTING ASSORTMENT

Consists of fifty-five straight, twenty 30 angle, ten 17 angle, and fifteen right angle ⅛" hydraulic fittings. A special deal that will save you several dollars.
Stk. No. LS100. Shlp. wt. 3 lbs. **$3.95**

GREASE GUNS

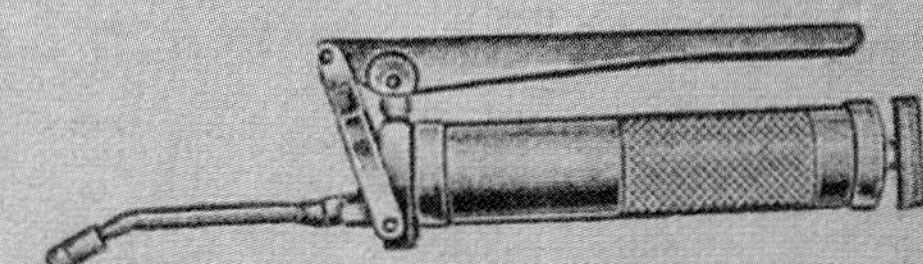

Stk. No. L35—18 OZ. LEVER TYPE GUN, as pictured. Develops 5000 lbs. pressure. Steel construction, "disappearing handle," ball check, and many other high priced features. Shipping weight 5 lbs. **$1.95**

Stk. No. L36—24 OZ. LEVER TYPE GUN, as pictured. Develops extremely high pressure for tough jobs, with any gun grease. Full spring pressure feed, all steel, a rugged and durable gun. 6 lbs. **$2.95**

Guns listed above are for "Zerk" push type or Hydraulic Fittings.

Stk. No. L33—SCREW TYPE GUN, for Pin Type Fittings. 8 oz. Capacity, complete with flexible metal hose. Shipping weight 3 lbs. **$2.25**

GREASE DISPENSER

FOR ALL STD. 25 LB. PAILS

The clean, simple way to transfer grease from pail to guns, etc. Replaces the orig. pail lid. Tightens with three set screws. **No dirt, dust, or water can get** under the lid, and into lubricant. **Handles any oil or grease.** Oil, Gun grease, transmission, etc. Fills pressure guns without air pockets or bubbles. Compl. with hose. For 11¼" to 13" pails. **Stk. No. L37.** 12 lbs. . **$2.95**

The evolution of the company's product lines is also depicted in the growing catalog. For the first few years, the cover is devoted almost exclusively to the tractor, as are the parts and accessories inside. The company is a tractor parts supplier. This product offering quickly expands in the post-World War II years, as did the overall retail market and consumers' appetite for merchandise.

By 1946 an automatic stock oiler finds its way onto the catalog cover. In 1962, a Tractor Supply Catalog just for Jeeps and military vehicles appears, indicating the company's continual attempts to broaden or redefine its niche. An occasional passenger tire finds its way on the front of the book and, by 1966, even simple kitchen and household appliances such as cake mixers and irons reside comfortably on the cover alongside the more traditional piston and sleeve kits. Screen doors, trash cans, air conditioners, boots, streetlights, and lawnmowers will follow as the company's products begin to edge past the once narrowly defined niche owned by Tractor Supply.

BEWARE THE BALLYHOO

It's also interesting to note the evolution of the company's merchandizing savvy. In the earliest days of the company – in the early '40s – it was important to differentiate itself from the branded parts sold by the original equipment dealers such

A Few Good Lines Here are a a few slogans the company has used over the years:
★ "You Save When You Buy from Tractor Supply" – the oldest slogan, of course.
★ "The Symbol of Savings to Modern Farmers across the Nation." ★ "Your Friend Since 1938."

as Deere and International Harvester. Tractor Supply fed the consumers' suspicions that they were paying more for the name and that the parts were no better than those supplied by TSC. The company made its point by purposefully avoiding a branded name.

On page 2 of the 1940 catalog, amidst the type outlining the company's shipping service, guarantees and ordering policies, this quaintly worded bit of copy appears:

"Tractor Supply handles only guaranteed new parts – honest merchandise, honestly advertised – for faithful, dependable service.

"Don't fall for the ballyhoo," warned the writer of the catalog – probably Charles Schmidt – "of the implement agent and machine dealer who is trying to sell you goods at high prices. The parts themselves are what counts, and we do not believe a trademark or the word 'genuine' adds anything in the way of service to the merchandise."

Ironically, Charles Schmidt would later market parts under the trademark name "Genuine Parts." Schmidt would win a lawsuit to retain this name before eventually selling it.

In 1941, the word "precision" is used as only a description of the quality of the company's parts, such as bearings, piston sleeves, and oil filters. But the descriptor had become a brand name as the company begins offering its own Precision brand parts. Trasco, sort of a techno-slang abbre-

"Where America's Farmers Shop," later changed to "Where America's Farmers and Ranchers Shop" which was later changed to "America's No. 1 Farm and Ranch Store." ★ "Whether You Have One Acre or a Thousand." ★ "The Stuff You Need Out Here."

viation of the company's name, will become the name of Tractor Supply's private label agricultural equipment.

Explained the 1946 fall catalog, "Our volume is so large we can deal direct with equipment manufacturers, thereby effecting big savings, but we cannot use the manufacturers' brand names. Therefore, in order to pass these savings along to you, we have adopted the 'Trasco' trade name."

The Trasco name would grow until by the mid-1950s it was slapped on everything from spray enamel paint to post hole diggers.

Regarding Precision parts, the same 1946 catalog stated simply, "Contrary to general opinion, Tractor makers do not make all the parts in their tractors, many are merely assemblers of parts made to their specifications by basic parts manufacturers. "The remarkable growth of our business gives us a terrific buying power, so that we, too, can order direct from the parts makers, specifying materials and finishes for improved service. To avoid conflict with brand names selling at higher prices, all of our parts are sold and guaranteed under our own 'Precision' quality labels."

Trasco

In a bit of a twist, the company that pooh-poohed the "ballyhooed" brands was creating and promoting its own. It was an early indication that the company was beginning to understand and embrace the power of brands. A brand could communicate fair pricing as easily as it could suggest the exorbitant.

Other names would follow. The Huskee brand would first be used as a rubber picker roller name. It was an extremely popular product, so Tractor Supply borrowed on the equity imbued in the brand by the picker and extended it to another rubber product. The Huskee name would eventually move to both tractor and passenger tires. Today, the brand still exists and can be found on a number of products including lawn tractors and parts for power equipment.

CONSTANTLY TINKERING

Schmidt and his friends weren't content to simply sit by and let their good idea continue its already prosperous run. There was expansion of outlets and distribution, merchandise and marketing areas, a thousand small and constant innovations that bolstered the brand's success for the future.

Schmidt mixed his ability to see and seize an opportunity with his natural ingenuity and desire to constantly tinker with things. Good was never good enough. Though he never set foot on a farm, Schmidt did share the farmers' tinkering spirit and ingenuity.

It may fly in the face of stereotypes, but farmers and people who work the land have always been early adopters of technology. They eagerly looked for any device, tool, or piece of equipment to help them in the hard work of subduing the land or providing feed for their livestock. In the early years of the twentieth century, "power farming" was all the rage.

"I think it safe to eliminate the horse, the mule, the bull team, and the woman, so far as generally furnishing motive power is concerned," announced W. L. Veile, director of Deere & Company, back in 1918.

American Inventor Henry Ford agreed in his autobiography, *My Life and Work*: "The farmer must either take up power or go out of business."

But power, as it always has, came at a pretty price. In 1915, a farm tractor could cost several thousand dollars. An International Harvester Titan 10/10 went for $900, a tough row to hoe for most farmers. A Ford Model T, on the other hand, could be purchased for just $450. Necessity being the mother of invention and farmers being more than blessed with their fair share of American ingenuity, the frugal farmer converted his Model T into a crude tractor. In the January 1919 issue of *Chilton's Tractor Index*, there were forty-five factory conversion kits that turned a Model T into a homemade tractor.

"Don't let your old Ford or Chevrolet go to waste," a 1939 Sears & Roebuck catalog urged. "Use it to make a practical general-purpose tractor that has the pulling power of from two to four horses, yet costs less than the price of one horse."

Very quickly, America's modern mechanized farmers knew as much about the internal combustion engine as they did composting and crop rotation. Not only did the need to maintain and repair your own farm equipment give birth to Tractor Supply, but it also continued to ensure the company's growth. Tractor Supply tapped into the frugal farmers' mechanically minded and independent attitude with products to deliver more to its customers for less. Tractor Supply's piston and sleeve sets were designed to give the old tractors more power and pop, and they proved a pretty hot commodity that helped power sales as well as old tractors. Most tractor engines were built with sleeves that acted as the cylinders for the piston. Because of the grit and grime that a tractor was forced to perform in and because of the rigorous stresses placed on equipment in the field, the sleeves were made to be replaced.

"If International Harvester came out with a tractor that put out 40 horsepower, putting a new Tractor Supply piston and sleeve set in could help you get maybe 50 horsepower out of the tractor," said Tom Burenga, Tractor Supply's former director of manufacturing.

"We were basically a hot rod shop helping the farmers soup up their tractors."

Heading the "hot rod" operation was an old hot rod aficionado – Mac McKittrick. McKittrick was an early product engineer who wound up an officer in the company.

"He was in engineering and ran Tractor Supply's manufacturing," said Max DeForest. "He was an old race car enthusiast. He was a hot rod type of guy, and he just loved powering up these old tractors and getting a lot out of them."

The piston and sleeve sets were manufactured by Richland Industries of Richland Center, Wisconsin. McKittrick, Tractor Supply, and Richland Industries also developed a power block.

Do-It-Yourself

With the advent of tractors and "power farming," there was more to working the land than planting. A good knowledge of engines and mechanics was a must. Tractor Supply's business was and continues to be built on the self-reliant nature of its customers.

Library of Congress

"It was basically a replacement block that the guys would install in their tractors," said Burenga. "It allowed for oversized pistons, and it would dramatically increase the tractor's power.

"In fact, one year, John Deere Model G won the pulling contest within its class, and it had one of these power blocks in it."

"When the power blocks left the Richland Industries factory, they were painted yellow," explained Burenga. "Of course, once the farmers installed them in their tractors, they would grab a can of paint and they would paint it green to go with their John Deeres.

"Now the block was already in the tractor when it was painted so they would paint the top of the block green but they never would paint the bottom. And so the tractors were called 'Yellow Bellies.'"

This is just one of many instances of Tractor Supply ingenuity. Although the products were engineered by McKittrick, many times they were dreamed up by Charles Schmidt.

"Charlie had an incredible feel for what would be next," said DeForest. "He might ask us, 'What should I be making? What do we need to give manufacturing?' We were out there in the field, but he was the one who always came up with the winner. He could sense some things like what might wear out on that manufacturer's tractor or that combine, and he developed improvement packages for them.

"They came up with a replacement husking roll for the old corn picker, too. He had it made and the engineering department had figured out how to do it. It was a great success story. He [Charles Schmidt] even bought his own factory and made sleeves and pistons and overhauled tractor engines."

Schmidt had an eye for materials as well as merchandise.

"Just after World War II, he figured out the Germans were going to be producing some pretty cheap steel," said Richard Schmidt. "I remember he had tremendous problems when he brought some of the products into the country. People would say, 'Oh, that crummy German stuff. We don't want that stuff.'

"Then within a few years the people began to recognize how well German steel was doing. It was doing fine. Then he replaced the German steel with Japanese steel."

THE BLUE BOOK IS BORN

In 1950, Tractor Supply began adding a bit more color to the cover of its fall catalog, adding a touch of blue to the face of what had been dominated by the brilliant barn and tractor red. The next year, in 1951, the company dropped the splash of red and printed a catalog with a blue and white cover.

The distinct blue cover must have caught the eyes of customers and, naturally, they began referring to the Tractor Supply Company catalog, the farmers' handy parts companion, as simply the "blue book." Tractor Supply has always availed itself of the wisdom of its customers; listening and learning have always been at the heart of the company's success. And so the very next year, in 1952, appeared the words "Tractor Parts Blue Book."

1950 CUSTOMER CATALOG

TRACTOR SUPPLY CO.

Guaranteed New Parts

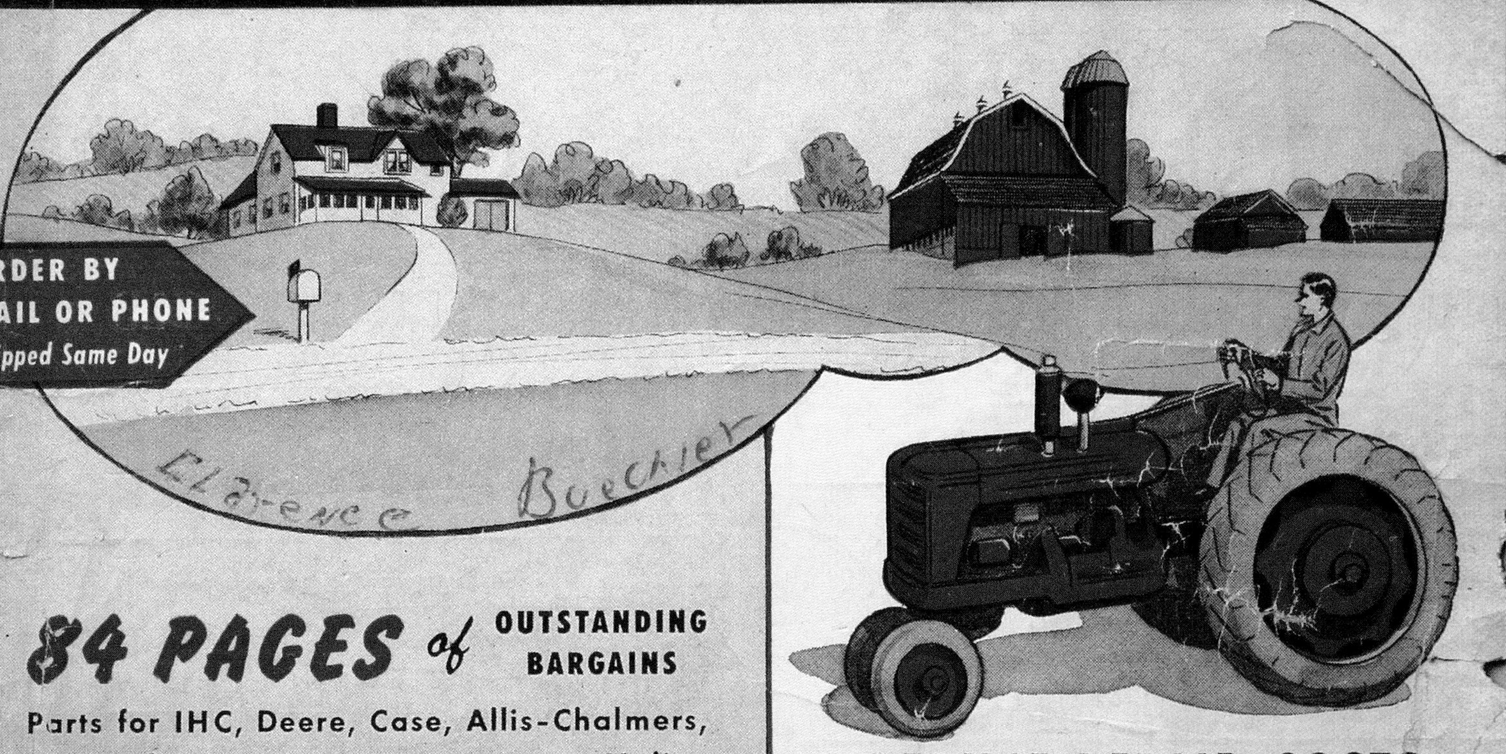

ORDER BY MAIL OR PHONE
Shipped Same Day

Clarence Boechler

REDUCE REPAIR COSTS

84 PAGES *of* **OUTSTANDING BARGAINS**

Parts for IHC, Deere, Case, Allis-Chalmers, Ford, Oliver, Massey Harris, Minn. Moline Tractors and Implements

COMPLETE STOCKS . . . ALL WITH SAME LOW PRICES

The Blue Book was the farmer, rancher and rural land owners' equivalent to the Sears Wishbook, a massive compendium of parts, accessories, equipment, and tools. It was everything that Tractor Supply had to offer to its customers, and it was mailed in addition to the fall and spring catalogs that carried more seasonal items. There's no telling just how many people have whiled away a long winter's night, poring over the dog-eared pages of the Tractor Supply Blue Book, plotting their spring repairs or dreaming of adding a nifty new device or increasing the power of their tractors.

1945 CATALOG

For the next fifty years, the Blue Book would be a Tractor Supply mail-order staple with only a brief respite during the late '80s for the company to come up with a more cost-effective means of delivering the Bible of Rural Lifestyle. Today the Blue Book supplements store circulars and is available annually through local Tractor Supply stores or online 365 days a year.

BOOM TIMES

In 1941, Tractor Supply Branch No. 3 opened in Williston, North Dakota, at 20th Main Street. It was the company's first retail-only outlet. Already, with the opening of just the third branch, Charles Schmidt could see that a retail operation had the potential to stand on its own two feet, independent of the already successful mail-order business. Branch No. 4, opened in Omaha by Wes Walker, moved Tractor Supply's retail operations out of North Dakota and into Nebraska for the first time.

The company's expansion slowed with the demands of World War II. Only one new store opened and carried the company into the fertile lands of central Texas. Branch No. 5 in Fort Worth was the beginning of what in a few short years would be described as a "Texas Institution." The Fort Worth store was located at 300 Calhoun, just a block south of the Tarrant County courthouse.

The years following the war saw immediate expansion. The desire to grow the business that had to be curbed during the wartime demands could now be fully realized. The number of stores nearly doubled in 1946, going from four to seven. Iowa and Minnesota joined the ranks of states with a Tractor Supply presence with stores in Sioux City and St. Paul. Nebraska added another in Columbus. In eight years, Tractor Supply had grown to $919,000 in sales, just shy of being a $1 million business. All of this happened despite the fact that half of its existence was under the restraints of a wartime economy.

In the economic boom that followed the war, over the next four years, Tractor Supply's sales would double, exceeding $2 million. These sales were even more significant given that they were generated by stores like Enid, Oklahoma, where manager Wilmer Wilson remembered the "sales floor" amounting to nothing more than six display tables. There were physical limitations, but Tractor Supply's potential seemed unlimited. With its six display tables, Enid did $150,000 worth of sales in its first year. It must have been an incredibly exciting time to be part of this burgeoning business, the boys back from the fight, everything moving and growing.

Four years after plowing past $2 million, Tractor Supply doubled its sales again and reached the $4 million mark. By 1958, sales more than doubled again at $9.6 million.

Tractor Supply still enjoyed plenty of opportunity. According to the United States Agricultural Department, the number of tractors on farms finally exceeded the number of horses and mules for the first time in 1954. Oddly enough, it would be the horses that the tractor supplanted in 1954 that would emerge fifty years later to account for a significant growth of Tractor Supply's business.

During the decade following the war, from 1947 to 1957, the company would open an average of three stores a year, adding Kansas, Ohio, and Minnesota to the growing list of states it did business in and towns with ag-rich histories such as Fond du Lac, Lubbock, Fargo, Salina, Sioux Falls, Waterloo, and Waco. It was a time of steady and controlled growth for the privately held company, a time of slowly amassing buying power, strengthening the supply chain, and gaining greater retail experience.

Every practical advantage was exercised. Instead of one massive company, for tax purposes, to reduce the overall tax burden, regions were incorporated as subsidiaries – Tractor Supply Company Illinois, Tractor Supply Company Texas, Tractor Supply Company Minnesota, and Tractor Supply Company California. And so this growing business was actually a collection of companies carefully multiplying across the Midwest, successfully transplanted in state after state. As the company grew, no matter how big the business got, one man could be counted on to know the ins and outs of Tractor Supply.

"There wasn't anyone who knew the hundred percent other than Chuck," said Paul Schneider, the auditor assigned to Tractor Supply for the Chicago accounting firm of Checkers, Simon & Rosner. "I'm not sure Gardner Abbott did. Chuck always did his homework. He was always prepared.

"He was the only guy who knew where all the bodies were."

There weren't many "bodies" to be buried. The company's growth to this point had been calculated and controlled, with expansion limited to the cash existing stores could generate. Its merchandise was expanding pretty much within the already established mix. It was still exactly what its name described it to be – a Tractor Supply store. And that was a successful commodity seemingly wherever it chose to open. The company's ability to grow faster was limited only by its financial resources and its founder's conservative approach. To grow faster and take advantage of the opportunity on hand would require a large infusion of cash.

Something that only the stock market could offer.

Tractor Supply storefronts from the 1948 catalog.

From left: Charles Schmidt, Charles Stern of Stern & Byck, G. Keith Funston, President of the N.Y. Stock Exchange and Wes Walker on the floor of the New York Stock Exchange on March 21, 1960

GOING TO MARKET

The year 1958 would be significant in the company's history for several reasons. Tractor Supply would add eight stores, more than doubling its normal annual increase in stores and adding one new state – Indiana – while strengthening its position in Iowa, Illinois, Nebraska, Texas, and Minnesota. It would also be the year Charles Schmidt prepared to take his company public.

On January 14, 1959, the previously privately held Tractor Supply Company would take the next major step in its corporate journey. It would go public, listed on the Over-The-Counter Market. A total of 800,000 shares were sold to the public. The initial offering was over-subscribed on the first day at a price of $12 per share.

A look at the 1958 prospectus provides an interesting portrait of the company on its twentieth anniversary. It's described as "a mail order and chain store merchandising enterprise in the sale of repair and replacement parts for farm tractors, other farm machinery, and tools and specialty items used by the American farmer."

The document described the general categories filled by the 6,000 catalog items supplied by 400 vendors. It noted, however, Tractor Supply didn't just carry parts, but that it also offered innovation to its customers.

"In many instances, the Company has made modifications and changes on various parts, believing its own designs to be superior in quality and performance," the document stated and used as an example the hydraulic accessories created for older tractors that had been designed for manual accessories.

"Another significant Company innovation," the prospectus pointed out, "is the design and sale of conversion kits, such as replacement engine blocks, cylinder sleeves, and piston assemblies which may be installed in older farm equipment engines to increase their power and economy of operation at substantially less cost than that of a new tractor or other complete farm machine."

The document went on to report that the company's sales were distributed among 400,000 current customers found in forty-nine states and Canada. Tractor Supply's distribution was comprised of two major warehouse facilities in Chicago and Omaha. And the company employed 220 people, with 45 working out of the company's Chicago office and warehouse.

The prospectus also succinctly identified the keys to the company's success: "Availability and favorable pricing are key factors in the success of the Company's sales program. Most farms are equipped with machinery of many different makes. Through the maintenance of stocks of parts for many makes and models of equipment in its branch stores and warehouses, the Company is able to attract the business of the farmer or mechanic who needs parts or service for machines of various makes. Another significant aspect of the Company's sales program is that it has from its inception refrained from using manufacturers' brand names or factory warranties. Rather, the Company has offered its merchandise under its own trade names ("Trasco," Precision," "Kleenite" and "Huskee") and guarantees, and its customers have come to rely upon the Company's reputation for quality merchandise. Local Company personnel in the branch stores are authorized to make adjustments and exchanges where called for rather than to refer complaints to the Company's manufacturing source."

Celebrating success in 1961, Mac McKittrick, Larry Schweik, and Max DeForest review the company's annual report.

Don't let that last sentence just slide by. Local stores were authorized to act on their own when it came to making sure the customer was treated right. It's an early echo of the sign that hangs in every Tractor Supply store today, reminding team members and their customers that "every team member has the authority to do whatever it takes."

The market potential was painted in glowing terms in the prospectus – or as glowing as these kinds of perfunctory corporate communications tend to get.

"Parts and supplies which make up the Company's major sale items tend to enjoy a relatively stable demand, reflecting more the amount of machinery in use than the volume of sales of new machinery," the prospectus explained. "The fact that farm machinery tends to have a substantially longer useful life than automobiles or trucks also contributes to the stability of demand for the Company's products. Many tractors in use today are 20 or more years old. The older machines require repair more frequently and in more substantial degree than the newer machines."

The company's relationship with its employees is discussed, noting Tractor Supply's policy of promoting from within the organization and that "substantially" all those in leadership positions are people who started at the sales counter or in warehouse positions. Group life insurance, the pension plan and profit-sharing are also mentioned and employee relations with the company are described as "excellent." Apparently describing it as a "family feel" would have been more

A stock certificate from Tractor Supply's first go-around on the New York Stock Exchange. It would later return to private ownership

LESS THAN 100 SHARES
CLASS A SHARES
NUMBER
N013919
CLASS A SHARES
SHARES
-15-
INCORPORATED UNDER THE LAWS
OF THE STATE OF ILLINOIS
TRACTOR SUPPLY CO.
THIS CERTIFICATE IS TRANSFERABLE IN THE CITY OF CHICAGO OR IN THE CITY OF NEW YORK
SEE REVERSE FOR CERTAIN DEFINITIONS
This Certifies that
GOODBODY & CO.
is the owner of
-FIFTEEN-
FULLY PAID AND NON-ASSESSABLE CLASS A SHARES OF THE PAR VALUE OF $1.00 EACH
of Tractor Supply Co. transferable on the books of the corporation by the holder hereof in person or by duly authorized attorney upon surrender of this certificate properly endorsed. This certificate is not valid unless countersigned by the transfer agent and registered by the registrar.
Witness the seal of the corporation and the signatures of its duly authorized officers.
Dated AUG 28 1963
SECRETARY
PRESIDENT
TRACTOR SUPPLY CO. CORPORATE SEAL ILLINOIS
COUNTERSIGNED: BANKERS TRUST COMPANY, (NEW YORK) TRANSFER AGENT
BY
ASSISTANT SECRETARY
REGISTERED: FIRST NATIONAL CITY BANK REGISTRAR
BY
AUTHORIZED OFFICER
TENS UNITS
SECURITY-COLUMBIAN BANKNOTE COMPANY

EARLY HAY DAYS.
Tractor Supply's 1962 Company Meeting at the Pick Congress Hotel in Chicago. Early executives seen in the front row from left, District Manager Carl Pietsch, Vice President Max DeForest, Treasurer Richard Schaefer, Vice Chairman Wes Walker, President Gard Abbott, Chairman Charles Schmidt, Outside Director Thomas King, Vice President Gordon Mac McKittrick and Assistant Secretary Larry Schweik.

1962 Company Meeting at the Pick Congress Hotel, Chicago

difficult for the prospective investors to understand, though certainly far more accurate.

What investors would appreciate – though probably not come any closer to understanding – were the results this seemingly simple company had generated in so short a history. The balance sheet attached to the 1958 prospectus shows the company's phenomenal growth over the last three years. From 1956 to 1958, Tractor Supply's net sales nearly doubled from $5.5 million to $9.6 million while its net income more than doubled from $500,000 in 1956 to $1.1 million in 1958. This rapid fiscal growth necessitated other physical expansions.

For the second time in its twenty-year history, Tractor Supply would be moving to a new company office. This time Tractor Supply was buying a building located at 4737-57 North Ravenswood Avenue for an estimated $275,000. The forty-year-old brick four-story building contained 110,000 square feet of space, of which Tractor Supply would fill 50,000 square feet when it moved in the late spring of 1959.

"He bought the building at 4747 North Ravenswood in Chicago," said Richard Schmidt. "I remember three dock-high lifts on one level of the warehouse and some pit docks next to the warehouse. I think altogether, there were five or seven docks for trucks to come in and unload and huge offices on one side of the warehouse building. I think there were four stories of offices that became the home of Tractor Supply. And there was a big water tower behind part of the plant that they put the Tractor Supply Company logo on.

"You could see it from the Northwestern Railroad as the train whizzed into downtown Chicago."

Ravenswood would prove the last Chicago address the company would ever have.

THE BIG BOARD

The excitement hitting the Over-the-Counter Market was short-lived. Less than two years later, on March 21, 1960, Tractor Supply would "hit the big board," as success propelled it to a listing on the New York Stock Exchange. If money was the tool Charles Schmidt had used as a measurement of his success to this point, the big board was the ultimate symbol of success. It must have been an incredible feeling for this former brokerage house board marker to see his own company's name emblazoned on the Wall Street ticker tape.

"He took great personal satisfaction in seeing Tractor Supply listed on the New York Stock Exchange," recalled Richard Schmidt. "That was a very big milestone for him. It was the housekeeping seal of approval on his business career, and he felt it legitimized him somehow.

"Later in life, when he would reminisce about his proudest moments in his life, he would remember playing for Mount Carmel High School as a seventeen-year-old in Chicago's City Football Championships at Soldier Field, and he would remember being listed on the New York Stock Exchange.

"That was an important moment for him."

It had been an almost meteoric rise aboard what might have seemed like the most unlikely vehicle…a humble tractor.

"What was amazing about him was he saw a future in the farm implement business, not electronics, not aviation, not one of the fancy businesses at the time," said Richard Schmidt. "Here was a guy in a meat-and-potatoes business, grinding it out each year to increase profits. And the company stock did very well."

The stock did very well for the young Richard Schmidt as well.

Ad and Brand Trivia Here are a few fun facts. Schmidt considered calling his company Tractors Owners Supply Company. Glad he didn't. TOSC doesn't have the same ring as TSC. Tractor Supply's first and longest running advertising was "You Save When You Buy from Tractor Supply!" And guess what? It's still true today. Finally, the Huskee brand, featured on lawn tractors and accessories today, was first used for rubber corn husking rolls. Huskee was derived from husking corn. The name also appeared on a line of TSC tires.

Today a successful businessman with interests in real estate and aviation in Boca Raton, Florida, Richard Schmidt had a bit of an adventuresome spirit as a young man that took some time for him to master. The younger Schmidt and his father had a falling out, because, according to Richard, he had not applied himself at the University of Florida. Later, after a stint in the army, when Richard decided to return to college, Charles Schmidt let him know that this time around, paying for school was Richard's responsibility. That's where Tractor Supply's stock came in.

"I had a little dividend income from some stock he [Charles Schmidt] had given me when Tractor Supply went public," remembered Schmidt. "It paid about $3,000 a year and, as I recall, that was enough to pay my tuition at Fairfield College.

"I got a job as a dorm proctor and that paid my room and board, but that still didn't give me any money to live on or do anything else while I was in school. So I drove around looking for a job and, in a college town, a job can be hard to find. Everybody is looking for work. I drove out of Fairfield, Iowa, about thirty miles to the next biggest town – Ottumwa – to inquire about a job, and I happened to see the Tractor Supply logo on a little store that was kind of tucked underneath an overpass toward the west end of town.

"I went in there and I met the manager and I asked if they could use any help. He asked me a few questions and I seemed to know a little bit about the stock. I remembered a few things from the stock room working for Tractor Supply as a young teenager. And so he hired me.

"I didn't tell anybody who I was," said Schmidt all these years later, shaking his head and grinning. "Not so much because I didn't want to take advantage of the family name as I didn't want the word to get back to my dad. I remember the manager after I was there about three weeks saying to me after work one day, 'Schmidt? Huh. You know I think the name of the guy that's the head of this whole kit-and-caboodle, I think his name is Schmidt.'

CHARLES SCHMIDT FROM HIS 1928 MT. CARMEL HIGH SCHOOL YEARBOOK.

"I said, 'No kidding?'

"One day Wes Walker came in the store on a trip visiting various stores and I was working back in the stockroom, trying to hide behind anything I could. He kept glancing at me. I knew I was busted, but I didn't say a thing. Toward the end of the afternoon, he said, 'Dick, Dick Schmidt, is that you?' I confessed, but I said, 'Please don't tell my dad,' and I don't think he ever did.

"So, without knowing it, my dad put me through college. And I got some pretty good first-hand knowledge of Tractor Supply."

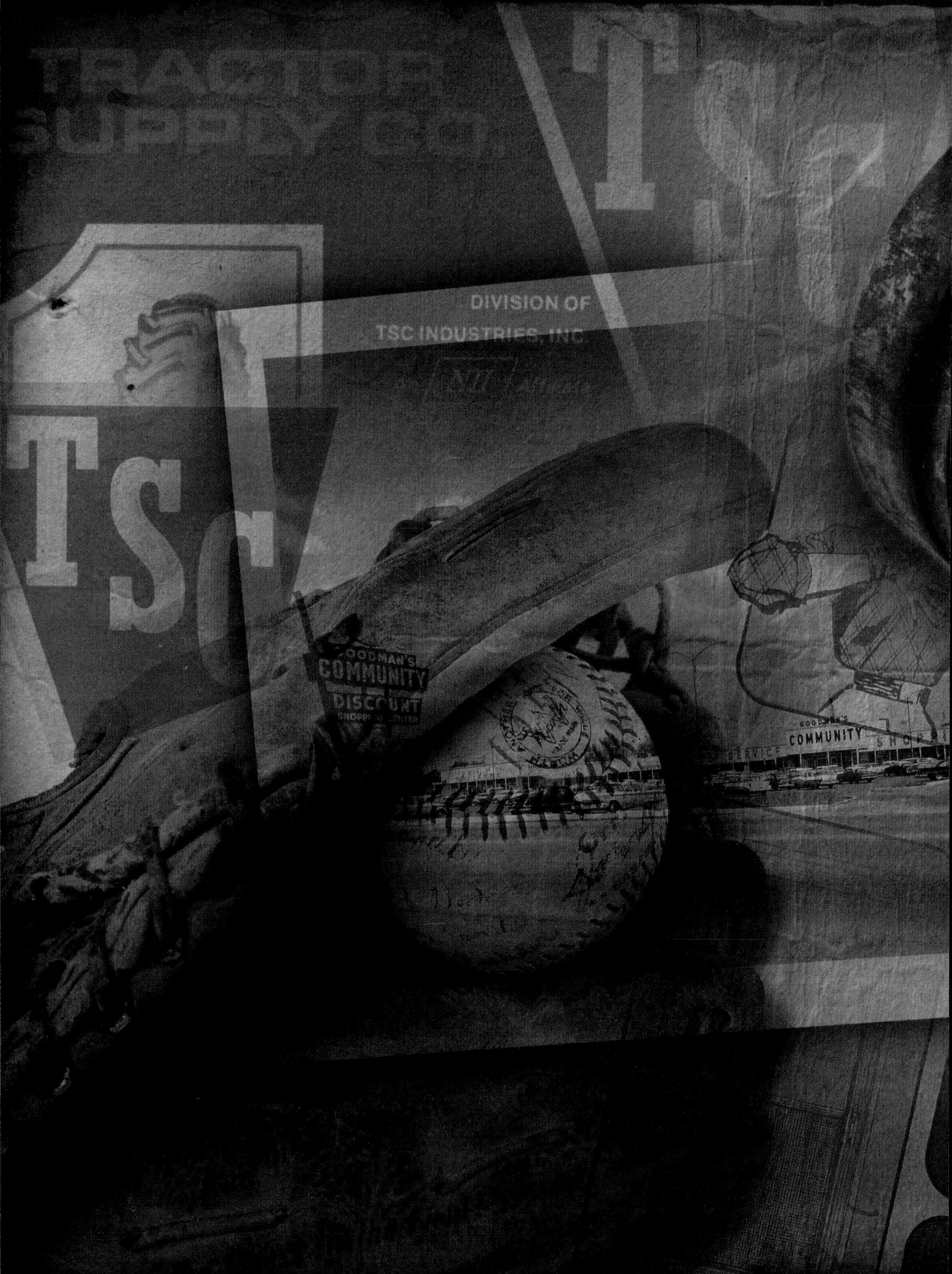

TRACTOR
SUPPLY CO.
TSC
DIVISION OF
TSC INDUSTRIES, INC.
GOODMAN'S
COMMUNITY
DISCOUNT
COMMUNITY

CHAPTER ★5★

GOING TO MARKET

LINCHPINS AND PISTON SLEEVES BECOME BIG BUSINESS

"FARMERS ONLY WORRY DURING THE GROWING SEASON, BUT TOWNSPEOPLE WORRY ALL THE TIME."

- EDGAR WATSON HOWE

THE UNCERTAIN '60s

America was a land in upheaval, torn by riots in the streets, protest over the protracted conflict in Vietnam, and a rapidly escalating arms race with Russia. Here, military police attempt to quell protestors outside the Pentagon building. It was a troubled time.

Wally McNamee/CORBI

THE TIMES THEY ARE A CHANGING The 1960s were a time of incredible upheaval. For America and for Tractor Supply. The two were forced to change to keep pace with a world that was spinning crazily around them. Both had outgrown their rural and agricultural roots and were more and more affected by big-city influences and attitudes.

Throughout America, the postwar euphoria of the jubilant '40s was over, as was the youthful exuberance of the rock-and-roll, TV-tray culture of the '50s. The '60s exploded on the scene with a little bleaker outlook than the previous two decades. It was the age of assassinations and race riots, Vietnam, the Cold War, and the arms race, all tearing America apart.

★

The rural landscape and Tractor Supply's customers were slowly beginning to shift, too. The number of farms in America was falling dramatically, from 5.3 million in 1950 down to 3.7 million just ten years later. Charles Schmidt, who had always kept close tabs on his customer – to the point of counting the number of tractors sold in any given county in the country – was well aware of the trends and recognized the impending challenge for his company.

The company continued to post impressive numbers. In its first full year as a public company, 1959, Tractor Supply passed $10 million in sales, and profits were reported at $1.51 a share. After hitting the big board in 1960, the company's share price quickly advanced from $12 to $22 a share. A little over a year later, the company's stock was selling at a record high of $62 per share and was celebrating with a 3 for 2 split.

Year after year, the opening sentence of the annual report read the same, repeating itself over and over like a broken record as it shattered sales record after sales record – "Tractor Supply Company set new highs in sales, earnings, and earnings per share, continuing the unbroken performance since the company's founding in 1938."

In 1963, among the 1,188 corporations listed on the New York Stock Exchange, Tractor Supply Company, since its founding, had achieved the longest history of uninterrupted year-to-year increases in volume and net income.

Between 1961 and 1965 – in just four years – the company's sales doubled from $14 million to $28 million. Four years later, they'd more than doubled again. By 1969, the company was enjoying thirty years of uninterrupted profitability.

The steady rise of the numbers – particularly sales – doesn't accurately indicate the ups and downs within the company and the mind of its founder. The '60s would prove a wild ride for Tractor Supply, filled with numerous twists and turns. Along the way, there would be acquisitions

both of retail competitors and parts manufacturers so that the company could now control the price of important items at the point of manufacturing.

There would be diversification both within the traditional Tractor Supply merchandising mix and by acquiring retail interests outside of the company's profitable farm and ranch store niche. The company would begin to move away from its farm store image as well as the word "tractor" in an attempt to broaden the newly named TSC Stores' customer base. The merchandise mix would follow suit, loading the shelves of TSC Stores with everything from passenger tires to guitars, chemistry sets to camper trailers.

Tractor Supply's sales and store growth would continue its steady rise through the decade. Even though profits would slip a couple of years during the mid-1960s, the company would still enjoy a profit, year after year, and continue to add more stores to the map, more space within the stores and more pages to the company's venerable mail-order catalog.

Kay Gorecki Walker recalled a special ceremony at the home office in Chicago that accompanied the opening of each new branch.

"As we grew, we used to make a big deal of pinning a star on a big map that was in our office," explained Walker. "It was like a party. We were so proud of ourselves. Mr. Schmidt and Mr. Walker would come in and say, 'Well, we've opened a store in Omaha. We've opened one in Wichita.' And on would go a star. It was one of our little idiosyncrasies. It was very important to us, very important that we see it growing.

"I got to pin the star on the map."

All during the '60s, Tractor Supply was definitely seeing stars. It was as if the heavens had opened for the company whose holdings once filled the space of a kitchen table and a small catalog.

Suddenly there were stars everywhere.

Drive to Survive

Passenger Tires would first roll into TSC Stores during the 1960s. Their introduction was part of a move by the company to draw new customers and extend the company's reach from the farm and into the home and auto markets.

"WE COULD DO NO WRONG"

During the '60s, stores opened at an accelerated clip like nothing Tractor Supply had ever experienced.

In 1960, the same year it began trading on the New York Stock Exchange, the company opened nine stores, more than it had ever opened before. This was the year it also ventured out west to California for the very first time, with stores in Bakersfield, Fresno, and Merced. Eight more stores would come on line in 1961, the company moving now both north and south with locations in Lansing, Michigan, and Greenville, Mississippi. Tractor Supply stretched from Michigan's cherry country to Mississippi's cotton fields. Colorado and Montana came on board that same year, too. Another nine stores opened in 1962. Notably, that was Nashville's first year. The year 1963 witnessed what one reporter called "an invasion of the East" with two stores opening in New York. By 1964, the company was celebrating with its customers "Our 100th Store Year" with a commemorative logo emblazoned on the pages of the annual Blue Book.

Tractor Supply's leadership saw growth as a means of insulating the company against severe weather or drought in any one region of the country. In its 1962 annual report, the company contended, "Tractor Supply's sales are related to the extent to which farm machinery is used, and poor growing weather limits employment of equipment. Therefore, expansion of markets served by branches acts as insurance against the effect of nature on volume."

In 1967, Tractor Supply would go international. A Canadian subsidiary opened two stores located in London, Ontario, and Regina, Saskatchewan, as TSC Stores, Ltd. In fact, the subsidiary would never call its stores Tractor Supply Co. Stores. They remain today TSC Stores. A year later, the company would more than double its Canadian presence, pushing the total to five stores. It was a logical progression for the company that had launched its retail fortune with its first store on the Canadian border in Minot, North Dakota, just to be a convenient drop-shipping distance from rich agricultural country.

By the end of 1967, Tractor Supply stretched across the country from the Atlantic to the Pacific, from the Great White North to the Gulf of Mexico. Including its Big Bear, Robertson, Western Mercantile, and TSC stores in Canada, Tractor Supply had 141 company-owned and franchise stores in operation. The company's mail-order catalog had grown to 194 pages, and its sales exceeded $46 million.

To a *Chicago Sun-Times* reporter in 1960, Schmidt said, "We expect the farm repair market to continue its long-term advance. Since Tractor Supply still represents only a small percentage of the total market, we expect to increase our shares by means of new stores and new product lines."

TRACTOR SUPPLY OPENED CANADIAN STORES IN 1967. A SEPARATE COMPANY TODAY, THEY CONTINUE TO THRIVE.

The reporter noted that the company was almost recession-proof, because it provided farmers with parts to repair old and failing equipment to see them through the lean times. Today these same dynamics of disaster are still at work, though they're spread over a broader array of rural home, farm, and ranch maintenance items.

ILLAGE TOOLS
MIDDLEBUSTER
& LISTER SHARES
100th STORE CELEBRATION
CUT 26% To 3
12" Was $7.29 ....NOW 4
TRACTOR SUPPLY
MINOT
SAGINAW
TSC Stores
TRACTOR SUPPLY CO.
STORES
U.S. ROYAL TIRES
TRACTOR SUPPLY Co.
LIMA
For John Deere
Fits Regular Or Trip
Covers Trash And Sta
Easy To Attach: Only
Bracket
GUARANTEED AGAIN
No Extra Drag On Tractor
Lifts With Disc For Easy Transporting
TRASCO TRI-BAR HARROW
SHIPPED PREPAID FROM FACTORY IN
8 FT. SIZE..............21-1383X—Shipwt.
9 FT SIZE..............21-1384X—Shipwt.
10 FT. & 11 FT. SIZES..............21-1385X—Shipwt.
12 FT. SIZE..............21-1386X—Shipwt.
13 FT. SIZE..............21-1387X—Shipwt.
14 FT. SIZE..............21-1388X—Shipwt.
NOTICE: Specify Make, Model and Year of DISC when ord
for IHC and JOHN DEERE Sold cultivator harrows.
86
NO MONEY

High Quality TILLAGE TOOLS

100th STORE CELEBRATION

Special!
DISC BLADE[S]
LOW AS 2...

- Highest Quality Imported Blades
- Satisfaction Guaranteed
- Star Punched—Fits 1" & 1⅛" Axle[s]

SHIPPED FREIGHT COLLECT FROM S[TORE] NOT PREPAID

16" DISC BLADES
10-1004—Shipwt. 7½ lbs. ....
LOTS OF 10 OR MORE ....Ea.

18" DISC BLADES
10-1007—Shipwt. 10 lbs. ....
LOTS OF 10 OR MORE ....

Quincy. Ill.

...79 Ea. ...more ...9 Ea.

...79 Ea. ...r more ...69 Ea.

...center hole for ... Stk.No.10-1013. ...5.19 Ea. ...r more ...99 Ea.

...hole for 1⅛" axle. 8 ga., 2½" concavity. ...—Shipwt. 17 lbs. 6.99 Ea. 10 or more 6.79 Ea.

...r hole for 1⅝" shaft, 8 ga., 3½" con... only in Memphis, Greenville and ...No. 10-1029—Shipwt. 20 lbs. 6.95 Ea. 10 or more 6.45 Ea.

...ULDE[R] ... pipe b... others ...-Shipw...

...ARE H... -Shipwt...

...TCHED DISC BLADES

...blades. Heat treated for hardest ... 10, 22" have 11. ...Prepaid.

...Widens The Cut of Your Disc

Now available for both front and rear gangs of tandem discs with ⅞", 1" and 1⅛" axles. Formed to fit properly. Fronts are concave and the rears are convex. Reduces ridging when used with smaller blade on rear gangs. Sold in pairs only. Extra bolts included.
REAR EXTENSIONS—10-1060—Shipwt. 21 lbs. Pair
FRONT EXTENSIONS—10-1061—Shipwt. 21 lbs. Pair 4.45

26" DISC PLOW BLADES

ONLY 12.95

- For Beam Type Disc Plows
- Plain type — $\frac{3}{16}$" thick — 4" concavity
- Save over 22% from comparable dealer price

Shipping Notice: Disc plow blades SHIPPED FREIGHT COLLECT FROM STORE — NOT PREPAID.

...LIS CHALMERS — 5-hole punching ...—Shipwt. 31 lbs. ....Ea. 12.95
...OHN DEERE — 5-hole punching—repl. #JDS-4448-A. ...—Shipwt. 31 lbs. ....Ea. 12.95
...ORD — 5-hole punching ...—Shipwt. 31 lbs. ....Ea. 12.95
...C — 4-hole punching, repl. #PO-12314 ...—Shipwt. 31 lbs. ....Ea. 12.95
...ASSEY-FERGUSON — 5-hole punching, repl. #660125M1 ...—Shipwt. 31 lbs. ....Ea. 12.95
BOLTS for above Plow Blades—Shipwt. 1 oz.— ...lis Chalmers, Ford, Massey-Ferguson 10-1069 ...hn Deere 10-1070 ...C 10-1071 12c Each

...ep dished ...for greater ...ID. 8.95 Ea. 6 or more 8.25 Ea.

24" 1-1/16" center hole ... 3-11/16" concavity. Stk. No. ... 10.95 Ea. 6 or more 10.15 Ea.

26" 1-1/16" center hole for 1" square axle, 3/16" thickness 4" concavity. Stk. No. 10-1045—Shipwt. 31 lbs. ....
1-19/64" center hole for 1¼" square axle, 3/16" thickness, 4" concavity. Stk. No. 10-1049—Shipwt. 31 lbs. .... 12.85 Ea. 6 or more 11.95 Ea.

SAVE MORE! Use Our Prepayment Plan

"In more than one way, we're at our best in bad weather," said Joe Scarlett. "Our sales continue because customers know we're there with exactly what they need to help them through the worst of circumstances – generators, batteries, emergency lighting, and fencing. They know, too, that we'll never jack up our prices to capitalize on their misfortune."

TRACTOR SUPPLY CO 25TH ANNIVERSARY Special

Back in 1961, this same sentiment, with perhaps a tad less color, was voiced in the company's annual report when it stated, "Product lines ranging from luxuries to absolute necessities mean business in good times and bad."

Said Charles Schmidt during the company's heady days in the '60s, "We could do no wrong."

Wes Walker seconded Schmidt's assessment of the company when he said simply, "It was a fairy tale from the beginning to the end."

Yet, even fairy tales come to an end.

HERE'S YOUR CHANGE

Even in the most fortunate of circumstances, it seems some nagging, nameless dread lurks on the periphery. Schmidt, who had painstakingly pioneered the company so many years before by carefully making sure he knew exactly what he was getting into, was now quietly amazed at the incredible numbers he was seeing, and he wrestled with doubts.

Charles Schmidt was beginning to feel the heat as early as 1964, something he alluded to in a presentation that he and Gard Abbott, then president of the company, made that year to the New York Society of Security Analysts. Schmidt told the analysts that Tractor Supply's incredible earnings and growth were a mixed blessing. It put an uncomfortable burden on him because of the expectations investors had. As recently as 1961, the company's stock was selling at more than forty times its earnings. Could such incredible numbers be sustained? Wall Street wondered. And so did Schmidt.

"Today we sit in the financial doghouse with our stock in the nineteen-to-twenty range, or about fifteen times earnings, compared to the Dow Jones average of nearly twenty times," Schmidt said in 1964. "We still feel uncomfortable; for despite a record of progress of which we are very proud, our below average multiple has investors believing we are 'has-beens' whose future is behind us."

Schmidt hinted that even a company with a stellar multi-decade record of success was not without chinks in its armor. Perhaps he had cut prices too low to maintain the company's valued reputation among its customers for having the

Sweetest the Second Time Around Not only has Tractor Supply enjoyed two separate periods of successful private ownership, it's also had lightning strike twice when it comes to success on Wall Street. The company has reached the Big Board in New York twice. The first time was in 1961 when Charles Schmidt led the company and then it did it again in 1994 under the leadership of Joe Scarlett.

best price. Tractor Supply's merchandise had been diversified with new items such as animal pharmaceuticals, paints, and automotive supplies. It was a move by the company to try to capture a greater share of its customers' retail dollar, to increase the amount of each register ticket, to broaden its offerings in other categories, and to keep its customers shopping at Tractor Supply even if they no longer came for tractor parts. However, these new items didn't provide the kind of profit margins the company had always enjoyed and, if not carefully selected, could confuse the customer and broaden the stores' immediate competition.

"About 1960…the farmer gradually began to slow up on the repair, overhaul, and modernization of some of his older machinery," Charles Schmidt announced with critical and straightforward insight in a presentation to security analysts. "Our rivals, the big farm equipment producers, were turning out ever larger new products which gradually began to make themselves felt. Smaller machines were not used as much. Little tractors were not rebuilt when they broke down, and the especially lucrative specialty business of TSC slowed a bit.

"Clearly," he concluded, "our customers were turning to the purchase of new and bigger equipment to increase efficiency so that they might keep alive in the big farm squeeze."

Schmidt looked at the possibility of expanding the size of his store and drawing from larger population areas to allow volume to make up for what he could no longer demand in margin. He explored this possibility with the acquisitions of two companies in 1962 – Robertson's Farm Supply, Inc., in East St. Louis and Western Mercantile Company in Kansas City, Missouri. These two businesses were larger, more established retail operations than any of Tractor Supply's stores at the time. Founded in 1918, Robertson's sold a broader array of products for farm and suburban use, including farm buildings and materials, feed, hardware, tools, and other equipment. Western Mercantile, established back in 1896, offered its customers merchandise for home and ranch as well as farm.

There were also the purchases of Town and Country Discount stores in Council Bluffs, Iowa,

PASSENGER TIRES ON DISPLAY AT THE ST. PAUL TRACTOR SUPPLY STORE

BIG BEAR WOULD KEEP ITS NAME EVEN THOUGH IT WAS PART OF TRACTOR SUPPLY.

and Carroll Wholesale Supply of Carroll, Iowa, in 1962. Five years later, in 1967, Tractor Supply acquired Big Bear, Inc., headquartered in St. Cloud, Minnesota, and its chain of eighteen farm supply stores in Minnesota and Iowa through an exchange of stock. At the time of the deal, Big Bear sales were nearly $6 million.

TRACTOR SUPPLY LOOKS MORE LIKE A JUNIOR DEPARTMENT STORE WITH THE GRAND OPENING OF THIS SIOUX FALLS STORE IN 1969.

Robertson's, Western Mercantile, and Big Bear would continue to operate under their traditional and long-revered identities. This was not the case for SAS, Inc., of Aberdeen, South Dakota. SAS was acquired by Tractor Supply in 1969, and its stores converted to the Big Bear brand.

What Schmidt and Tractor Supply couldn't accomplish through expanded market coverage, they tried to accomplish through expanded product offerings.

Just how far could Tractor Supply stretch itself in terms of product lines and customers until it was no longer Tractor Supply? The company answered the question itself when in 1967 it began changing its name and signage to TSC stores to shed the "farm" image and better reflect its diversification into broader categories of products and customers.

"Through the '60s, we changed our image a lot," Max DeForest said. "We were changing from the old parts store to more of a farm and home place. We started adding some things. We sampled a lot of things. Some clothing items. Maybe appliances didn't work here, but they might in this store. Tractor Supply was slowly changing its image.

"We went from Tractor Supply Company to calling ourselves TSC Industries and TSC Stores so we'd be broader. So customers would recognize it as more than tractor parts."

Even what the initials stood for – Tractor Supply Company – was changed to Town, Suburb and Country to broaden the stores' appeal.

While Schmidt had seen the number of tractors on farms grow from about 1 million to 5 million over the company's twenty-six-year history, he also admitted to the analysts that he'd seen the number of farms in the United States shrink dramatically from 5.2 million to 3.7 million.

"But even more significant, in 1960, a mere 800,000 farms – 22 percent of the country's total – sold over 70 percent of the total farm products," said Charles Schmidt in a presentation.

THE UNINVITED COFFEE GUEST

The world was changing. Agriculture was changing. Tractor Supply's customers and their needs were changing. And during the '60s, Charles Schmidt would undergo a change, too – from calculating upstart to free-wheeling success.

Tractor Supply was in more-than-capable hands under the proven leadership of Wes Walker and Gard Abbott and the emerging leadership of others like Max DeForest. Schmidt was freer now to spend time at his home in Florida and play the new role of successful businessman, entrepreneur, and investor. Perhaps restless or maybe looking for new opportunities, Schmidt began looking for other mountains to scale. He started to broaden his focus and business interests. Take his company public. Consider and make acquisitions. Control the pricing of products in his stores by identifying and acquiring key suppliers. To help him navigate this more fiscally demanding landscape, Schmidt looked, as he always had, to the right people.

He would begin with Richard Schaefer.

In 1959, Tractor Supply placed an ad in the *Wall Street Journal*, looking for a forty-year-old financial expert who had corporate experience. It didn't matter that he was eleven years under the ad's age requirement or a public accountant with no real corporate accounting experience. Dick Schaefer was aggressive and confident, so he applied anyway.

"They thought I was too young and didn't have enough experience," said Schaefer. At the end of the interview, they said they'd call him back. But they never did. Not ever one to simply see what would happen, the twenty-nine-year-old Schaefer made things happen. He picked up the phone. And he was rewarded with another meeting.

At his second meeting with the company's chairman, Schaefer was bombarded with hypothetical "what-ifs" to try and gauge how this relative corporate novice would fare at Tractor Supply. To Schaefer, the meeting seemed to be going nowhere and so he spoke up and stirred the pot.

"Chuck was going to get up and leave," Schaefer recalled. "And I said, 'Before you leave, where do we go with this thing?'

"He said, 'Well, this isn't my responsibility to fill this job. This is Gard's responsibility.' "

The persistent Schaefer then turned to Gard Abbott and asked him what he would do if it were his responsibility. Abbott said that he would probably hire him. Persistence, poise, and tenacity served Schaefer and would ultimately serve Tractor Supply well.

From two rather inconclusive and innocuous meetings, Schaefer managed to emerge with a job. He was hired as assistant treasurer for Tractor Supply Company. Schaefer's combination of assertiveness and financial acumen would complement Schmidt's need to venture out.

"I developed a pretty good relationship with Chuck pretty quickly," Schaefer said. "Chuck was open and forward-looking all the time.

FOUNDER CHARLES SCHMIDT

A PIPING HOT CUP OF COFFEE SERVED AS A CATALYST FOR TSC EXECUTIVE MEETINGS.

"I started out and the company was reasonably well controlled. It had a rudimentary accounting system," Schaefer explained. "In my initial role as a CPA, I sort of took over the accounting and organized it for bigger and better things, and I think shortly after that we brought in the first accounting or computerized system and developed that for inventory control.

"I was coming up with ideas. I don't know if they were exclusive or anything but I pushed things. I think we got into the credit business, then we started acquiring companies, and very quickly I was the guy in charge of accounting."

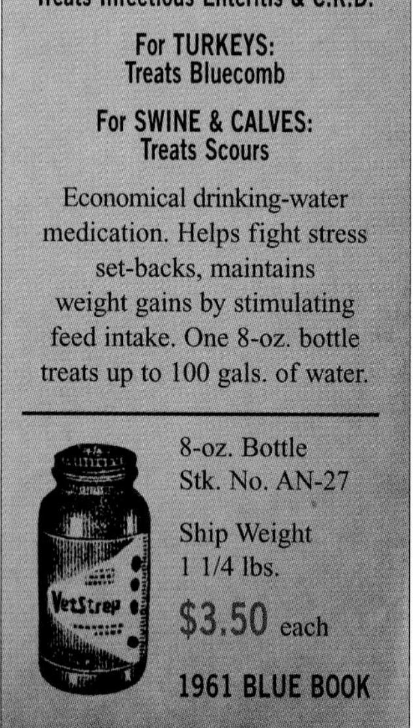

Schaefer's fire and drive played well with Schmidt's growing vision.

"I think Chuck had the vision that they had something good, obviously, and that there was no reason they couldn't grow because the money was there. Once you were public and making money, it was easy to finance the growth, which we did several times," Schaefer said. "I think he [Schmidt] knew that while Gardner had a lot of strengths, he needed help, as everyone does, as you expand. You need new disciplines and new thinking. So it just developed. And it wasn't hard to do because Chuck was quite progressive.

"He wasn't wild by any means, but he had vision. He did it all his life."

Vision in any business venture is a must. But it's rarely enough. It's an unplanted seed. The right soil – a working environment that appreciates, recognizes, rewards, and empowers vision – is equally necessary for vision to come to fruition and business to achieve success.

Dick Schaefer had stepped into just such an environment, an environment open to ideas and empowering people to do whatever it takes to make it right, an environment that would become the capstone of the Tractor Supply culture.

A part of the Tractor Supply culture in Schaefer's day was an informal coffee session that started each day with the company's top executives in Charles Schmidt's office. Today the coffeepot has given way to the rental car. The same kind of easy, freewheeling exchange of ideas over coffee is now part of the legendary road trips the company's key executives take together to visit stores, theirs and competitor's, while gathering, sharing, and spinning ideas as they travel cooped up in a car together.

But back in the late '60s, Tractor Supply's vehicle of choice was coffee rather than a car, caffeine rather than octane. Schmidt, Walker, and Abbott would all gather for coffee each morning. Schaefer, as was his way, showed up for coffee, too. Though never officially invited, he was also never asked to leave.

"The atmosphere was pretty wide open," said Schaefer. "Chuck was open, Chuck had ideas.

"Here's a little anecdote. Chuck and Gardner and Wes and I were at this little coffee thing we had every day, it was ten, fifteen minutes, no agenda, informal. We would talk about ideas: where to take the company, what should we do, should we get into manufacturing, and all this kind of stuff. After quite a few weeks of talking about this one subject we had sort of worked it all out and beat it to death and were going nowhere.

"One of us said, 'Let's do something about this or quit talking about it and talk about something else.'"

In response, Charles Schmidt gave everyone a piece of paper and asked them to write down what they thought they'd agreed to do. As you might expect, everyone had a different answer. In that open and informal atmosphere, over a cup of coffee and among friends – sort of like a small town coffee klatch – the ideas that propelled Tractor Supply into the next phase of its evolution were born.

BATTLE-FORGED BONDS

With competitors taking a run at Tractor Supply's low-price position, an edge the company had built its reputation on from the beginning, controlling the manufacturing and, therefore, controlling the pricing of replacement parts became more attractive. And so in 1960, the company's first major acquisition took place, and the relatively new Dick Schaefer was part of the deal.

"We acquired a company out in Bakersfield, California, that made spindles for cotton pickers – Spindle Specialty Company," said Schaefer. "Chuck went out to make the deal. Then he called me and I went out. We got our heads together and made the deal."

The details of what actually took place offer insight into the character and relationship of the young Schaefer and founder Charles Schmidt. Schaefer had developed a plan for how the acquisition of Spindle Specialty should be handled for tax purposes. He turned the proposal around in one long night of work. Before the deal was closed, Schmidt had a revealing conversation with Schaefer.

"He said something to the effect of, 'You know, this plan you've got has got some flaws in it. I think that was a very stupid thing for you to do,' " remembered Schaefer. "I exploded internally when he used that word [stupid], but I had enough good sense to sit back and probe a little bit."

It turned out Schmidt had taken the young and relatively new employee's plan to his auditors for a second opinion, and he was really expressing their thoughts about his plan.

"Chuck didn't carry things," Schaefer explained.

"He researched it and once he was satisfied, boom, it was there, right in front of you. That was a big part of the atmosphere.

MAC AND MAX, TWO OF THE HARD WORKING EARLY EXECUTIVES

SIOUX FALLS, SOUTH DAKOTA, GRAND OPENING IN 1969

"You were never worried about what anybody thought because what anybody thought is what they told you."

Now that he had the facts, Schaefer fired back as directly as Schmidt had.

"I responded by saying, 'Don't you ever call me stupid again,'" said Schaefer. "'And you'd better research what your auditors told you because I don't think it's right.'"

Schaefer's plan proved correct and, tested by fire and honest responses, the relationship between Schaefer and Schmidt grew closer.

"I can remember how he reacted," recounted Schaefer. "Chuck said, 'Well, if you feel that way, why don't we just strike that word as if it never happened and let me do my research on this.'"

ALL SMILES

A happy group of Tractor Supply executives gather for lunch after the 1962 Shareholders meeting. From left to right, seated, are Richard Schaefer, Charles Schmidt, G.W. Sullivan, Tom King, Wes Walker and Gard Abbott. Standing from left, Max DeForest, Mac McKittrick and Larry Schweik.

So began a relationship that would see the company through a series of key acquisitions during the '60s and ultimately make Schaefer president of what would become TSC Industries.

"I think we had a superb relationship," said Schaefer. "I could pretty well keep up with him. I understood the finances. I understood the goals. There was no question of loyalty on his part, of me I'm sure, or anybody there. It was a group that was really tied together because of this oneness thing."

It's no surprise in a business as people-oriented and driven as Tractor Supply that this "oneness thing" among top management and, at times, its lack, would prove to define the company's pivotal successes and failures.

PISTON SLEEVES AND MINI-BIKES

In November 1961, Tractor Supply acquired Richland Industries of Richland Center, Wisconsin. For years, one of Tractor Supply's more popular items had been the sleeve and piston replacement kits developed by Schmidt and engineer Mac McKittrick. The kits were used by customers to "soup up" or enhance their tractors' engines in order to squeeze just a little more horsepower out of their older equipment. The parts for the kits were produced by Richland Industries. So when the owner of the company neared retirement, it was only natural for Tractor Supply to acquire it.

This move strengthened Tractor Supply's reputation as "the only chain store with an engineering department."

Along with power blocks and sleeve and piston kits, Richland Industries would engineer and produce other parts and assemble equipment for Tractor Supply, such as mini-bikes and air compressors. While Tractor Supply was 85 percent of Richland Industries business, it did supply parts under other labels.

"We made sleeve sets for Ford for some of the Ford tractors, so when we packed them, we packaged them in plain white boxes and they were shipped out of the factory under seven different labels, including Ford Motor Company," remembered Tom Burenga, who became director of manufacturing for TSC in 1969. "It always used to tickle us when once in a while the story would

Powering Sales

In order to better control the price of its own private label products, Tractor Supply purchased Richland Industries of Richland Center, Wisconsin, in 1961. Richland manufactured the company's popular sleeve and piston replacement kits and Power Blocks.

get back to us that a guy would come into a Tractor Supply Store and here would be the sleeve set for forty dollars. He'd look at it and he'd say, 'I probably ought to go down to the Ford dealer and get original parts.'

"You know he'd go down to the Ford dealer and pay seventy dollars, and it was the same damn part."

While some opted to pay for the "original" parts, many more were content to use Tractor Supply parts to save money or soup up their equipment.

"If International Harvester came out with a tractor that put out 40 horsepower, well, if you put Richland Industries/Tractor Supply pistons and sleeves in there, you could get maybe 50 horsepower out of that tractor," explained Burenga. "We also made power blocks. This was basically a whole replacement block that the guys could install in their tractors that would allow oversized pistons and give you more power. They would dramatically increase the power of John Deere's two cylinder tractors.

"In fact, one year a John Deere won the national pulling contest within its class with one of our power blocks."

Burenga may be remembering a victory recorded in the company's 1961 Tractor Parts Blue Book.

"I was thankful for the EXTRA POWER my Tractor Supply POWER-BLOCK gave my John Deere Model 'A' while at the World's Lightweight Tractor Pulling Contest at Givson City, Ill., September 10, 1960, where I won FIRST PRIZE," wrote Bill James of Ada, Ohio. "I also have a John Deere Model 'B' with a Tractor Supply POWER-BLOCK with which I have won more than 50 trophies."

Richland Industries would prove a profitable part of the Tractor Supply portfolio through the '60s. Under Burenga's leadership, the Tractor Supply subsidiary would triple its size, adding more than 40,000 square feet to its existing manufacturing area.

Unfortunately, a tax quirk, a pricing strategy, and two rounds of ownership would lead to Richland Industries' demise.

QUESTIONS OF THE HEART

During the '60s, Schmidt showed early indicators that he was restless and perhaps ready to venture outside farm maintenance parts and supply retailing where he'd sown his first success.

CHARLES SCHMIDT SR. AND JR. SHARED A LOVE OF SPORTS THAT EVENTUALLY LED TO SCHMIDT SR.'S ACQUISITION OF THE MAGES SPORTING GOODS CHAIN IN CHICAGO.

His vision was broadening as a businessman, and he looked to other fields of retailing.

His first major venture outside of Tractor Supply was made with one of his sons' futures in

MAGES SPORTING GOODS WAS A CHICAGO INSTITUTION WHEN CHARLES SCHMIDT PURCHASED A CONTROLLING INTEREST IN 1961.

mind. Since the very beginning, Charles Schmidt made a conscious effort not to bring his boys into the business at Tractor Supply. He'd worked hard to build an organization in which people were rewarded for their own merit, and he didn't want any question of nepotism. There would be no advancement because of who you were, only for what you could do.

Other than summer jobs and Richard Schmidt's brief covert employment at a TSC store while he was in college in Iowa, Schmidt's two sons weren't part of the company. But that didn't mean he didn't want to see his sons following in his footsteps as businessmen.

CHARLES SCHMIDT JR. AND THE GAME HE LOVED

In 1961, Schmidt purchased Mages Sporting Goods in the hopes that his oldest son, Charles Schmidt Jr., would take an interest and work with him in the venture. Because both father and son shared a love and a natural gift for sports, the acquisition seemed a natural to Charles Schmidt Sr.

"My brother was drafted right out of high school by the Yankees organization," explained Richard Schmidt. "But my father was insistent he go to college. That was one of my brother's regrets – that he never got to pursue Major League Baseball – although he went to Florida Southern on a baseball scholarship and did very well.

"In an effort to try and bring my brother into the business, my dad bought Mages Sporting Goods. It was about a fifteen-store chain in Chicago. It turned out to be a financial disaster and he was scrambling around trying to make that work," Schmidt said.

"My brother stayed with the company during all those years, but I'm not sure that was the direction he wanted to go in."

Mages was a Chicago institution. A family-owned sporting goods chain in a blue collar town with an insatiable appetite for athletic competition. Even after selling to Schmidt, the Mages name would later resurface when brothers Morrie and Sam Mages made a comeback in the sporting goods business.

To say Mages proved a disaster for Schmidt is to put it mildly, as most associated with the company would agree. It was the beginning of several financial missteps and emotional decisions by Schmidt that would ultimately see him leave the company and mistakes behind.

To put it simply, Mages proved unprofitable and had problems.

It's hard to imagine that the otherwise cautious Charles Schmidt would have wandered into such a financially difficult circumstance, unless he was led by his heart instead of his head. Is it possible that Charles Schmidt felt some personal guilt for not allowing his son to pursue his baseball dreams? Except for sustaining a serious injury playing football, would Charles Schmidt have given himself so entirely to the pursuit of business while at the University of Chicago? Or was it all just an honest mistake made by an overconfident businessman who thought he could apply his considerable firsthand learning and success in one retail environment to the challenges of another? We'll never know. The two people who could answer this question are no longer with us.

What we do know is that Schmidt quickly looked for a business solution to Mages' financial challenge. According to Richard Schmidt, his father thought that Mages wasn't big enough to reach the critical sales and purchasing mass that would make it profitable. And so he bought and merged it with another popular Chicago retail name, a chain of discount stores called Community Discount Centers.

SMALL TOWN MEETS DOWNTOWN

The successor to a number of retail companies founded in 1947, Community Discount Centers' chain of stores was an early pioneer in an industry that would later be developed and dominated by Kmart and revolutionized by Wal-Mart. Headquartered in Chicago, Community Discount was a much bigger retail operation than Tractor Supply. Its store at Forty-Seventh and Halsted was approximately 120,000 square feet, a far cry from Tractor Supply's 4,000 to 8,000 square feet at the time. Some of the properties were so large they also housed bowling alleys, and one location even sold powerboats. It was an odd mix for what was at the time essentially a farm-equipment replacement-parts retailer. All told, between Community Discount and Mages, Schmidt acquired approximately 45 stores, primarily located in Illinois.

Plainly Schmidt didn't know anything about the discount or sporting goods businesses. But then, when he first ventured out in 1938, he didn't know anything about farming or retail either. The difference with Community Discount was, in a word, people.

"Community Discount was a nightmare," explained Tom Burenga. "There were serious operating problems throughout the company."

JOE SCARLETT WOULD BE PART OF A LEADERSHIP TEAM THAT RETURNED TRACTOR SUPPLY'S FOCUS.

Today, Chairman Joe Scarlett is quick to reply to any question about the company's greatest asset, secret of success or most important consideration for the future with that same single word – people. At the heart of the Tractor Supply mission and three-part mantra of "working hard, having fun and making money" is the unspoken and understood element of people. None of the three other elements of the mission can happen without that one necessary ingredient, the vehicle that drives the company's success – attracting and developing good people. Perhaps inherently, because of the nature of the business, its closeness to the land, and the values drawn through an association with natural world and the hard work that living on the land entails, Tractor Supply has enjoyed a long history of good people in the stores.

"Tractor Supply is a people business," Joe says. "It's about the people in the stores – customers and team members – and keeping those good people happy and satisfied."

The importance of people is certainly borne out by the contrasting fortunes of Tractor Supply and Community Discount Centers. It would prove a valuable but costly lesson for Charles Schmidt and perhaps, ultimately, the reason he sold Tractor Supply.

"Chuck was really struggling with Community, and that whole thing was nothing like Tractor Supply," said Paul Schneider, an executive with Tractor Supply's Chicago accounting firm of Checkers, Simon & Rosner. "It was the total antithesis of Tractor, which was run with precision."

Mages Sporting Goods, Community Discount – Schmidt's solution to getting out of the hole he found himself in was to dig the hole a little deeper. In 1968, Schmidt acquired Shoppers World and Gamble's Department stores out of Minneapolis, Minnesota. Shoppers World was a higher image retail operation than Community Discount, and Schmidt hoped that folding it into Community Discount would bolster the sag-

ging retailer and make “a significant marketing impact” in the Chicago area.

“Chuck was really struggling with Community,” said Dick Schaefer. “He called me one morning, about two o’clock in the morning, and said ‘I’m out at such and such motel by O’Hare so come on out here.’

“It was highly unusual for him to call me at 2 a.m. So I got up and went.”

Schmidt was getting ready to travel to Minneapolis and see Burt Gamble, the owner of Gamble’s and Shoppers World, the next day and wanted to know what Schaefer thought about acquiring the Gamble’s Shoppers World stores in Chicago and merging them with Community Discount.

“I’m going to see Burt Gamble tomorrow, how are we going to finance this?” Schmidt asked Schaefer.

Schaefer suggested borrowing the money to buy Gamble’s stores by using Tractor Supply as collateral.

“My charge was to raise $5 million that day so we could make the deal,” remembered Schaefer. “I told him not to worry about it. I’d do it.”

So he went to Minneapolis and went to the bank and raised $5 million for the joint venture.

Four decades later, the excitement generated by the spontaneity of making the deal is still fresh for Dick Schaefer. He shakes his head and laughs.

“This is the kind of guy he was,” Schaefer said. “I loved every minute of it.”

GOODMAN’S COMMUNITY DISCOUNT, CHICAGO, ILLINOIS, IN 1961

A former senior executive at Goldblatt's Department Store, Samuel P. Sharfman, was brought in to head up the merged retail chain. Finally, the addition of the right person helped improve Community Discount's financial situation. Even so, Community Discount would never prove to be the success Schmidt had hoped, and his son would venture out to pursue his own business career. Charles Schmidt Jr. would go on to become very successful in a sports business, of sorts, with a successful horse farm in Lexington, Kentucky.

Effective February 19, 1968, Tractor Supply Company and Community Discount Centers, Inc., would merge to become TSC Industries, Inc., to form a new mini-retail conglomerate of approximately 207 stores. Headquarters for the two companies was located in the same building at 4747 North Ravenswood Avenue, but with the two entities now operating as separate divisions. The Tractor Supply Division was comprised of 162 stores in twenty-six states and Canada, plus four subsidiary manufacturing companies. The Community Discount Division operated 45 retail stores in seven states, with the heaviest concentration being in Chicago and Illinois. Along with its discount department stores, Community Discount controlled eight sporting goods stores under the names of Mages and M & H Sporting Goods.

Was the move to bring Schmidt's two business interests together a means of consolidating certain functions and facilities as well as cover for Community Discount's lagging profitability? Or was it all an effort to create a mini-retail conglomerate big enough to catch the eye of one of the "conglomerateurs" who were then the darlings of Wall Street? Was he putting everything together so he could sell it all and walk away from a hodge-podge of investments that were making Schmidt increasingly uncomfortable?

Despite the occasional egg and Schmidt's nervousness, the golden goose proved healthy enough to continue to thrive through its third decade. As 1968 drew to a close, almost thirty years to the date of opening his first retail store in Minot, North Dakota, Charles Schmidt stood at the helm of a small but surprisingly vibrant retail, service, and manufacturing mini-conglomerate crafted from the creation of one business and the acquisition and melding of eight or more individual businesses and retail operations. TSC Industries was a growing enterprise listed on the New York Stock Exchange, generating more than $165 million in sales, and employing thousands of hard-working rural and urban people across America.

Perhaps compensating for the fiscal tensions that tore his family apart as a child, Charles Schmidt had poured his life into creating a successful business with "a family feel." So why did he simply walk away from all he'd built so quickly and so completely?

In December 1969, National Industries, a large diversified company headquartered in Louisville, Kentucky, purchased all of Charles Schmidt's stock in TSC Industries, a one-third stake in the company, for a reported $35 million.

It was a shocking move that devastated many of the people who were closest to Charles Schmidt.

A move the company nearly didn't survive.

Famous Brand APPLIANCES

14.88 (1) 8.88 (2) 24.88 (3) 28.88 (4) 12.88 (5)

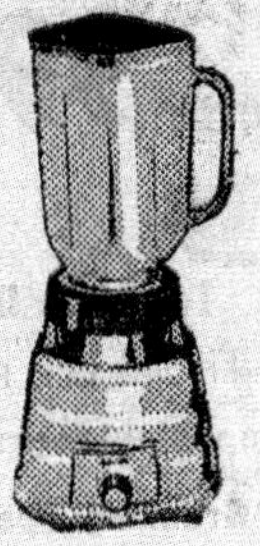

13.88 (6) 8.88 (7) 10.48 (8) 17.88 (9) 12.88 (10)

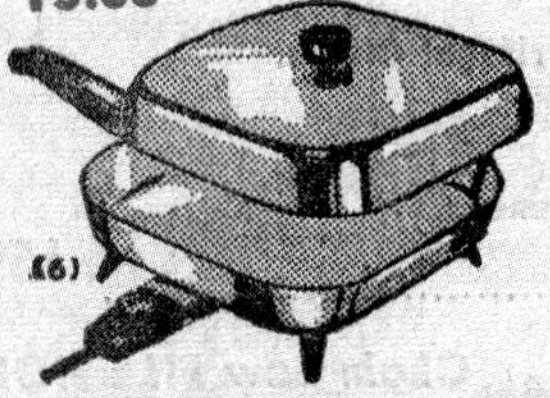

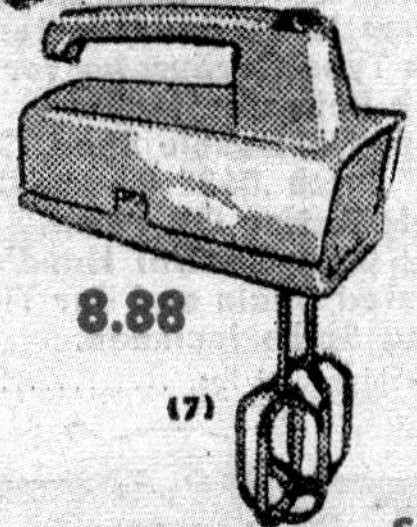

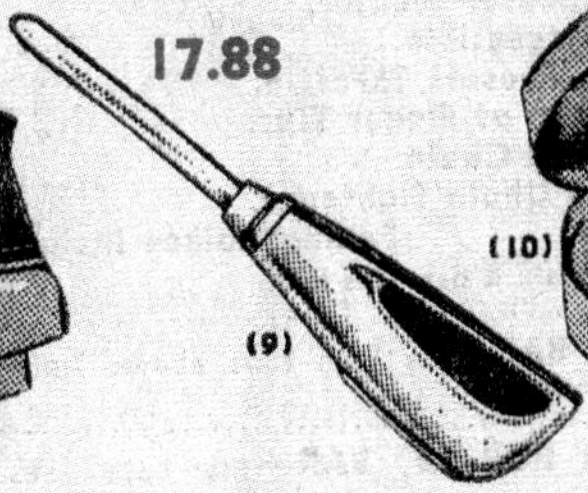

(1) SUNBEAM AUTOMATIC PERCOLATOR
Sunbeam Model AP11A 60-0176—Shipwt. 3 lbs. 14.88

(2) Hamilton Beach CAN OPENER
Model 238 60-0204—Shipwt. 5 lbs. 8.88

(3) Sunbeam MIXMASTER MIXER
Model EM 60-0162—Shipwt. 13 lbs. 24.88

(4) Oster BLENDER
Model 235-01 60-0233—Shipwt. 12 lbs. 28.88

(5) Sunbeam TOASTERS
2-SLICE—Model T46 60-0144—Shipwt. 2 lbs. 12.88
4-SLICE—Model T55A 60-0149—Shipwt. 4 lbs. 19.88

(6) Sunbeam FRY PAN
Model 61PL-C 60-0194—Shipwt. 4 lbs. 13.88

(7) Westinghouse MIXER
Model PM581 60-0156—Shipwt. 3 lbs. 8.88

(8) Sunbeam STEAM or DRY IRON
Model S-22 60-0128—Shipwt. 4 lbs. 10.48

SPRAY, STEAM or DRY IRON
Sunbeam Model SSA 60-0130—Shipwt. 5 lbs 13.88

(9) Hamilton Beach ELECTRIC KNIFE
Model 270 60-0240—Shipwt. 2 lbs 17.88

(10) Lady Sunbeam HAIR DRYER
Model HD-11 60-0220—Shipwt. 6 lbs. 12.88

Lady Sunbeam HAIR DRYER
Model PHD-1 60-0222—Shipwt. 3½ lbs. 21.88

Presto HAIR DRYER
Model HD6 60-0218—Shipwt. 4½ lbs. 9.88

2.88 (Plus Tax)

(1)

18.88

(2)

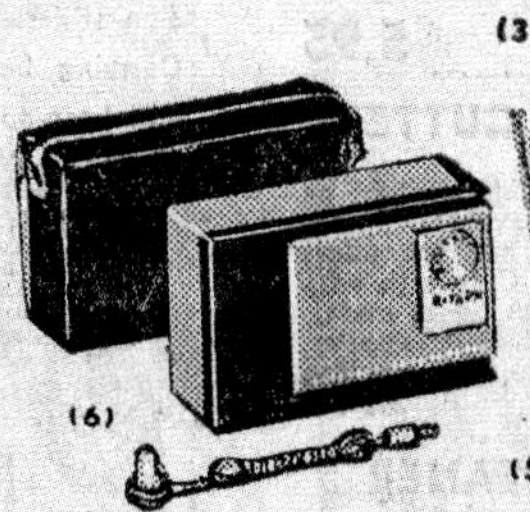
(6)

(3)

(5)

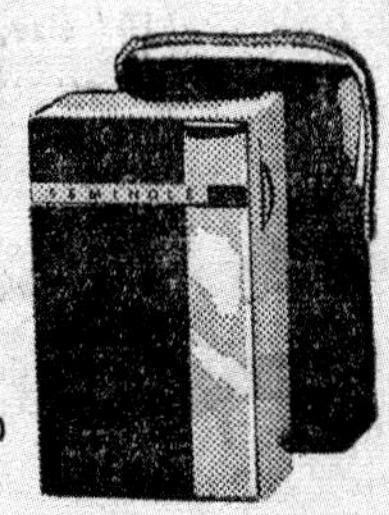
(4)

(1) Sunbeam ALARM CLOCK
Model B016 60-0556—Shipwt. ¾ lb. (Plus 29c FET) 2.88

Sunbeam LADIES' SHAVER
Model LS4 60-0504—Shipwt. 2½ lbs. 6.99

Sunbeam MEN'S SHAVER
Model 333A 60-0507—Shipwt. 1½ lbs. 12.57

(2) Sunbeam SHAVEMASTER
Model NS6 60-0509—Shipwt. 1½ lbs. 18.88

(3) WEATHER STATION
Thermometer, Barometer, Humidity Meter mounted on wood grain wall panel. Metalized finish has glow of polished brass. Dials of etched aluminum. 44-0108—Shipwt. 3 lbs. 9.49

(4) 6-Transistor Pocket Radio
Full 90 day Guarantee. Ideal for local reception. 2¼" speaker. Standard AM broadcast band (535-1605 KC). Use one 9-volt battery (included) for up to 150 hours. Size 4¼"x2½"x1¼". Leather carrying case and earphone included. 60-0253—Shipwt. 1 lb 6.88

(6) 10-Transistor AM Radio
Guaranteed for One Full Year! Standard broadcast band (535-1605 KC). Sensitive vernier tuning. Dynamic 2½" speaker. Long ferrite core antenna. Use 4 standard penlight batteries for up to 400 hours use. Size 5"x3"x1⅜" Leather carrying case and earphone included. 60-0259—Shipwt. 1½ lbs. 13.88

(5) 11-Transistor FM-AM Radio
Standard broadcast AM and static-free FM bands. Big 3½" Dynamic speaker. Vernier pinpoint tuning dial. Two antennas; ferrite core for AM built into carrying handle, and side telescopic rod type for FM. Uses four "C" cells for 6-volt power (included). Automatic volume control and frequency control. 10¼" long, 7½" high, 3⅛" deep. In smart silver, gold and black color. Earphone included. Guaranteed for One Full Year! 60-0262—Shipwt. 5 lbs. 29.88

Batteries for Transistor Radios
High Quality Zinc Carbon Batteries, National Brand Mallory. Avg. Shipwt. 4 oz.
1½ volt "C" Flashlight 60-0304 .... Ea. 16c; 2 for 29c
1½ volt, "AA" Penlight. 60-0306 .... Ea. 16c; 2 for 29c
9 volt Transistor Radio Battery. 60-0318 .... Ea. 59c

TRACTOR S

Huskee

METAL CABS

COMBINE CAB

LOW AS 502.50

Shipped freight collect from central Kansas, allow 7 to 10 days plus transit time. State delivery carrier and delivery point on order. Store prices higher by amount of freight.

- High capacity Fan-Blower circulates 450 C.F.M. of filtered air constantly. Some charge $60.00 to $80.00 additional for this equipment.
- Highly efficient Filter can be serviced from inside cab.
- Flat roof, ribbed for extra strength. Large Visors front and rear.
- Tight, weather-stripped construction keeps out dust.
- Sectional construction simplifies installation.
- Luxurious NYLON Floor Mats—not just rubber.
- ATTRACTIVE BAKED ENAMEL FINISH—OFF-WHITE COLOR
- Exclusive Interlocking Frame—stronger than many other cabs.
- Two full size doors on most tractor cabs. Automotive type la…
- Urethane insulation for greater thermal protection and noise reduction.
- Tinted and Tempered Safety Glass—not just plate glass or plas…
- Windows may be removed, if desired.
- Dome Light and two Mirrors included.

METAL TRACTOR CABS

Specify the following on order: (1) Stock Number (2) Make, year and model of tractor (3) Whether 6, 12 or 24-volt (4) Whether Row Crop or Standard (5) Type of fuel (6) Type of Hitch (standard or 3-point).

FOR ALLIS-CHALMERS 190, 190XT; CASE 930, 931, 1030, (state whether gear or chain drive); 730, 731, 732, 830, 831, 832, 932, 1031, 1032. JOHN DEERE, 3010, 3020, 4010, 4020, (with standard hitch). FORD 6000, OLIVER and COCKSHUTT 1750, 1800, (Series C only), 1850.

2-9285—Aver. Shipwt. 650 lbs. 579.50

FOR ALLIS-CHALMERS D-21; DAVID BROWN 990; IHC 560, 706, 756, 806, 1206, 1256; MASSEY-FERGUSON 95, 97; MINN.-MOLINE 704, 705, 706, 707, 708, G6, (without 3-pt.), 1000. VERSATILE 118, 125, 145.

2-9286—Aver. Shipwt. 650 lbs. 598.50

CAB FOR OTHER TRACTORS

For makes and models of farm tractors not listed above. Cab construction almost identical to Cab pictured above at left, but supplied with flat bottom. Rubber floor mat instead of Nylon. 44½" wide at front, narrowing to 40" wide 12 inches from front. 56¼" from front to back. Purchaser must design and construct axle mounts for row crop tractors, or fender mounts on standard tractors where there is sufficient room for side doors. Write to: TSC, 4747 N. Ravenswood Ave., Chicago, Illinois, 60640, for illustrated sheet showing dimensions and suggestions for designing mounts. Shipped freight collect from Central Kansas.

2-9284—Specify all information requested above. 399.50

METAL COMBINE CABS

Specify the following on order: (1) Stock Number (2) Make, Year and Model of Combine (3) Whether 6, 12, or 24-volt. For John Deere, also state serial number.

FOR ALLIS-CHALMERS A, A2, C2, E; IHC 303, 403, … 45, 55, 95 (ser #20,001 up), 105 (ser. #3,001 up) … DEERE 95 (To Ser. #20,000) 510.50

2-9040X—Aver. Shipwt. 390 lbs.

FOR ALLIS-CHALMERS C (Thru 1964), E3, F, G; …

2-9041X—Aver. Shipwt. 390 lbs. .... 510.…

FOR CASE 600, 660, 700, 900, 960, Grain; IHC …, 93, 203; MASSEY-FERGUSON … 80, 82, 90, 92, 300, 410, 510; MINN.-MOLINE 2890, 2890, … OLIVER AND COCKSHUTT 430, 431, 525, 535, 545.

2-9287—Aver. Shipwt. 480 lbs.

HOT WATER HEATER FOR TRACTORS, COMBINES, TRUCKS

For cabs and trucks—Compact, efficient. Only 6¾" square by 7¼" deep. Powerful blower. Mount it almost anywhere in metal tractor or combine cab, truck or car. Two ¾" … Includes 30 ft. of hose, switch and fittings. For 12-volt systems only.

2-9083X—Shipwt. 12 lbs. 41.99

ADJUSTABLE WIDE FRONT AXLES

Low as 232.50

For IHC M, Super M, 400, 450

Convert your row crop tractor to Wide Front. Gives greater stability, safety, easier steering and stops wheel clogging. Imrpoves flotation. Easily adjusted in 2" increments from 58" to 84", for rows of various widths. Easy to install. Just remove original spindles and pedestal, and replace with new mounting bracket and steering arms. If not in stock at your T.S.C. Store shipped freight prepaid from factory.

FOR IHC M, SUPER M, 400, 450

Hubs not included. Use original wheels, hubs, bearings.

2-7150—Shipwt. 280 lbs. 232.50

FOR OTHER TRACTORS

Includes bearings and hubs for original 6-bolt wheels or new flotation wheels.

For the following tractors:

CASE 400, 700, 700B, 730, 800, 800B, 830, 900, 930; FORD 701, 740, 900, 901, 2000, 4000 (before 1965), 6000; IHC H, Super H, M, Super M, 300, C, Super C, 200, 230, 300, 340, 350, 400, 404, 450, 460, 504, 560, 656, 706, 806; DEERE 50, 60, 70, 520, 530, 620, 630, 720, 730, 2510, 3010, 3020, 4010, 4020; OLIVER 77, 88, (on OLIVER 77 and 88 front pedestal must be left attached to tractor). State Make, Year, and Model of Tractor.

2-7151X—Shipwt. 260 lbs. 254.95

For ALLIS-CHALMERS WC, WD, WD-45.

2-7148X—Shipwt. 260 lbs. 276.95

For OLIVER 770, 880, 1550, 1650, 1750, 1800, 1850; (models with power steering)

2-7149X—Shipwt. 260 lbs. 276.95

For MINN.-MOLINE M-5 and 5 Star.

2-7176X—Shipwt. 260 lbs. 254.95

For OLIVER 77, 88, 770, 880 (models without Power Steering). Permits pedestal to be removed from tractor.

2-7177X—Shipwt. 280 lbs. 306.95

EXTRA HEAVY DUTY WIDE FRONT AXLES

For Deere and IHC models (listed below) when equipped with loader.

… 3020, 4010, 4020. .... 349.95

… 706, 806, 856. .... 349.95

63

FRONT FENDERS FOR WIDE FRONT TRACTORS

…ERS

CHAPTER ★6★

SOLD!

BIG BUSINESS PLOWS UNDER TRACTOR SUPPLY'S FAMILY FEEL

"WHAT GREATER GRIEF THAN THE LOSS OF ONE'S NATIVE LAND."

- EURIPIDES

COLORFUL AND CONTROVERSIAL

Everywhere he went, Stanley Yarmuth created quite a buzz. During the Golden Age of Conglomerates, he was touted for taking a used car lot public and attempting a takeover of one of Louisville's most beloved institutions – Churchill Downs. Yarmuth acquired more than 26 companies in his meteoric career. One of them was Tractor Supply.

Louisville Courier-Journal, 196

GARDNER IS GONE

Shock. Surprise. Outrage. Disappointment. Deep personal hurt. Those are some of the emotions registered by many of the individuals who'd worked with Charles Schmidt the closest and longest when they learned he was selling Tractor Supply.

People like Gardner Abbott, Max DeForest, and others who had exhibited an amazing loyalty to the company and to Charles Schmidt were first shocked and then hurt that the decision was made without them. People who had worked hard without complaint, finding a personal sense of fulfillment and joy in the work and the obvious success of this company they had built together, found out after the fact that Tractor Supply had been handed to an outsider.

Their disappointment and surprise was, perhaps, made even more poignant given that Tractor Supply had always been a place where honest and informal discussions among the company's leaders regarding its future were the norm. Decisions and plans were typically discussed out in the open. All except this most important of decisions. It seemed counter to the company's culture and certainly its values.

"It came as a complete surprise," said Max DeForest, a vice president and director of the company at the time of its sale to National Industries in 1969. "Dick Schaefer worked closely with Charlie in putting it together. I think it was just between those two.

"It was a shock when the rest of us found out it was sold."

TSC's 30th Anniversary
The celebration of Tractor Supply's thirtieth birthday in 1968 as a successful retail operation had barely finished before the company learned it had been sold. It signaled a changing of the guard, for not only would the ownership of the company change hands, but so would many key executives and critical team members.

Schmidt's son Richard remembers that the emotions that rocked his father's closest friends and associates also reverberated through the family.

"There were some strong feelings when he sold the company to Stanley Yarmuth in Louisville," said Richard Schmidt. "There was a sense that he'd abandoned the people working there.

"I know that it was a decision that my mother didn't agree with, and they fought about it for years afterwards. 'How could you do that to our friends who have been working for us for so long?'

Schmidt's closest friend and associate may have been the hardest hit by the sale of the company.

"I don't think Gard Abbott knew it was coming," said Larry Schweik, secretary of the company at the time of the sale.

"He was very unhappy with how the thing was handled, because he told me that during his first meeting with National, they never talked about any future, they just talked to him about when he was leaving," Schweik explained. "There was never any indication that they wanted to keep him. And he was chairman of the board and one of the guys who had been with Charlie from the very beginning.

"He was a wonderful guy and well loved. And he was pushed out."

"Charlie and Gard were very close friends," said Max DeForest. "Gard was badly hurt over the sale. And, of course, when National took over, Gard was out."

The sale of the company must have been an incredible blow to Gard Abbott. During the '60s, occupied by acquisitions and mergers and the squeaky wheels of Community Discount, Charles Schmidt had become less and less involved in the day-to-day business of Tractor Supply. In 1964, Schmidt made the decision to retire as Tractor Supply's chairman, a decision the board of directors "accepted with regret." Schmidt's departure meant that Abbott, in addition to being president, took on the responsibilities as chairman of the board. It must have seemed a vote of confidence. But it only served to make Schmidt's ultimate decision to sell and get out of the business even crueler.

Louisville Courier-Journal, 1969

STANLEY YARMUTH AND CHARLES SCHMIDT WERE CUT FROM VERY DIFFERENT CLOTH.

Schmidt wasn't blind to the obvious pain his decision inflicted on his close friends and business associates. The fact that he'd made his decision with such secrecy and suddenness may have been an indication of the tremendous personal pressure he was feeling at the time.

"THE AVENUE IS NOW CLOSING"

"He was scared," Richard Schmidt said with candor. "That's why he sold. He had one company that was threatening to go under and another one whose incredible string of successes he couldn't see continuing."

For the man who had meticulously planned the creation of his company and had painstakingly created its first mail-order catalog line by line, the man who knew the company inside and out, it was not knowing what might lay ahead that seemed to frighten him the most.

"I remember he used to come home and he was scared to death at how high the stock price was," said Richard Schmidt. "He said, 'I don't know why people are buying this stock.' And he was very nervous about it. He almost felt like, you know, he was pulling something over on them.

"'People are paying too much for our stock,' he said. 'The company's not worth that much!' He said, 'This is the same company that sold for $8 a share. Now it's going for $35 and it's not possibly worth $35.'"

Schmidt wasn't so enamored by his success that he didn't appreciate certain economic realities. He saw during the 1960s what so many on Wall Street refused to see. Stock prices were over-inflated, the Street was running amuck. The '60s bull market and the excess of the conglomerateurs would give way to the bear market and "stagflation" of the 1970s. Schmidt didn't have to look that far ahead to see that now was the time to get out.

"This avenue is now closing," Schmidt said simply of the successful farm store business he'd built over the last thirty years of his life.

"A lot of the employees were bitter about it, because they thought they were sold down the river," said Kay Gorecki Walker. "But if you could get the money, wouldn't you take it, too?" Walker seems to have summed up the heart of the matter. Yarmuth made Schmidt an offer that, given the circumstances of Community Discount, he couldn't refuse. As shocked as Schmidt was by the prices that the market was paying for TSC stock, he was even more floored by how much his controlling interest in the company was worth.

"Frankly, when Stanley Yarmuth came down to see him and put a number on the table and said this is what he'd buy the company for in cash, it had never occurred to my father that it was worth that much money," said Richard Schmidt. "He never imagined that someone would come and put a check in front of him and say, 'I'll give you this if you'll give me your stock in this company.'

It was a very difficult decision for him. But it was a decision he made on strictly business terms. He'd seen what money issues could do to a family growing up. He must have known what they could do to his "family" company. Rather than rely on those he shared deep emotional ties to and a long history with to help him make the decision, Schmidt turned to the person who'd helped him make so many of his recent financial decisions – Dick Schaefer.

"Chuck never discussed selling out," explained Schaefer. "It just happened to him.

"The story goes he was at a cocktail party and talking to a broker type person. We had a stock offering under way at the time, and Chuck was raising maybe $5 million for himself and the company was raising maybe $5 or $10 million.

"So this guy says to him 'Instead of raising $5 million what you ought to do is cash in.' And that's when he was told about National Industries."

"That's the type of guy he was," said Schaefer. "It really amazed me. He had this meeting like on the evening of day one and on day two he called me and he said come on down to Boca [Boca Raton].

"He said, 'I got an offer to sell the company, and I don't want to sell the company unless you agree, because you've been a very important part in the recent development of this thing and its growth and all the things that have been going on. I want you to think about it, and I want to know how you feel about me selling out.'

"I was very flattered by that," said Schaefer. "I said, 'What you own you can sell, and you have the right to do what you feel you should do. And I don't think it involves me.'"

According to Schaefer, Schmidt replied, "Well, if you're really opposed to me doing this, I might reconsider."

Would he really have reconsidered? Or did Schmidt go to Schaefer already having a good idea what his advice would be and wanting some type of affirmation rather than facing the guilt he might have felt approaching someone like his old friend Gard Abbott or Max DeForest? One can only speculate. Why didn't Schmidt go to one of his longtime business associates to make the important decision to sell the company?

Schaefer, obviously, never asked Schmidt to reconsider his decision, acknowledging that what Schmidt owned, he was free to sell. And so Schmidt sold the company.

MAX DEFOREST WASN'T CONSULTED ABOUT THE SALE OF THE COMPANY.

MINOT, NORTH DAKOTA, STORE BEFORE THEY ADDED ON.

TAKING A USED CAR LOT PUBLIC

It wasn't just that Charles Schmidt decided to sell the company. It's whom he sold the company to that heaped insult onto injury for many of those he left behind. Had he sold TSC Industries to anyone but Stanley Yarmuth, what follows might have been a completely different story.

Stanley Yarmuth was no Charles Schmidt. The two were polar opposites, as were the cultures of the companies they had built.

YARMUTH HOLDS COURT FROM HIS LOUISVILLE OFFICE.

"Schmidt, Walker, and Abbott were dignified guys," said Larry Schweik, who worked at the company's headquarters in Chicago under both administrations. "You'd go to a board meeting and the first time you met Stanley Yarmuth, you were greeted with some kind of a curse word. And that shocked everybody.

"It was really a culture shock. I mean those guys [Schmidt, Walker, and Abbot] never talked like that, and this guy talked that way all of the time."

It seems everyone who knew Yarmuth had a colorful Stanley story. His powerful confidence, perhaps born from a relatively rapid rise from obscurity to the *Forbes* list, seemed to just breed stories of personal eccentricity.

"Yarmuth came in and he was a big bag of wind," said Kay Walker, with the classic candor of a long-time executive secretary. "He had to have his cashmere coat put on by someone. Someone would light his cigarette for him. He was mister big."

"Tractor Supply people were always pretty classy people," Max DeForest explained. "Then National Industries got involved. They were a different breed. A lot of the class was gone, and it just wasn't fun anymore."

And without the fun, working hard would become even harder and eventually making money would go by the wayside.

The differences between Schmidt and Yarmuth went far deeper than language. Their language and personal manners were simply a reflection of character, attitude, and their approach to doing business – qualities they projected into the character and culture of the businesses they created. Where Schmidt had imbued his business with a "family" feel, Stanley Yarmuth viewed business as being all about business. He was a self-professed "economic opportunist" and "wheeler-dealer." He didn't mind being labeled in the press as "the black sheep of the Louisville business community" or derisively pointed to as the man who "took a used car lot public."

This was a reference to how Yarmuth entered the world of business. He got his start selling used cars at National Auto Sale in Louisville, a business owned by his father-in-law.

Born in New York City and raised in New Jersey, Yarmuth settled in Louisville after a World War II tour of duty in the army as a medical corpsman. He participated in the D-Day Invasion of Normandy and was held by the Nazis for ten months in a German prison camp. The decorated veteran came home and soon married Edna Klein, the daughter of Samuel H. Klein, the president of Louisville's third largest bank.

It wasn't long before Yarmuth bought his father-in-law's car lot with a minimal investment of his own money. According to a *Business Week* article on the entrepreneur, Yarmuth purchased other lots so that his sales people could tell a prospective car buyer, "Look, if my boss won't give you a deal, I know a guy across the street who will."

He incorporated his business as Globe Industries and went public in 1963, billing his company as "the used General Motors."

National Industries was born when Globe Industries merged with Kentucky Industries Trust Co. This was followed by a rapid series of mergers and Yarmuth piling up debt as he amassed more and more companies in the divergent worlds of insurance, retail and leisure, petroleum, transportation, metals, and food and beverage. Yarmuth's Dixie-headquartered corporate dynasty controlled everything from Yellow Cab Co. of Louisville to Cott Corp, a New Haven, Connecticut, soft drink company; from Retail Centers of America Inc., a discount store operator, to Vanguard Industries Inc., maker of sports headgear.

A COTT DISPLAY FROM I.G.A FOODLINER DURING THE '60s

The bold and colorful Yarmuth once unwittingly stirred up the disfavor of his adopted hometown by attempting to take over the venerable Louisville institution – Churchill Downs, home of the Kentucky Derby – with the purchase of Churchill Downs Corp. His advances were met with shock, vehemently criticized in the papers, and ultimately fought off.

Cott

A WILD RIDE THROUGH THE GO-GO YEARS

In spite of losing his Churchill Downs bid, Yarmuth rode the crest of young conglomerateurs who captivated Wall Street investors' collective imagination and fiscal resources during the 1960s, merging and acquiring more than twenty-six companies in what has been described in the media as his brief but "wild ride." Yarmuth's many mergers were a commonplace occurrence, part of the fiscal landscape of the time in which he operated.

In 1960, there were 844 corporate mergers in America. Seven years later, by 1967, the mergers in a single year numbered nearly 3,000.

This urge to merge during the '60s was heralded as the "Go-Go Years," and was led by companies such as ITT, Textron and Gulf + Western. During this time, the Wilson Co. was referred to as "Meatball, Golf ball and Goofball," a humorous attempt to make sense of its diverse holdings in meatpacking, sports equipment, and drugs. A 1972 *Time* magazine article commenting on ITT pointed out that a consumer who wanted to boycott the company "could not rent an Avis car, buy a Levitt house, sleep in a Sheraton hotel, park in an APOCA garage, use Scott's fertilizer or seed, eat Wonder Bread or Morton's frozen food; he could not have watched any televised reports of President

CD
FINISH
FINISH
3

OUR OLD KENTUCKY HOME

Eventual Triple Crown winner Seattle Slew leads the field to the finish line to win the 103rd running of the Kentucky Derby at Churchill Downs, May 7, 1977. The venerable track caught the eye of Louisville's Stanley Yarmuth, but when the dust finally settled, Yarmuth had lost his bid for control.

THE KENTUCKY DERBY AT CHURCHILL DOWNS

Nixon's visit to China, he would have had to refuse listing in *Who's Who*; ITT owns that too."

Also known as "multi-form" or "free-form" companies, conglomerates were considered the wave of the future. Putting together diverse business interests was viewed as a way of spreading risks, a means of moderating and averaging out the peaks and valleys naturally experienced by cyclical business operating as individual companies. This same logic had been part of Charles Schmidt's move to bring Community Discount Centers and Tractor Supply Company together. According to conglomerates, one plus one equaled three – the whole company was greater than the sum of its individual businesses.

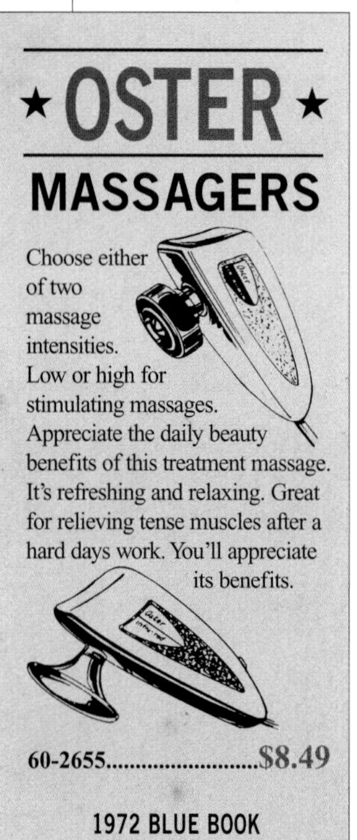

Cocky, confident and oh-so-quotable conglomerateurs like Stanley Yarmuth made for good copy in the media and became the darlings of reporters. Investors embraced the romantic and rather naïve notion that the stodgy single business managers of old were being replaced by fast and farsighted modern-age entrepreneurs who were free to look at the big picture, unfettered by detailed knowledge and the day-to-day demands of any one specific business. Wall Street and the media's blind fascination with the conglomerates and their swashbuckling captains felt more like the dazed devotion of a rock groupie than the dispassionate interest of business analysts.

It was all too good to be true – a pleasant dream from which "the Street" would eventually wake.

According to one study, investors who bought shares of a dozen budding conglomerates in 1965 got more than three times the return than the *Standard & Poor's 400* industrials by 1968. Just six years later, by 1974, those gains were wiped out. In fact, those who bought at the peak in 1968 lost more than half of their investment by 1974, while the rest of the market was up 10 percent over the same period.

The problem, of course, was that most conglomerates were highly leveraged. Many of their acquisitions were financed by debt and warrants. The first winds of a slowing economy and heightened inflation would collapse this house of cards.

The winds were about to blow.

SPEED KILLS

At the time Charles Schmidt made the decision to sell his shares in TSC Industries, the bubble had yet to burst, and conglomerates were still enjoying their brief but brilliant glory days.

As described in newspaper accounts at the time, the proposed transaction between TSC and National would involve 439,575 shares of TSC convertible preferred stock and 427,840 shares of common, giving National Industries 33 percent of TSC Industries, a controlling interest in the company. According to the reports of the day, the deal between Yarmuth and Schmidt had been struck rather quickly. The *Louisville Courier-Journal* reported the stock purchase deal "began with a call from a finder on January 8 [1969] to inquire whether National would be interested in buying control of a New York Stock Exchange listed company with 1968 sales of $168 million.

"Eight days later, National officials met with the prospective seller....By January 21, company officials had visited key TSC retail operations and were ready to interview key management the following week. Negotiations were settled about February 1."

Said National Industries Executive Vice President Charles F. Simonelli in the story, "National is a mobile, opportunity-oriented company."

The speed with which the self-avowed and gleeful opportunist Yarmuth moved in on TSC would later come back to haunt him and might well be one of the missteps that ultimately led to the demise of National Industries.

Yarmuth moved too quickly in two respects – in his impatience to take control of TSC Industries and the speed with which he later asked the company to add more and more stores in order to deliver more and more sales.

In hindsight, a February 3, 1969, story in the *Wall Street Journal* announcing National Industries' plan to buy Schmidt's controlling interest in the company is revealing. The story reported that, according to Stanley Yarmuth, National had no immediate plans to recommend a merger of TSC and National. It's obvious, though, that acquiring TSC Industries' 213 retail stores would help bolster National's retail division of eleven department stores operated by Retail Centers of America and would significantly advance National from an estimated $300 million conglomerate to one with annual sales approaching a half-billion dollars.

Not exactly calling Yarmuth a liar, but also not entirely buying into Yarmuth's announced plans for TSC Industries, the *Wall Street Journal* reporter pointed out that "ownership by National of large blocks of stock in other companies often has led to a merger after a period of time. Such was the case with Retail Centers of the Americas, Cott Corp., Crescent Corp. and others."

And that was precisely what Mr. Yarmuth planned to do in the case of TSC Industries. He intended to merge the company with his own. His intention is suggested in TSC Chairman Gard Abbott's statement to the newspapers after the announcement of National's purchase of Schmidt's stock. Gard said TSC's directors would be meeting early that same week to consider "a National Industries request for proper representation on the TSC management's slate of directors for the next annual meeting."

This "board representation" was the first step in several National mergers. National would get its representation on the board. Stanley Yarmuth would, in fact, take Gard Abbott's seat as chairman of the board, a move that also made Yarmuth, according to the company's bylaws, CEO of TSC Industries. Four additional National representatives would be placed on the board. Of the ten

TSC STORE, LANSING MICHIGAN, 1969

GARD ABBOTT WOULD LEAVE AFTER THE SALE OF TSC.

board seats, five were filled by National. Next, the board quickly approved the sale of TSC to National through an exchange of stock. Because of National's presence on the board and an alleged incomplete disclosure on the proxy statement to its shareholders, the merger couldn't be considered an arms-length deal. Or so one shareholder contended before filing a lawsuit that would be argued in the courts for years. There were also charges filed by the shareholder asserting that National had manipulated to National's advantage.

LARRY SCHWEIK AND TOM FLOOD SERVE TRACTOR SUPPLY DURING THE NATIONAL YEARS.

A lower court ruled in favor of TSC Industries/National Industries but was reversed by the Court of Appeals. Finally, in 1976, the case came before the U.S. Supreme Court, where Justice Thurgood Marshall delivered the opinion of the Court that "none of the omissions… were, so far as the record reveals, material misleading as a matter of law, and Northway was not entitled to partial summary judgment."

Because the case was one of the first dealing with securities fraud in a takeover, *TSC Industries, Inc. v. Northway* has become an important ruling and has been cited in numerous cases since.

Beyond the legal implications and mounting years of legal fees, the lawsuit impacted TSC in other ways. It tied up precious mind power at the leadership level at a time of uncertainty and change.

"I was the first person to be called for a deposition because I was secretary of TSC Industries at the time," remembered Larry Schweik, who would later serve as Tractor Supply president and chairman of TSC Industries during the National years. "Schaefer was president then and he called me one Saturday and said, 'Larry, they'd like to have you on a deposition on Monday.'

"I said, 'You know I've got plans to go out of town.'

"He said, 'Well, just tell our pilot to sit there at the airport with the motor running because you'll only be in there about twenty minutes with the record books and all of that stuff.'

"So, I said, 'Fine.' Well, I went there and I was there for two days. All for a 'twenty-minute deposition.'"

The legal intrigue surrounding the Northway case would be the introduction for a young bookkeeper who would later play an important role in the life of the company. Hired in September 1969, Tom Flood was assigned to help reconstruct the books at the time of National's takeover of the company.

"When the lawsuit came about, one of National's financial people came down from Louisville. His name was Ed Burke," remembered Tom Flood. "I was picked to work directly with him to build all of this information. That's why I'll never forget the date of the purchase."

This would be the first of two purchase dates Flood would never forget. He would be a part of the second one.

Besides the lawsuit, the exchange of TSC stock for National stock was costly in other ways. It hit at the pocketbooks of the company's most valuable resource – its people.

"Tractor Supply had a stock bonus trust plan," Larry Schweik explained. "Most employees participated. It was a wonderful plan. You put 5 percent of your earnings into a pension plan and the company matched that. So that gave you 10 percent. And then the company made a 10 percent contribution to the stock bonus trust depending upon the profitability of the company.

"The company always made sufficient profit to pay out the 10 percent. So, if you participated, you paid a 5 percent contribution and you were given 15 percent more. You had 20 percent of your salary being put away, of which 10 percent went into stock."

Schweik paused. "Of course, when the merger took place, the stock was transferred from Tractor Supply stock to National stock and warrants, and [because of the performance of the National stock] those warrants eventually expired worthless," he said.

"When National bought out the company, they closed our stock bonus operations," said Jack McCracken, an eighteen-year store and district office veteran with the company whose career stretched from the early '60s to the early '80s – the company's highest and lowest points.

"They froze it. And the only way to get the money you had worked for and put in profit-sharing for years was to leave the company. It started out as Tractor Supply Company stock and it split and split. That's where people made their money, you know, back in those days," said McCracken. "Then when National bought Tractor Supply, the stock was converted to National stock, and we lost a lot of what we'd worked for."

WE LOST A LOT OF GOOD PEOPLE

The highest levels of power at National were awhirl in whispers and innuendo. In retrospect, most assume Stanley Yarmuth's "unusual" behavior was the result of the brain tumor that would later claim his life in September 1975. But the myriad abuses weren't easily excused.

Rumored infidelities and jet-setting trips to New York for a fling away from home. IRS investigations. Sales gatherings held at the Playboy Club. A Hollywood consultant once brought in by Louisville management, who told Max DeForest that rather than giving away trips to the annual sales winner, he should give him a starlet. Even the whisper of one of these happenings would have been unheard of under the former leadership at TSC. Under Yarmuth and National, there seemed no end to the wild tales.

These are the sorts of things whispered about by the rank and file who saw the company through the National years and remembered what it had been and what it still might be again.

NATIONAL INDUSTRIES EXECUTIVE VICE PRESIDENT JOE GAMMON, BIG BEAR EXECUTIVE VICE PRESIDENT JIM FRIEDERICHS AND TSC PRESIDENT LARRY SCHWEIK PAUSE FOR A PICTURE AT A CONVENTION IN 1973.

Former Tractor Supply President and TSC Industries Chairman Larry Schweik acknowledges Yarmuth's excesses, but contends that the majority of folks in the company were shielded from Stanley's erratic and abusive behavior by TSC's leaders. And, Schweik recalls, other National executives, like Joe Gammon and Jack Segal, were "stand-up guys."

Even if they weren't subjected personally to the abuse absorbed at the top levels of the company, even if they didn't hear the stories, gossip, and innuendo, the people on the floor, in the field, the folks who served the customers and made sure that the registers continued to ring – they could

TSC in Canada? Tractor Supply, who strategically placed its first store in Minot to be close to the farmers of Canada, finally crossed over the border and made TSC an international company in 1966. It was known as TSC Stores Ltd. in Canada and Joe Parkey from Texas served as the first Canadian General Manager. The first store opened in London, Ontario, in 1966. Four more stores quickly followed. In 1987, the Gang of Five gave the Canadian management team of Murray Cummings, Doug Schneider, and David Street the same opportunity to buy the company. The three purchased the Canadian company. In 2004, there were twenty-one TSC Stores throughout Ontario doing more than $80 million under the slogan "The Incredible Country Hardware Store." Although there are no ownership ties to Nashville, TSC Stores spokesperson is country music star Michelle Wright.

see the results of the outrageous activity and dissatisfaction at the top. They could see people leaving – good people who had long careers with the company, people who embodied the character and values of the company. The heart and soul of TSC's leadership team were leaving. Gard Abbott and Wes Walker, people who were with the company almost from the beginning, respected leaders who worked their way up from the store floor, were gone. When TSC Vice President Max DeForest left, one by one, the zone managers he'd trained left, too.

LARRY FRENCH

"It wasn't a good time," said Jack McCracken. "We lost a lot of really fine guys in the home office. We were hoping they could find some way for it to be bought by them and other employees.

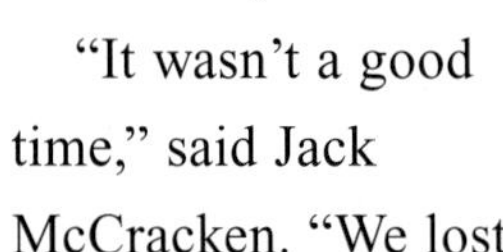

"That, of course, fell through when National came along."

They couldn't help but wonder about the turnover at the very top of the company. There were five presidents during the '70s: Dick Schaefer, president from 1969 to 1973; Larry Schweik, briefly Tractor Supply president and the chairman of the company from 1973 to 1978; Larry French, president of Tractor Supply from 1973 to 1978; and Jack Segal, an executive down from National in Louisville as a brief interim president of Tractor Supply until the company hired Ed Savage, president from 1978 until 1980.

Such turnover at the top had never been a part of the TSC culture and character prior to National's ownership and is generally not the mark of a company enjoying success.

For several reasons, the decade of the '70s has proven the most difficult TSC era to document. During this period, the company was led by five different presidents and two different ownership groups. The two companies that acquired TSC are no longer in existence. Turnover among employees was very high during this time. The company itself is difficult to define, expanding to become something of a miniature retail conglomerate before contracting and returning to its core business during the successful decade that would follow. At the end of the '70s, the company's headquarters moved from Chicago to Nashville.

And, finally, the '70s was an era of decline for the company. People prefer to recount successes rather than be reminded of their failures. We tend to forget, gloss over, or reinvent mistakes and missteps as the forerunners of ideas that paved future successes. In fact, often more is learned and retained from the challenges we face.

Interviews with the four primary leaders of the company during the decade of the '70s – Schaefer, Schweik, French and Savage – tend to center on the positive contributions that were made during their tenures. And, in their defense, there were honest attempts made to strengthen the business. But, in some cases, the decisions being made had more to do with preserving the health of the parent company than ensuring the success of Tractor Supply.

"It was no longer a personal company," said Jack McCracken with a note of sadness in his voice, as if reminiscing of the passing of something or someone dear to him. "It was a conglomerate, a company owned by another company.

"You wondered if your company really mattered to them."

SQUEEZING EARNINGS AND DICK SCHAEFER

Dick Schaefer, the CPA Charles Schmidt had hired back in 1959, was the first to lead the company through the National decade.

Schmidt valued Schaefer for his financial mind. He'd assisted with many of his and the company's acquisitions and helped him to structure what became TSC Industries. During his years with the company, Schaefer did a number of things to improve TSC's financial backbone. He led the modernization of the inventory systems and introduced Tractor Supply's first primitive computerized financial system, developed for inventory control. Prior to that, the company's inventory was all done on handwritten cards. Schaefer also led work on TSC's first early warehouse automation. He instituted the company's first finance credit program and set up the infrastructure for TSC to start carrying its own receivables.

Schaefer was obviously a numbers guy whose talents helped TSC as its treasurer and through the tremendous growth period during the '60s.

"We were broadening our products and broadening our customer base," said Schaefer. "It was working. But once Chuck sold out, the whole thing changed. You had this umbrella over you, which was National Industries."

But it was more than the switch to National. The people at the heart of the company were changing, too.

"Under Schaefer, we really started pushing, expanding the merchandise mix, and we brought in more outside merchandise managers," said French. "That's probably why he had a falling out with a lot of the – I'd call them – farm boys.

A TSC Charge Account

LETS YOU BUY *TODAY* WHAT YOU NEED *TODAY*

THE MOST CONVENIENT WAY TO SHOP.

✔ BY PHONE ✔ BY MAIL ✔ IN PERSON

CHOOSE A PLAN THAT SUITS YOUR NEEDS.

★ ***PAY IN 30 DAYS WITH NO FINANCE CHARGE OR WITH A FINANCE CHARGE YOU CAN SPREAD YOUR PAYMENTS OVER 24 MONTHS.***

Your Satisfaction Guaranteed at TSC

Mail to your nearest TSC store or TSC., 4747 N. Ravenswood, Chicago, Illinois 60640

ACCOUNT NO. ______

PLEASE PRINT ALL INFORMATION

TSC CHARGE ACCOUNT APPLICATION

LINE

NAME First Initial Middle Initial Last Name

AUTHORIZED BUYERS 1. 2.

ADDRESS				PHONE NO.						
CITY	STATE	ZIP CODE	HOW LONG AT PRESENT ADDRESS	OWN	RENT	AGE	MARRIED	SINGLE	DEPENDENTS	
PREVIOUS ADDRESS (IF LESS THAN 2 YEARS AT PRESENT ADDRESS)									HOW LONG	
Acres Owned	Net Farm Income Past Year	Previous Year	EMPLOYER	ADDRESS					HOW LONG	
OCCUPATION	BUSINESS PHONE	WEEKLY EARNINGS	FORMER EMPLOYER (If less than 1 yr. with present employer)						HOW LONG	
EXPLAIN OTHER INCOME IF ANY				NAME AND ADDRESS OF BANK						

CREDIT REFERENCES

1. NAME ______ ADDRESS ______
2. NAME ______ ADDRESS ______
3. NAME ______ ADDRESS ______

TSC CHARGE ACCOUNT AGREEMENT

TSC
In consideration of your selling merchandise to me on a TSC Charge Plan, I agree to the following regarding all purchases made by me or my Charge Indentification Card.

1. I have the privilege of a charge account, in which case I will pay the full amount for all merchandise purchased within 30 days from the date of each billing statement with no finance charge.
2. If I do not pay the full amount for all merchandise purchased within 30 days from the date of each billing statement, the following terms shall be in effect.
   (a) I will pay the time sale price for each item purchased consisting of the cash sale price and the finance charge of 1½% on the monthly balances of my account until the full amount of all purchases and finance charge thereon are paid in full. The finance charge is computed by a single periodic rate of 1½% applied to my "previous balance" without deducting current payments and/or credits appearing on the face of the statement.
   (b) I will pay the merchandise purchased in monthly installments which shall be computed according to the following schedule, determined by the highest balance of my account.

If the Unpaid Balance Is:	The Scheduled Monthly Payment Will Be:
.10 - 10.00	Balance
10.01 - 100.00	5.00
100.01 - 120.00	6.00
120.01 - 140.00	7.00
140.01 - 160.00	8.00
160.01 - 180.00	9.00
180.01 - 200.00	10.00
200.01 - 220.00	11.00
220.01 - 240.00	12.00
240.01 - 260.00	13.00
260.01 - 280.00	14.00
280.01 - 300.00	15.00
OVER 300.00	1/20 of Balance

   (c) I will pay each monthly installment computed as provided above upon receipt of each statement. If I fail to pay any installment in full when due, the entire unpaid balance shall, at your option, become immediately due and payable.
   (d) You will send me each month a statement as of a specified billing date determined by you which will show the previous balance as of said billing date, the finance charge based upon my balance on the preceding billing date, the dates and amounts of each purchase, payment, and credit, the minimum monthly payment and the new balance.

NOTICE TO THE BUYER

Do not sign this credit agreement before you read it or if it contains any blank spaces. You have the right to pay the full amount due or any part thereof in advance.

CUSTOMER'S SIGNATURE x ______ DATE ______ ACCEPTED: TSC BY ______

TSC CREDIT CARD APPLICATION

He had a lot of new products coming in that they didn't really like or believe in.

"Tractor Supply was becoming a more sophisticated company, and it was outgrowing some of the people."

Schaefer's view differs. In his estimation – beyond the issue of clashing cultures – part of the difficulties under National was created by the parent company's focus on the bottom line and a lack of understanding of the farm store business.

"They [National] weren't too knowledgeable," explained Dick Schaefer. "They wanted to change things in Tractor Supply and me being me, I wouldn't do it. I just refused to do it."

"They tried to make pronouncements that they didn't know anything about," said Schaefer. "You'd sit down and have a rational discussion about what you wanted to do and why you thought you should do this or do that. And they may have comprehended it, but they didn't like the result, so they didn't support it."

The "result" National was looking for was earnings and happy shareholders. It was a focus that proved counterproductive for the company and is something that is markedly different from today's Tractor Supply.

"Our focus is people," said today's Chairman Joe Scarlett. "Our people first, the customer second, vendors third, and our communities fourth. We don't focus on the investor because if we center our energy and attention on our team members, customers, vendors and the communities where we do business, then we're going to have good results.

"Wall Street will take care of itself," Joe explained. "Their primary interest is results. And we'll get the results they're interested in only if we focus our attention on the key elements of the business. A lot of companies focus too much of their attention on the words they deliver to investors, providing 'good stockholder value.'

"We don't spend a lot of time talking about stockholders."

It's interesting to note that Joe came to leadership of the company through human resources, while Schaefer came to leadership through the financial end of the business. Ultimately, the focus on people would prove more profitable.

CHAIRMAN JOE'S CUSTOMER FOCUS ULTIMATELY BENEFITS INVESTORS.

Schaefer's focus wasn't just on the bottom line, but also on the long-term success of the business. He would stand his ground when National kept trying to squeeze the business.

"They wanted me to increase the margins and I just flat refused," said Schaefer. "We've got 12,000 SKUs or whatever the heck we had and they didn't know anything about it. They were just looking at numbers and someone said to Stanley, 'If we could get higher gross margin out of Tractor Supply, this is what it would do to our bottom line.'

"They wanted to squeeze out more earnings. They didn't really care about the business."

Obviously, Schaefer excelled at the monetary side of the business and the company grew under his leadership. However, the people side of the business seemed to suffer. Perhaps it was the pressure put on him from above or the change in the company's management team.

Before taking over the reins at Tractor Supply, Schaefer had always been a part of a management team and partnered with leaders who had great people skills. But, with Schmidt, Walker, and Abbott gone and DeForest leaving a few years later, it was the people side of the business, the culture of the business that seemed to suffer.

"We had a familiar situation," Schaefer said. "I was the upstart guy.... I think that we could have gone along under my leadership okay, but with Chuck being in the background. But I think when it became evident that Chuck was no longer going to be involved.... I think there was probably disappointment."

"When Gard was president of the company, he wouldn't do anything that involved me without checking," said Max DeForest. "If something came up, he'd say, 'What do you think about this?' And we made a decision.

"I thought a lot of Dick and I was a great promoter to get him to be president," said DeForest. "He'd been treasurer and he was very, very aggressive. I worked closely with him before. But the attitude changed quite a lot when Dick Schaefer became president. He got into everybody's business."

Eventually, DeForest, another farm boy who'd worked his way up through the store to a leadership position within the company, a man who commanded tremendous respect among the store people, left.

"I just had to get out of it," said DeForest, by all appearances pained to this day by the difficulty of the decision. "If I'd stayed in, pretty soon my word wouldn't be any good and that's what was important – my word to the people I worked with.

"And so I left."

Schaefer, too, would leave just a few years later in 1973. He won't discuss the specifics of his departure from TSC Industries other than to say he was treated fairly, but there were differences of opinions on how the business should be run and he had other opportunities. Long in the middle of deals made at Tractor Supply, ironically, Schaefer would play a minor role in the business again when the company was sold to Fuqua.

GROWING PAINS AND A TALE OF TWO LARRYS

Larry Schweik and Larry French, the two men who led Tractor Supply through the last half of the National years, provide an interesting contrast that serves as a subtle indicator of the disparity within the company.

Schweik was a lawyer; French, an ag grad. Both rose relatively quickly to leadership in the company, partly because of their individual talents, partly due to the turnover in leadership that plagued the National years. Schweik's career began in Chicago at the headquarters while French began out in the field as a manager trainee. Their viewpoints reflect their differing experiences. Schweik focused more on the financial aspects of the company while French's merchant eye seemed to pay more attention to what was happening in the store. French's memories from the period are more personal, while Schweik's are more oriented to the business.

Schweik was hired in 1958 as assistant to Gard Abbott who was then a vice president at Tractor Supply. Like Abbott, Schweik's background was in law. In fact, Schweik received his law degree from DePaul University in 1963 while he was also working at Tractor Supply.

"Larry Schweik was a hard worker," said Max DeForest, a real compliment coming from the hard-working DeForest. "He went through law school while he was working full time at Tractor

★ 3 H.P. ★

MINI BIKE

Great fun off the road at the farm or in the field. The 127cc. engine drives it up to 20 MPH, with automatic governor for safety. Twistgrip throttle, adjustable internal shoe brake, automatic clutch, ballbearing wheels, 5" knobby tires, spark arrestor muffler, front and rear fenders, fold up foot pegs, and kickstand give you a super bike at a super price.

1-9301......................$129.95

1973 BLUE BOOK

Supply. He had to be a real hard worker to get through school like he did. "

Schweik, who served as the company's attorney in the real estate department, was known for driving a hard bargain. In 1962, when Gard Abbott became president of the company, Schweik was promoted to assistant secretary of the company at the same time that Dick Schaeffer became treasurer. He was named secretary a year later, executive vice president and, finally, president of TSC Industries in 1973.

The man Schweik chose for president of TSC Industries' Tractor Supply division was Larry French. French was born and raised on the farm. He went to college at Illinois State University to become an ag teacher. Instead of teaching, however, French joined Tractor Supply's store manager training program in 1959. A year later he opened Branch No. 39 in Quincy, Illinois.

"It was fun," said French. "It was a great company, good people. It was like family. You felt like you belonged. It was never a high-paying company. We never made a lot of money, but you had camaraderie with other people and a tremendous esprit de corps that was hard to beat."

Yes, it was a fun time. French still looks back on his introduction to his boss, Max DeForest, with a smile and an undimmed memory, because it was a colorful meeting.

"The stores had always been gray, kind of blah-looking, and so I decided they needed to be a little brighter," French said, pausing occasionally to chuckle, the memories still fresh forty years later. "I was doing a monochromatic color scheme with three different colors, which ended up being nine different shades of these colors, when Max walks in.

"We're hustling along, and I turn around and say, 'Hi, Max,' and dump the paint pan right down my front.

"Those are the things you'll never forget."

DeForest referred to French fondly as "the ninety-day wonder." It was a telling title, perhaps more than Max knew. French moved quickly up the company ladder. Store manager at twenty-one. Zone manager at twenty-five. Vice president by thirty. Tractor Supply was moving quickly and so were many of the people leading it.

LARRY SCHWEIK

LARRY FRENCH

THE TWO MEN WHO LED TRACTOR SUPPLY THROUGH THE END OF THE NATIONAL YEARS

"When National first took over, they loved Tractor Supply, because we were profitable," French said. "So they really pumped us to grow as fast as we could grow.... We opened so many stores that we had an awful lot of young managers.

"We'd select managers before they were ready."

Like Dick Schaefer before him, Larry Schweik tended to focus on what he knew best – more emphasis on the numbers and financial concerns than on people matters. In Schaefer's and Schweik's defense, the heavy financial orientation of the company at the time was a direction that trickled down from the top. Almost immediately after the sale of Tractor Supply to National, the conglomerate's fortunes began their downward slide during the '70s, and anywhere cash could be squeezed from holdings like Tractor Supply to cover the debts of the highly leveraged parent company, it was.

"They [National] wanted a lot of growth," explained Schweik. "But they also had cash needs. They had a tendency to draw money out of the company, too. On one hand, you were pushed to grow and then on the other hand you're delivering cash to them, which is kind of hard to do, but the farm stores did grow."

QUINCY, ILLINOIS, STORE

And grow they did. The company that had never added more than seventeen stores in any single year of its previous thirty-one years in business, grew by twenty-two stores in 1970 and another twenty stores in 1973. During four of the first six years of National's involvement, the company grew at a record clip of nearly twenty stores a year, but it was not by choice.

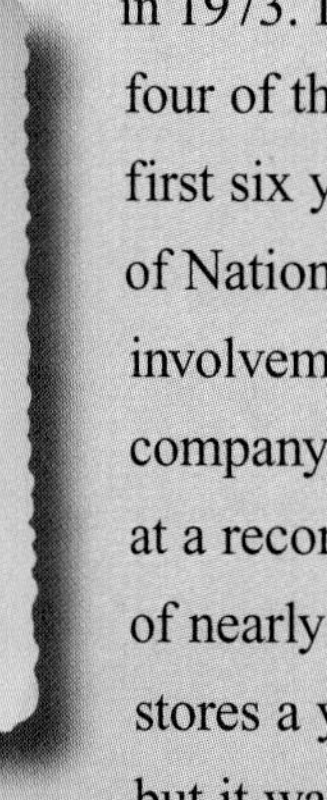

MINOT, NORTH DAKOTA, STORE

"The expansion plans were dictated by National Industries, saying you have to open this many stores and so on," said Tom Flood, who was working for the controller at that point in his career. "They were requiring us to grow at a minimum of twenty-five stores a year and we did that, but it was tough. It was real hard to do.

"In fact, as I remember, there were some stores we opened the doors on December thirtieth with virtually no inventory just to say we opened the twenty-fifth store that year."

National was burning the Tractor Supply candle at both ends, drawing cash from the company while at the same time demanding growth.

"The company suffered for a lot of reasons," said Tom Flood. "Growth was one, because we didn't have the financial wherewithal to do all of the growing. We had to borrow a lot of money from National Industries, and so we carried a pretty heavy debt load. Things weren't great, but the company still managed to hold its own for awhile."

The growth spurt put additional pressure on the company's infrastructure and magnified problems with inventory, delivery, and keeping merchandise on the store shelves. In addition, there were growing personnel issues, and the company had made major acquisitions of competing farm store chains with Big Bear and SAS. And, while buying these competitors brought additional talent and experience to the quickly expanding company, it did not create a unified company with a shared focus, mission, and values. Unlike the days of Schmidt and Walker and Abbott, there was no one to promote the culture of the company. The company's focus had shifted to earnings and growth and serving the financially troubled conglomerate that controlled it.

"Part of the charge by National was for us to grow," said Schweik. "We also began to streamline the merchandising program at the farm stores and get a better handle on keeping the merchandise replenished.

"We were working with Touche Ross to develop an electronic inventory system along the lines of what you see almost anywhere today. Go into a retail store today and they scan the merchandise and know what and where everything is.

"I think one of our major problems was one of keeping merchandise properly replenished, trying

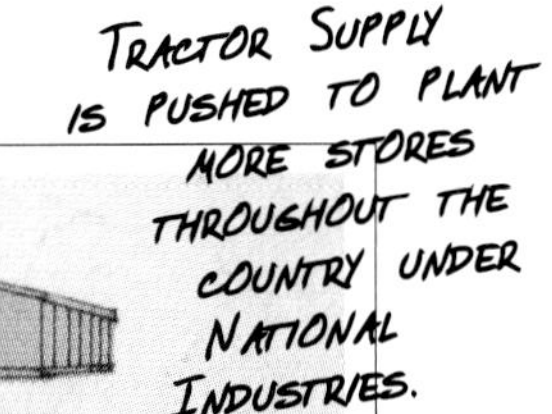

to have the right mix of lines and not a proliferation of lines," said Schweik. "All of that and at the same time build the stores.

"National was always interested in having a lot of stores. We probably needed to close more stores than we did. The tendency was to keep stores going because they delivered something to the bottom line."

Larry French left Tractor Supply in 1978 over a dispute about Touche Ross handling the inventory control system. He wanted the job handled internally. Instead, Schweik and Gammon opted to go with Touche Ross, a decision that resulted in a half million dollar expenditure for a system that was never implemented, according to French.

But French doesn't blame the company's poor performance completely on inventory control. He points to the problems of leadership, a loss of contact in the field, and a company trying to be too many things to too many people.

"I think the combination of not staying focused on our core business and trying to get into too many things caused us problems," said French.

"I was telling my wife, you know, I look back on my career and I think I would take some of the blame because I didn't really have any support from the top," explained French. "We were so fragmented. Larry Schweik was a bright guy, a lawyer by education, but not a merchant.

"As I told many people, I became a corporate dropout because all we did was go to meetings and talk about what we should do. We weren't out in the field seeing what we really had to do. We stayed in the office more than we should.

"We had lost touch with the field, I think."

While it had continued to grow, almost without interruption, for nearly forty years, there was a limit to what Tractor Supply could deliver. National couldn't keep squeezing earnings and forcing growth. It couldn't last. And it didn't. Tractor Supply's growth spurt came to an abrupt halt in 1976. For the next three years, the company would only open a store or two annually. It was a time of double digit inflation, rising interest rates, and high energy costs. It was a time of a slowing economy and recession and the bold excesses of the conglomerates had lost their luster on Wall Street. National was struggling. The huge debts it had piled up while amassing its broad

September 1969, South St. Paul, Minnesota

conglomeration of the companies was now crushing National under the weight of soaring interest rates. And, because National didn't show the same aptitude for running the companies it was so good at acquiring, its individual holdings were less and less able to produce the earnings National needed to survive. And so it didn't.

Schweik stepped down and remained a vice president with the company, leaving TSC Industries when it moved its headquarters from Chicago a year later.

The search was on for a new leader for Tractor Supply. In the brief interim, Jack Segal, an executive at National Industries, presided over the company. Before they could find a replacement, National would be acquired by another conglomerate – Fuqua Industries.

ED SAVAGE SEES AN OPPORTUNITY

If there's a lesson in the Fuqua years, it's that in the depths of failure are often sown the seeds of success.

ED SAVAGE CONGRATULATES KAY GORECKI ON HER FORTIETH YEAR WITH TRACTOR SUPPLY.

What may seem like Tractor Supply's lowest point after forty years of operation, actually sets the stage for its greatest growth.

It must have seemed to everyone involved that Tractor Supply's glory days were long passed. But as we shall see, the very best was yet to be.

In 1978, at the same time the company was looking for an executive to lead it, Tractor Supply was being sold for the second time as part of a crumbling conglomerate. In the next two years, it would post the biggest losses in the history of the company, nearly $13 million in a single year. TSC Industries would be dismantled, its discount stores and manufacturing and construction businesses sold. The Tractor Supply chain would give every indication of retreating: stores closed, franchisees bought out, its geographic area shrunk. Most of its leadership would quickly abandon what they thought was a sinking and hopelessly wrecked ship. Hardly the kind of moves that would herald success and the beginning of a billion-dollar business. But these trying and uncertain times would provide the foundation for the rebirth of Tractor Supply, rising amid the ashes of two major conglomerates that are no more. These times would serve to test the mettle and burn away the impurities and imperfections that had served to distract the company's focus.

But first, things had to get a whole lot worse.

To put Tractor Supply's ruined house in order, the company turned in 1978 to the home building materials industry. After all, the company had moved so far from its farm store roots, it made sense to find someone with a background in an industry that broadened the company's customers. And Ed Savage was the man the company turned to.

Ed Savage was a personable leader of a building materials chain, Moore's Building Supplies, headquartered in Roanoke, Virginia. Moore's was owned by Evans Products Co., a company listed on the New York Stock Exchange, and Savage had been with Evans twenty-four years. Prior to his nine years with Moore's Building Supplies, Savage had been at another Evans company – Grossman's Lumber. He was promoted to general manager of Moore's to help turn the failing company around.

"It was a turnaround situation," explained Savage. "The company was losing about $2 million a year when I started. We had thirty-five lumberyards and I immediately closed three. When I left nine years

The Schmidt Legacy When Charles Schmidt sold Tractor Supply to National Industries in 1969, his business career was far from over. Schmidt settled with his wife, Dorothy, and son Richard in Boca Raton, Florida. He operated two area golf courses and in 1975 went into banking. His Gulfstream Banks, Inc. became a twenty-seven-bank holding company that was listed on the New York Stock Exchange. He sold the banks to NCNB which today is Bank of America. Late in his life, Schmidt was known for his philanthropy. A $10 million gift to Florida Atlantic University in 1991 helped build the school's Dorothy F. Schmidt Center and endowed two eminent scholar chairs. Charles Schmidt died May 1996 at the age of eighty-three. The Schmidt Family Foundation continues his good work. In September 2001, the Charles E. Schmidt Biomedical Science Center officially opened at Florida Atlantic University, built with a $15 million gift from The Schmidt Family Foundation.

later, we had eighty-two building centers and were highly successful and very, very profitable."

Because of his turnaround experience, Savage was contacted by an executive recruiter for the Tractor Supply job. At first, he was reluctant to take the job so he simply offered only to visit a few stores.

"I visited the stores, and I could see some real opportunities," Savage remembered. "They didn't have what I felt was the merchandising technique. They didn't have the displays, the signage and things that could have made their stores much more vibrant and probably could mean more sales."

Savage, who has a penchant for always looking at the positive, saw an "opportunity" at Tractor Supply and so he decided to learn more about the company. At the time, TSC Industries was comprised of about 225 Tractor Supply Stores in twenty-two states and southern Ontario, Canada; twenty or so franchise stores; several manufacturing facilities for cotton picker parts, engine sleeve kits, pumps, compressors and three-point equipment for tractors; a construction company for pole barns and environmentally controlled structures for raising hogs; and a chain of discount stores mainly in the Chicago area. Savage was taken by the size of the opportunity and chance to be the company's president and CEO.

"I told my boss at Evans, 'This is an opportunity that I will never have again,' " said Savage. "And I took the job."

Savage also learned that the company that owned TSC Industries, National Industries of Louisville, was in the process of being purchased by Fuqua Industries. He was interviewed by Joe Gammon of National and one of Fuqua's executives, Don McClinton.

"At first, it [Fuqua's purchase of National] troubled me," said Savage. "But I said, 'Well, I see opportunity here, so I'm going to go.'"

Little did Savage know that the opportunity would be far less than he envisioned once Fuqua had dismantled TSC Industries.

Welcome to Nashville, Tenn

CHAPTER ★7★

THE UNDERTAKER CALLS

TRACTOR SUPPLY EXPERIENCES ITS BIGGEST LOSSES

"DON'T IT ALWAYS SEEM TO GO
THAT YOU DON'T KNOW WHAT YOU'VE GOT
TILL IT'S GONE
THEY PAVED PARADISE
AND PUT UP A PARKING LOT."

- JONI MITCHELL, "BIG YELLOW TAXI"

THE MOVE TO MUSIC CITY

The celebration of Tractor Supply's thirtieth birthday in 1968 had barely finished before the company learned it had been sold. It signaled a changing of the guard for not only would the ownership of the company change hands but so would many key executives and critical team members. The company would also make the move from its longtime home of Chicago to the relative wilds of Nashville, Tennessee.

FUQUA AND FARMVILLE John Brooks Fuqua, multimillionaire confidant of several U.S. presidents, international business leader, highly regarded philanthropist, and founder of Fuqua Industries, began his life on a struggling farm. His mother died shortly after he was born in 1918, and J. B. was reared by his grandparents on a farm near Prospect, just a few miles away from Farmville, Virginia.

"I was raised on a tobacco farm in Prince Edward County, Virginia, in very unhappy circumstances," wrote Fuqua in a recent autobiography.

Ironically, given the later acquisition of Tractor Supply that helped him reach his lifelong goal of being head of a billion-dollar company before the age of sixty, J. B. Fuqua sought his fortune by leaving farm life behind.

"…I decided early on that I was not suited for farm life and began preparing myself for a different occupation," wrote Fuqua.

Fuqua, like Charles Schmidt before him, was largely a self-made man. Though he graduated from high school, Fuqua was self-educated, borrowing books by mail from the Duke University Library. He would make the most of this opportunity and later pay back the debt of gratitude he felt by endowing Duke's business school.

WJBF-TV
Not only did Augusta television station WJBF-TV play an important part in J. B. Fuqua's early business career, but it was also Tom Hennesy's first job with Fuqua. His last job with Fuqua would be at Tractor Supply.

From an interest in radios as a child and a twenty-five-cent pamphlet entitled *How To Become an Amateur Radio Operator*, Fuqua would go on to build a media empire. He started as an engineer at a radio station, and within three years, at the age of twenty-two, he ended up owning WGAC, Augusta, Georgia's second radio station. Fuqua would come to control several media outlets, including WJBF-TV, a station that still operates in Augusta and still bears J. B. Fuqua's initials as its call letters. In 1946, at one of his radio stations, Fuqua hired a young man to be an announcer. This new hire would go on to make quite a name for himself. His name was Tom Hennesy.

"He proved to be an invaluable addition to my team," said Fuqua of Hennesy, "and moved with me as I acquired other businesses over the years.

"I could depend on Tom to use his judgment in handling any job," Fuqua reflected in his autobiography. "When I acquired the Claussens bakery, I put Tom in charge of the operation, even though his previous experience had been in radio and television. In the early years at WJBF-TV, he worked a variety of jobs, from station manager to on-air announcer. His versatility was a great help to me."

For his part, Hennesy would describe his relationship with Fuqua in emotional terms rather than the business terms Fuqua used, simply saying, "J. B. was like a father to me."

This close relationship between the two would prove pivotal in the later rebirth and resurgence of Tractor Supply and critical in creating a favorable deal and even some of the funding required for the leveraged buyout of the company in 1984. It's safe to say that without Fuqua's purchase of National Industries, Tractor Supply would have been relegated to history rather than still thriving and celebrating a history of success.

LIKE YARMUTH AT NATIONAL, J. B. FUQUA HAD A SOFT DRINK COMPANY AS PART OF HIS PORTFOLIO.

In 1965, J. B. Fuqua purchased controlling interest in Natco, a brick and tile maker, and Great Lakes Industries, a small over-the-counter business, and began building what would become Fuqua Industries.

"My approach to getting into a public company," wrote Fuqua, "was to buy control of a company with a listing on the stock exchange and then use this as a vehicle to swap stock for other companies and thus build a conglomerate.

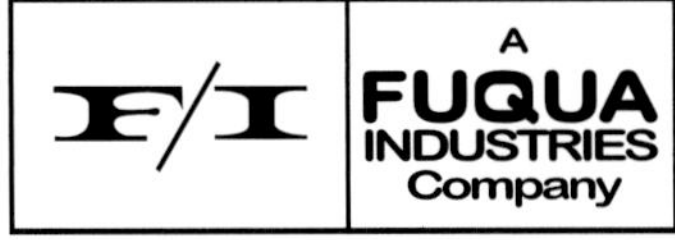

"This was in the 1960s when the conglomerate era was beginning to peak."

According to J. B. Fuqua, the deal with Natco "closed on September 30, 1965. At the beginning of 1966 we changed the name to Fuqua Industries and put my name in the newspaper stock listings every day."

WJBF-TV, Fuqua Industries – J. B. Fuqua liked to put his mark on a business in the form of his signature. Later in life, he would pay $1 million to buy back the name Fuqua Industries in order to protect his reputatiom.

Through the years Fuqua's interests and the breadth of his holdings in companies would broaden to include the Royal Crown Bottling Company, insurance, banking, a coal mining company, and others. Fuqua Industries' three most profitable divisions were also its oldest – Snapper brand lawn and garden equipment, Colorcraft wholesale photo finishing, and a network of sporting goods manufacturers.

A FRIENDLY $65 MILLION WEDDING

As the market for conglomerates soured during the early '70s and a recession during 1974-75 cooled the economy, Fuqua began selling off the least profitable of his subsidiaries and slimming down the company.

"I discovered I didn't have the company I thought I built," said Fuqua in a *Forbes* interview. He sold off operations with $70 million sales and kept the money-makers. With his new liquid position, he was ready to identify a takeover bid.

"Many of the conglomerates stumbled during the recessions of the early 1970s, and Wall Street's fascination with these types of companies began to fade," wrote Fuqua in his autobiography, appropriately entitled *Fuqua, A Memoir: How I Made My Fortune Using Other People's Money.*

"One of the problems was that entrepreneurs who were good at making acquisitions were not necessarily good at running companies," explained Fuqua, accurately pinpointing the problem at National. Stanley Yarmuth was all about the art of the deal and expressed disdain for day-to-day business. Consequently, the infrastructure for running the individual businesses together as a conglomerate was never put into place. Even after Yarmuth passed away in 1975, the die had already been cast for the corporation.

According to a *Fortune* story written in 1979, Fuqua's initial takeover target, prior to the acquisition of National, was Avis. He dropped out when the bidding went through the roof. Fuqua would make sure his next takeover bid was carefully engineered to avoid outside competition.

He turned his sights on National Industries.

National was one of the many companies that didn't fare well during the market's shifting attitude towards conglomerates. It also didn't do enough of the right things to put its house in order. That would be left to Fuqua and it was why he saw National Industries as an attractive takeover target.

"National was in the state Fuqua was in before our 1975 write-off," said Fuqua. "It takes a lot of courage to sell, very little courage to buy. That's the reason so much is lost in the stock market."

National Industries was, according to the *Fortune* piece on Fuqua, "another grab-bag conglomerate not unlike the one he himself had built, but one still beset by the kinds of problems he had just solved."

"We began looking for an acquisition target that would be a conglomerate, much as Fuqua Industries had been in 1975, with a broad base of operations," wrote Fuqua. "If we could acquire such a company, we knew we could create value by selling off the bad companies and keeping the good ones."

National fit the bill perfectly. At the time, it was earning about 1 percent on sales. And so Fuqua moved in.

Reports vary as to what happened next. In his autobiography, Fuqua makes it seem as if it was a relatively agreeable transaction. He simply sat down with the longest tenured director on National's board, a Louisville attorney by the name of Bernard H. Barnett, and negotiated the deal. But newspaper accounts from the time cast a different light on the acquisition.

"The impending corporate marriage of National Industries, Inc., to Fuqua Industries, Inc., has been portrayed as a harmonious arrangement – a friendly $65 million wedding of two big conglomerates," wrote *Louisville Times* Business Editor Mike Kallay in an article dated November 29, 1977.

"But the courtship was rapid-fire and disquieting, if not stormy, according to sources close to National."

Truck toolbox It may be the most highly visible product Tractor Supply has. You see them stopped at intersections both in the city and the country. You see them at the parking lots of country fairs, music concerts, and around the courthouse square. It is, of course, the shiny metal toolbox stretching across the bed behind the cab of a pickup truck. Emblazoned on the box is the distinctive, bright red Tractor Supply logo. Not only is it a great seller for the company, it's a highly targeted communications vehicle (yes, the pun was intended) for reaching the Tractor Supply customer.

The Louisville newspaper, after interviewing "nearly a dozen individuals close to National… including board members" for the story, contends that Fuqua gave National an "ultimatum" to either go along with his proposal or prepare for a hostile takeover.

DISMANTLING NATIONAL

Fuqua Industries' merger with National was a case of the fish swallowing the whale whole. Fuqua Industries' 1976 revenues were $535.8 million while National's were $881.2 million. But National's earnings on sales were only about 1 percent. The National acquisition was a major coup for J. B. Fuqua. While he paid a premium over the market, purchasing it for $65 million, only half of it in cash, the purchase price was 40 percent under book. Because National had $45 million in cash assets, Fuqua had, as he was fond of saying, "bought them with their own cash."

As one writer put it in an article entitled "Buying Them with Their Own Cash," "You should go naked when you deal with J. B. Fuqua…because that way you won't feel the draft when you're coming home."

Reported *Fortune*, "Almost from the moment he took control of National in January 1978, Fuqua began to dismantle it, following the pattern he had used on his own company three years earlier. National units that had $230 million in sales but no earnings were sold for $34 million in cash, more than the amount [in cash] Fuqua had put up.

"By breaking the company apart, we got what you might call reverse synergism," said then president Kay Slayden, meaning that the parts turned out to be worth more than the whole. "Fuqua's 1978 earnings jumped 82 percent, to $29.9 million…."

"…Because the National businesses we wanted to sell were so visible and we were in a period of easy financing, buyers lined up in a hurry," Fuqua wrote. "Within a year, we had recovered all of the cash we had put into the deal and we still owned the most valuable assets."

One of those valuable assets turned out to be Tractor Supply Company.

Shortly after the sale of National to Fuqua, *Forbes* wrote that instead of selling National's money-losers, he might opt to turn a few around, such as "the 153-store Tractor Supply Corp. retail chain, which now loses money. But TSC's thirty-six-store Big Bear subsidiary makes pretax $2 million to $3 million yearly selling the same products. J. B. Fuqua, figuring logically that the parent's problem is bad management, has also hired a new president. But even if he fails, the worst that could happen would be selling off the parent and adding the subsidiary's profits to Fuqua's."

They turned out to be prophetic words. Tractor Supply survived Fuqua's dismantling of National but TSC Industries did not. For all intents and purposes, TSC Industries – the mini-conglomerate of two retail divisions, franchisees, and a manufacturing arm of the company – would be dissolved.

In essence, Fuqua did for National and TSC Industries what they should have done themselves – cut them down to their most profitable entities.

"They have some units that should be disposed of, but they can't bring themselves to do it," said J. B. Fuqua to *Forbes* magazine. "The write-off would mean a reduction in the stock price and reflect on management.

"It would make a better company, but only after a one-year disaster."

Fuqua did Tractor Supply a favor when it finally divested the company of the discount retail chain that had so long put a burden on the company's financial sheet. It spun off the manufacturing companies and franchisees and forced the company to focus. Though it focused on the wrong things, the initial moves made sense. A far more focused company would emerge with a more defined geography and business. Within months of the Fuqua sale, Community Discount was sold to its president, Don Lazar. Without the strength of Tractor Supply to support it, Community Discount would eventually disappear. Next came the manufacturing and construction businesses with the sale of Richland Industries, Huskee Construction, and Thrive Centers. Then the franchisee operations were sold. These stores tended to be on the fringes of Tractor Supply's real distribution area, outposts too distant from warehouses to make delivering inventory cost efficient. The company was slimming down, refocusing on its core stores, returning to its traditional geography. They were all good moves for the company. But Tractor Supply still lacked a solid strategy and a mission.

And that lack at the core essence of the company – a clearly understood and communicated definition of who it was and what it was about – negated all that was good.

MEANWHILE BACK AT THE RANCH...AND FARM STORE

COMMUNITY DISCOUNT'S DONALD A. LAZAR

Ed Savage's place in the company's history is difficult to assess. His time at TSC, from 1978 until the end of 1980, was brief. It was near the end of a long string of leadership changes – three presidents in just shy of ten years and Savage would make number four. He arrived in the middle of uncertainty and instability that naturally accompanies a major ownership change. Fuqua moved quickly to dispose of National's assets and some of the companies that surrounded Tractor Supply, like Community Discount, and that created some tension.

ED SAVAGE AND KAY GORECKI ARE WELCOMED TO NASHVILLE BY GRAND OLE OPRY STAR MINNIE PEARL.

Savage was fully aware of what was transpiring, but he chose to step into what he called an "opportunity." Small in stature, a shock of thick black hair capping his head, his eyes framed by an oversized pair of glasses that gave him an air of intelligence underscored by his ease in conversation, Savage was generally considered a "good guy."

"He was strictly a PR guy," said Tom Flood, who made the move with Savage and the company from Chicago. "If you were to walk around the building and you saw him, he would talk to you. He was a nice person. Most people liked him."

"I think some of the people were very shocked when he was let go. Being the nice guy and let go."

Putting things in the best light was Savage's greatest strength. It also proved to be his greatest weakness.

"Ed Savage was a very fine man, a nice person," said Joe Scarlett. "But he put together a strategy that just didn't cut it, getting into the building materials business.

Two Guys

"To his credit, he moved the company out of a terrible location in Chicago and he hired me," Joe said, laughing. Joe laughs partly out of modesty but also laughs because it truly is funny. Funny the way things work out. Funny because who would have thought Joe Scarlett would have wound up where he is today. Who would have thought this retail refugee from Two Guys, an early super discount chain on the brink of disaster when Joe left, would wind up leading a team and chain of stores whose success story has graced the pages of everything from *Chain Store Age* and *Discount Store News* to the *Wall Street Journal*, the 2004 *Forbes* list of best managed companies in America, and an Associated Press feature story that ran in 160 newspapers across the country.

ED SAVAGE CUTS THE RIBBON STANDING NEXT TO J.B. FUQUA, CHAIRMAN OF FUQUA INDUSTRIES.

"I couldn't get a job anywhere else," said Joe. "I guess it was the first offer that I had from a company that I thought I wanted to work for. I liked Ed Savage. I thought he was a good guy. I really didn't understand the business."

Joe would come to understand the business by just jumping in and doing whatever needed doing. And the biggest thing that needed doing at the time, according to Savage, was moving the company's historic Chicago headquarters.

"When I was hired by Joe Vega, Tractor Supply's controller, in 1969, he said to me, 'Before you accept the job, I want you to look at the offices because they're not the nicest offices in Chicago,' " remembered Tom Flood.

"I said, 'OK, but it shouldn't make any difference. I like what you told me.'

"Well, I go into this building on Lawrence Avenue and Ravenswood. It was an old four-story building that was mostly warehouse. The floors were wood with some linoleum. There were old wood pillars throughout the building. Wood beam ceilings that were just painted and the paint peeling off of it. It wasn't the best environment. You sat at your desk and were afraid if you sneezed it would fall apart."

There was no question Tractor Supply needed to leave its headquarters in Chicago. In fact, the move from Chicago was one of the conditions Savage made with Joe Gammon before taking the job with Tractor Supply.

"'I want to tell you, Mr. Gammon, I'm going to move the company out of Chicago,'" said Savage, recounting his conversation with Joe Gammon before coming to Tractor Supply.

"He [Gammon] said, 'Don't you like Chicago?'

"Tractor Supply doesn't have a store in Chicago," Savage replied to Gammon. "The nearest store they have is in Wisconsin. How can marketing and merchandising people have a test tube laboratory store to experiment in, to visit, to change, when they have to go all the way to Wisconsin?"

Nashville was selected from among five prospective cities where Tractor Supply had stores. The others were Charlotte, Indianapolis, Omaha, and Louisville. Because Louisville was the prior home of the now defunct National Industries, Fuqua wanted to sever Tractor Supply's ties to its former owner, and Louisville was quickly out of the running. Because the company had warehouses as well as stores in Indianapolis and Omaha, many thought they would be the frontrunners. So the choice of Nashville was a bit of a surprise.

"At the time, I thought it was a bad decision to come to Nashville," said Joe. "In the long term, I'm thrilled we're in Nashville and wouldn't have it any other way. But at the time, we didn't have any stores farther south or east of here. This was the southeastern end of the business, so it just didn't make geographic sense at the time. But it's turned out to be great."

Why was Nashville selected?

"Ed had lived in Roanoke when he was with Moore's," Joe explained. "He loved the small Southern city. And the parent company was Fuqua out of Atlanta, so it made sense. Ed wanted to be in the South. Fuqua was in the South. And Fuqua also had two other businesses here at the time."

The move of Tractor Supply's headquarters would accomplish several important things for the company. It would, as Savage had suggested, move the company's headquarters closer to the heart of the business and where things actually happened – in the stores. And, as Savage also contended, given the decaying part of Chicago where the company's headquarters were located and the dilapidated condition of the building in which the headquarters were housed, Nashville was a definite plus in terms of executive recruitment. The move to Nashville also allowed the company to secure favorable interest rates on a development bond issued by the city for 7 percent at a time when interest rates were in the double digits.

JOE SCARLETT DURING THE TWO GUYS ERA

Finally, the guise of moving would also allow Savage to trim staff and build his own team. And that's exactly what he did – trim staff and assemble his team. Only forty or so families were asked to make the move to Nashville. Two were those of Joe Scarlett and Tom Flood.

At the time, 240 people worked for TSC Industries' headquarters in Chicago. That meant

GRAND OPENING OF THE FIRST NASHVILLE OFFICE
IN 1979, TRACTOR SUPPLY FINALLY SAYS GOODBYE TO ITS FOUNDING CITY OF CHICAGO AND MAKES ITS NEW HOME IN NASHVILLE AT 915 MURFREESBORO ROAD.

So Why the Odd Shape? Everyone has his or her theory about the odd, little shape that frames the Tractor Supply logo. Former TSC Vice President Max DeForest says it reminds him of a tractor grill. Others say a plowshare. Officially it is called a trapezium – a four-side figure with no two sides that are parallel. According to Charles Schmidt's son, Richard, it all

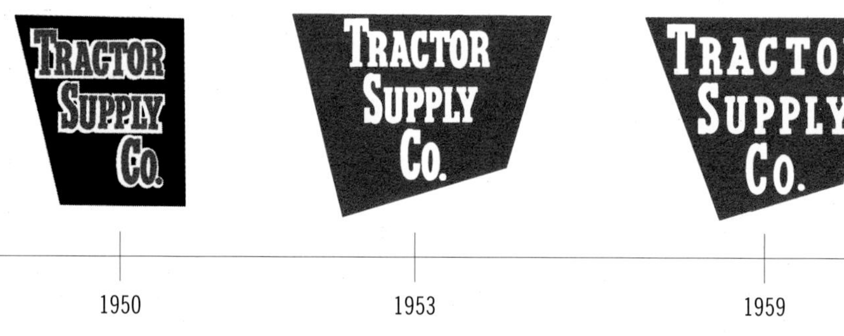

recruiting and developing a new office staff in Nashville. The new headquarters ended up with a total of 180 people, so sixty jobs were cut in the move. The loss of experience would prove costly to the company, as there were fewer people knowledgeable about Tractor Supply to challenge some of the moves Savage was about to make. And closest to Savage would be the people he brought with him from the building materials business.

"He brought with him several people from his previous company," said Joe. "He brought with him a fellow named Bill Van Note who ran store operations. He was Savage's number two guy, a real driving force in the organization. He also brought with him a fellow to run data processing, Dave Owens."

Bill Van Note was Savage's executive vice president of operations and Dave Owens, his vice president of management information systems. His executive vice president of merchandising was John Roe, a regional operations manager at Tractor Supply that Savage promoted. Larry Hall was the vice president of distribution. Then, finally, there was the person he'd hired as vice president of personnel and manpower development – Joe Scarlett.

"My role here was to be vice president of personnel and whatever else needed to get done," said Joe Scarlett. "There were a whole lot of things that needed to get done because Ed had decided to move the company. So I just grabbed a leadership role and just did what needed to get done."

Doing what needed to get done, Joe would follow in the footsteps of Tractor Supply's most successful leaders – Charles Schmidt, who got a job during the Depression because he was willing to sweep the floor in addition to posting the stock numbers and wound up bundling catalogs in the mail room as well as leading the company; Gard Abbott, who gave up law to manage the company's first store for his college friend; Wes Walker, the man who always had time for customers and employees, collected their letters, and realized their value to the company; and Max DeForest, who regularly went back to the store after dinner just to get the stock on the shelves because he had some began as a doodle. TSC engineer Mac McKittrick sketched the shape at a meeting one day and Schmidt happened to see it. He was fascinated by it. It was a simple four-sided shape, yet complex because none of the sides were of equal length or parallel. It was both common and uncommon - sort of like his company. And so it stuck.

1967 1982 1993

time on his hands. Joe went them one better. He made the can-do attitude a part of the company's culture. He did it by not only setting it down in the company's written mission and values statement, but also by living it whenever he straightens a shelf in a store or greets a customer. Joe jumped headlong into the move, helping Savage develop the organizational chart and decide what staff would be in Nashville. He helped determine the list of those who'd make the move. He organized the severance programs and how announcements would be made. He set up the recruiting operations in Nashville and arranged for some public relations.

"In the absence of anybody else, I sort of took charge of the relocation process," admitted Joe. "I filled the vacuum. It was there and so I just did it."

More important, unknowingly, just doing what came naturally to him, he kept alive a remnant of the Tractor Supply culture and the can-do attitude.

Savage describes the move as proceeding smoothly: "It was absolutely the smoothest move. We never missed a beat."

This may have been true from Savage's point of view. The move would be the calm before the enveloping storm. Along with physically moving the business's home office, Savage also shifted the company's emphasis in the very same year. This proved one move too many.

LOOKS GOOD ON PAPER

Ed Savage saw what Charles Schmidt had seen now almost a decade before – the number of farms in America was continuing to decline and so Tractor Supply's potential customers were declining. The company had to increase its customer base or extend the line of products it offered its customers. Quite naturally, Savage's response was to turn to what he was most comfortable with and introduce building materials to the company's merchandise mix.

"I wanted to bring building materials to Tractor Supply," said Savage. "Not to convert the company but to have that as an adjunct, an added category.

"In the building materials business, you're looking for owner-occupied households," Savage explained. "What intrigued me at Tractor Supply was the farmer was more than an owner-occupied household. He owned a house. He owned a barn. He owned out buildings. He owned fences.

"Wow, maybe if we put in a few building materials items in certain selected markets, it would be an adjunct to our business!"

On the surface, it seemed to make sense. But in reality, the strategy was flawed. Perhaps because the introduction of building materials wasn't clearly communicated in the field among store managers who saw it as a move away from farm supply. Perhaps because it became entangled in so many other major initiatives Savage had taken on at the same time – moving Tractor Supply's headquarters, putting in place a new management team, getting a new financial and inventory system up and running, and delivering profits to Fuqua as quickly as possible to demonstrate the company's success under Savage. There may have been some good ideas in this mix. But taken all together, it proved to be a disaster.

J.B. Fuqua in his office

TSC Executive Vice President of Operations Bill Van Note at the managers meeting in 1980

"The end of '79, Savage pitched his theory of turning Tractor Supply Stores into a hybrid of farm stores and building materials," explained Joe Scarlett. "The premise is the number of farmers in the country is declining. Therefore, our business is declining. Therefore, we need a strategy. Savage's strategy was to meld a building products program in with a farm store program.

"That may have looked good on paper but, the fact of the matter is, it didn't work."

Adding building supplies was an easy sell at company headquarters, but then there were a lot of new faces at the new Nashville headquarters who were new to Tractor Supply's business. And many of those closest to Savage, in particular his right-hand man, Bill Van Note, had moved with Savage from the home building products industry. So, Savage was probably exposed to very little opposition.

In the field, however, Tractor Supply's shift in emphasis wasn't as well received.

"The people who managed the stores grew up in the farming business," said Tom Flood. "They didn't want to believe the farming business was going the wrong way. They still worked there in their local towns. They probably grew up on farms. It was a good business in most of the towns they were still in. That's why they [Savage's team] lost good people. They lost people, and they lost control of what was going on. And, they lost control of the inventory, which was the biggest asset the company had. When you lose control of that, you lose control of everything."

The company began converting stores in Kentucky and Tennessee, beginning with five locations and then adding another five. Eventually the company would have as many as twenty Tractor Supply Stores, branded TSC Stores with building materials, according to Gerry Newkirk. Newkirk, like Ed Savage and Bill Van Note, had

TSC Landmarks In 1965, Tractor Supply opened its 100th store in Hutchinson, Kansas. In 1996, the 200th store opened in Hamilton, Ohio. In September 2000, the 300th store opened its doors in Triune, Tennessee. The company finally cracked the 400-store barrier in 2002, when it acquired eighty-seven locations from Quality Stores.

come to TSC from Grossman's, but he was honest enough to see that the move to more building materials wasn't working.

"After about a year and a half," said Newkirk, "instead of improving, things were worse."

Those fifteen or so stores with building supplies were the core of a million-dollar loss in 1980, according to Tom Flood. Why didn't something that looked so good on paper work?

"I don't think we had enough of a presence in terms of our size in a particular market to be meaningful in the building materials business," Joe explained. "And I don't think we ever had an assortment that was powerful enough to compete with the other building materials stores.

"We didn't have a big enough presentation. We had some resentment internally about it and those individual stores were losing a lot of money. And we made some other poor strategic decisions that year. We used to sell farm toys and model tractors. We just decided not to buy any that year, because they [Savage and Bill Van Note] didn't like the business."

Savage may not have liked the toy business but the field didn't like the building materials business. They didn't like the fact that faucets now filled the space once filled with high-margin clothing items.

"Everything just went in the wrong direction at that point," said Flood.

"Because most of the people at our stores were farm community people, and they thought we're getting out of a business we knew. So it hurt sales in all the areas around the company.

"In fact, we didn't really support the inventory in those stores, so they lost sales that way."

To try to offset some of the losses, Savage began laying people off. In May 1980, the headquarters staff was reduced from 180 to 150. Six months later, there was a second layoff. Another fifteen to twenty people were let go.

"The unfortunate thing is, between the two layoffs, fifteen of the forty families that moved from Chicago were let go," said Flood.

Things were getting bad. And then they got a whole lot worse.

KNOWN FOR HIS EASE AT A PODIUM, ED SAVAGE, PRESIDENT OF TSC, SPEAKS TO THE COMPANY AT THE 1980 MANAGERS CONVENTION.

THE BIG WRITE-DOWN

Beginning as far back as late 1978, Tractor Supply's financial people were reporting significant losses on physical inventory reconciliations. The problem was brought to Ed Savage's attention by Tractor Supply's controller, Kevin Fitzgerald, and the CFO of TSC Industries, John Brack.

"Ed Savage said to them, 'I don't believe those numbers and neither does Bill Van Note," explained Tom Flood, who was in charge of reconciling inventory at that time.

"They didn't believe them so they didn't record them on financial reports."

Bill Van Note was Tractor Supply's executive vice president of operations, the number two person in the organization and someone Ed Savage trusted.

Always thinking positively, Savage wouldn't see it as anything but a problem with the company's financial and inventory software. This might have made some sense given that the software was new and didn't have reliable documentation.

In 1980, Tom Flood's boss, Kevin Fitzgerald, went to Ed Savage and said, "These are real inventory write-downs and they've gotten worse. If you don't book them, I'm leaving."

"So finally in October 1980, the company recorded well over a million and a half dollars in inventory write-downs," explained Flood.

The gross inventory loss was probably the result of shrinkage and disenfranchised employees disappointed at the prospect of the company moving away from its core business. A lack of experience may have also contributed to the problem. In the wake of the ownership, management, and merchandise changes, experienced store personnel had left the company, leaving new employees unfamiliar with the inventory systems.

To save face with Fuqua, Savage's executive team decided to start funneling cash back to Fuqua. To do this, they had to reduce inventory replenishment and, of course, that hurt sales even worse, especially going into the end of the year.

"At the end of 1980, the company did $93 million in sales and lost $13 million before taxes," said Tom Flood. "At this point, if you didn't have a big brother like Fuqua, you would have been filing for Chapter 11."

"In 1980, if we'd have been a stand-alone company, we would have been out of business," said Flood bluntly. "It was that critical."

Tractor Supply didn't file Chapter 11, but Ed Savage was released.

"December 1, 1980, I'll never forget that date," remembered Joe Scarlett. "Two men came up from Atlanta – Tom Hennesy and Fuqua Industries President Kay Slayden.

"They arrived and two hours later Ed Savage was finished."

Savage has very little to say on this matter today. He points only to the good footing he placed the company on before turning over the reins. He talks of being part of the effort to sell off Community Discount and the other entities that clouded the focus of Tractor Supply. He talks of "pruning" the company, reducing its geographic focus, spinning off stores that didn't make sense in California and other outlying regions, and getting rid of an ill-conceived franchise organization. He remembers instances when Fuqua President Kay Slayden suggested Savage sell off some more stores to bring in money, to which he responded, "No. I know when to close stores. I know how to do that. But I'm in the store opening business and not in the store closing business.... Sometimes you have to cut good branches off beside dead ones to shape the tree. I understand that, Kay. But from the way I understand the angle you're coming at, you're asking me to preside over the disillusionment of the business, and that's not my cup of tea."

Savage speaks of specific instances of getting out of product categories that no longer made any economic or practical sense for the company – like tires and sprayer equipment. He points to the hire of Joe Scarlett. He says Tom Hennesy's replacing him at Tractor Supply was part of a larger coup d'état to oust J. B. Fuqua from Fuqua Industries.

"Tom Hennesy was really like J. B. Fuqua's right hand," began Savage. "He treated Tom almost like a son. And Tom, when he started to work with me and we talked about the businesses to get rid of [the divestiture of Community Discount, etc.] and what we should do, he said, 'You know, I really like this farm supply business. It's really interesting. I like all of these little gadgets.' So he liked the business. He did his job and we collaborated, and I helped him and he helped me, and we got rid of those businesses.

"Now, Kay Slayden and Dave Fraser, who was treasurer at Fuqua, wanted a coup d'état," explained Savage. "They wanted to actually take the company over and get rid of J. B. Fuqua. And one of the things they had to do was get Tom Hennesy out of Atlanta. So what do they do? They send him to Tractor Supply in Nashville.

"You don't need two high-priced guys in the six figures, do you?

"So they said, 'Ed, you've done a hell of a nice job but we're really not happy about this. You want to open more stores. Maybe it's time we make a change. It isn't that you did anything wrong. You did a good job with the move and all this blah-blah-blah. But you know I think it's time for a change.'

"Of course, when I saw Hennesy, I remember what he said to me back in Chicago when we first started – 'Oh, boy, I'd love to be in this business,' Savage said. "So he wanted to get into it. I think they just tried to ease me out the easiest way they could and he was the messenger.

"That was the first time in my life that I was ever let go," Savage admitted. "First time in my life. But, you know what, I'm a positive person. I tell my children this. I tell my friends this. It's sort of my credo. If you have an adversity, you have the three As. Number one, accept it. Number two, adjust to it. Number three, have a positive attitude going forward."

In Savage's mind, he's more than proven his own business worth since leaving Tractor Supply,

ED SAVAGE AT A BIG BEAR MEETING

FUQUA INDUSTRIES PRESIDENT KAY SLAYDEN SPEAKS TO GUESTS AT THE GRAND OPENING OF WHAT WAS THEN TSC INDUSTRIES EXECUTIVE OFFICES.

working in prominent positions at several companies and finally helping grow Crown Bolt, a fledgling company, from $5.6 million in sales in 1989 to $139 million in 2003.

"I did leave the company [Tractor Supply] better than I found it," Savage said.

CHAPTER

★8★

THE LUCK OF THE IRISH

TOM HENNESY AND THE GANG OF FIVE

"A GOOD FARMER IS NOTHING MORE NOR LESS THAN A HANDY MAN WITH A SENSE OF HUMUS."

\- E. B. WHITE

GROUNDBREAKERS

Tom Hennesy's assignment to lead Tractor Supply during the '80s came at a critical time in the company's history. Hennesy was given the choice to help the company dig out from under its $13 million loss or simply plow it under. He opted to try and turn it around. It proved to be a groundbreaking decision.

SO WHEN DO WE GET TO THE GOOD PART? At this point in the Tractor Supply story, you're probably wondering, "How in the world do we get from here to a billion-dollar company?" And for good reason. As a new decade dawned on the more than forty-year-old company, it found itself $13 million in the hole on $95 million in sales, its fifth president in the last ten years gone, very little inventory on the shelves to pull it out of its slump and in the middle of a building supplies merchandising strategy that frustrated its store managers and confused its customers.

Everyone still at Tractor Supply was wondering at this point, too. But not how they were going to reach a billion dollars in sales. They were just hoping for a miracle to keep the company afloat long enough for them to jump ship. Tractor Supply would get its miracle. Though, at the time, most didn't recognize the firing of the popular Ed Savage and the arrival of the intimidating Fuqua liquidator Tom Hennesy as any cause for celebration.

"Tom Hennesy was a big guy, six-foot-four-inches, well over 300 pounds, a physically very intimidating individual," remembered Flood. "People noticed when he walked through the building with Kay Slayden to see Ed Savage. All of a sudden, the rumors were flying around the office.

"When the people Ed Savage brought in found out he'd been terminated and this new individual [Hennesy] was in charge, the *Wall Street Journal* was ripped to tatters from so many people cutting out employment ads."

Tom Hennesy

No one person is more responsible for the immediate turnaround of Tractor Supply following its $13 million loss in 1980 than Tom Hennesy. He was a big man who made a huge difference because he understood the little things. He knew how to listen. He knew you had to keep customers happy, not just satisfied.

The executive team was familiar with Hennesy. They'd already been exposed to a little bit of his handiwork with the dismantling of TSC Industries by selling off Community Discount Centers shortly after Fuqua took over National. There was no reason to believe Hennesy wouldn't continue his demolition of the poorly performing Tractor Supply now that Ed Savage was out of the way.

"I remember seeing him [Hennesy] for the first time when he came to Chicago," said Flood. "He came to spin off Community Discount Centers, to get rid of it. It couldn't have been a month after Fuqua bought the company."

Hennesy had been charged with figuring out what to do with Tractor Supply – sell it, get rid of it, or fix it. According to Hennesy, a top Fuqua executive had told him, "I want you to go to Nashville next Saturday morning and pack a bag, because you're not coming back for a long time."

Tractor Supply's fate was in Tom Hennesy's hands, as were the fates of everyone involved in the failing company.

OMAHA, NEBRASKA – OWEN HALLORAN (SECOND FROM LEFT) RECEIVES HIS SERVICE AWARD FOR "25 YEARS OF DEDICATED SERVICE" FROM JOE SCARLETT. ALSO PICTURED ARE HERMAN STATUM AND TOM HENNESY.

"Oh, yes, my resume was ready," said Joe Scarlett with a broad smile. "We were all fearful that we were all going to lose our jobs. So we were all looking for something. I was lucky enough not to get a job when some of my peers had already left the company.

"Tom had a reputation. He was called the Undertaker because he liquidated companies for Fuqua. So we all thought we were going to get liquidated.

"But that's not what happened."

Far from it.

It speaks volumes of Fuqua's trust in Hennesy that the company wasn't immediately sold as were so many of National's failing assets under Fuqua.

What Tom Hennesy did instead of liquidating the company seemed to catch everyone at Tractor Supply off guard. His approach to deciding the fate of the company wasn't remarkable, but it was refreshing to the people who had become accustomed to simply following orders that trickled down from above. Joe Scarlett, Tom Flood, Joe Maxwell, and Gerry Newkirk – the four people Hennesy would eventually elevate as leaders of a re-born farm supply chain – distinctly remember how Hennesy decided what to do with the company. He began by listening.

"Tom came in and, instead of talking to people like me, he talked to the store managers and the district managers," said Joe. Even more than twenty years after the fact, Joe's voice is still touched with a bit of wonder at the sheer simplicity of what Hennesy did – simple, yet powerful.

"He talked to people in the field and he said, 'What's wrong?' And he listened to what they had to say, listened for a month or two and then said to all of us, 'We have two problems. We're confused, and we don't have any inventory to sell.'

"'So first of all,' he said, 'Buyers start buying the goods, putting the inventory back in the stores and start taking care of the customers. And, second,' he said to everyone in the company, 'we're going to be a farm store chain,'" remembered Joe Scarlett. "'We're farm stores. Here's the merchandise. Get out there and sell it.'"

That's what they did. And it worked.

"We went from a huge loss of $13 million in 1980," said Joe, "to cutting that loss to around $5 million in '81, to breaking even in '82. We've been profitable ever since."

LEADING BY LISTENING– ACTION RATHER THAN EDICTS

Because of its simplicity on the surface, it's easy to overlook the significance of what Tom Hennesy did in those first few months at Tractor Supply. He didn't suppose that he had the answers. Even though he had a wealth of experience at a host of different companies while working all those years with Fuqua, he didn't assume that he knew more than the people closest to where the business of retailing really takes place – in the stores. He began leading by listening.

"I knew nothing about the retail business or about farming," Hennesy said.

"I interviewed every manager and asked them the same question – 'What's wrong?'"

Hennesy's approach sent a powerful message. Not only to the people in the field but also to the people at the home office. Hennesy – through actions rather than edicts – sowed the first seeds from which would blossom the company's new culture, a culture that fostered open dialog and thought, a culture where ideas could be shared and everyone is empowered to have ideas and work to make the company better, a culture in which the customer was truly the organization's reason for being and disappointing the customer by being out of stock or not providing exceptional customer service was considered a cardinal sin.

"During the '70s, we had an erratic history of being out of stock and really 'alienating customers,'" commented Joe Scarlett. "Tom had a great passion, picked up by the rest of us, to always be in stock and take care of our customers. Don't disappoint the customers.

"Tom used to say, 'We want our customer, America's farmers, when they roll over in the morning and say I need something from a farm store, we want them to think the very best place to go and find that item in stock is Tractor Supply.'"

By April 1981, Hennesy was confident that Tractor Supply was viable. The company could be saved, and he wanted to be the one to do it.

"I was encouraged by the fact that, at the time, TSC had existed for over forty years," Hennesy would later write in an annual report as he looked back on the "bleak" days when "TSC was struggling to survive."

"There must be something worth saving here, I thought, if our customers have stayed with us for four decades."

Given his customer emphasis, it's appropriate that Hennesy believed in Tractor Supply because customers still did. And so he presented a plan to Fuqua management based on his findings from the field. Fuqua's management endorsed Hennesy's strategy: Put him at the helm to lead the company in its turnaround attempt and provide funding in order to get inventory back in the stores. Instead of selling the failing company for cash, Fuqua now agreed to plow more into the farm supply chain at the urging of Hennesy.

It's hard to imagine that anyone other than Tom Hennesy – with his powerful personal ties to J. B. Fuqua and other important lieutenants in the Fuqua organization – would have fared as well. And without the infusion of cash for inventory, there's no doubt that Tractor Supply would have ceased to exist.

As Hennesy's longtime executive secretary, Gwen Herald, so succinctly put it – "There would be no Tractor Supply if Mr. Hennesy hadn't come along."

HOW AN UNDERTAKER BECAME THE WORLD'S GREATEST LEPRECHAUN

It's a credit to the power and breadth of his personality that Thomas Hennesy III was known by so many colorful nicknames. The man who was described as the "Undertaker" because of his frequent role as a corporate liquidator for Fuqua was eventually dubbed the Savior of Tractor Supply and the company's second founder. He was also beloved as the World's Greatest Leprechaun – a title emblazoned on a brass plate that hung on his office door at Tractor Supply, recognizing his deep cultural pride in being Irish and the good luck the company enjoyed with his arrival. This whimsical title was also an obvious tongue-in-cheek reference to his anything but "wee" leprechaun stature. Something about Hennesy's warmth and caring attitude allowed people to once again have fun at Tractor Supply. They could enjoy a smile about their newfound, 300-pound leprechaun.

★ MAC 320 ★

CHAINSAW

- 2.1 cubic inch engine
- 12.1 pounds complete with bar and chain
- 16" laminated sprocket tip bar
- Safety trigger
- Automatic and manual chain sharpening
- Wraparound chain brake/hand guard
- Anti-vibration system
- Muffler Shield
- Solid state ignition
- Non-metallic components
- Throttle latch
- All-position carburetor
- Chain catcher

McCULLOCH

44-60464

$199.00

1983 BLUE BOOK

Finally, many also referred to him as "a true Southern gentleman," and he was.

Tom Hennesy hailed from Charleston, South Carolina. His childhood wasn't without difficulties. His father and mother separated when he was young. Later, when his father died, Hennesy's mother would enter a convent in Canada and become a nun. She would remain there the rest of her life. Like his mother, Hennesy held deep religious beliefs.

His annual holiday message in the Tractor Supply internal newsletter, *The Voice*, didn't shy from blatantly Christian references. His acts of benevolence and generosity were many and, though he tried to keep them quiet, they were simply too numerous to remain undiscovered. From providing private counseling for workers in financial straits to taking care of the funeral expenses for a single parent's young child, from sponsoring a child in the Dominican Republic to actually traveling down to the country to find out what happened to the child he was supporting when the child mysteriously disappeared. Tom Hennesy was a man who would go the second mile. Quite literally. This level of caring was a stabilizing force in a company that had undergone so many years of confusion, misdirection, and the distrust and disappointment that undirected effort just naturally generates.

In the wake of a decade of glib big business maneuverings, Hennesy's personal touch and ethical approach to business was a refreshing change. Doing the right thing – for customers and for fellow team members – was a Hennesy mantra at the heart of the company's reemerging culture.

Hennesy's big heart was also complemented by an equally well developed business mind. Like his business mentor J. B. Fuqua, Hennesy was largely self-educated, leaving the College of Charleston before finishing his freshman year in 1947. He left to take a $25-a-week job as an announcer at a local radio station owned by Fuqua.

"I realized the school was charging me to go, and the radio station was paying me," Hennesy said in a newspaper interview.

Hennesy was an innately intelligent individual. "He was very smart," recalled Joe. "Intuitive for the most part."

"Tom was a genius," said Gerry Newkirk, who was perhaps closest personally to Hennesy. "He never graduated from college, but he was a genius. I'm sure his IQ was off the charts. He was a Renaissance man. He could talk sports. He could talk about classical music. He would read three, four, five books a week."

Hennesy would move from announcer to program director, take a couple of years off for military service, and then return to Augusta as a program director and then general manager of a new Fuqua-owned television station – WJBF. Eventually, Hennesy would earn the title of vice president at Fuqua Industries. He was the man sent to Nashville to sort out the situation at Tractor Supply.

"He'd been a part of Fuqua for about thirty years," explained Tom Flood. "He'd gone off to run a bakery company that Fuqua spun off. He did that and it didn't work out. I think he wanted to do something of his own.

"He was very close with J. B. Fuqua, so he said, 'I'd like to be the one to run the company,' and evidently they agree to do that, and that's when he stepped in as president."

FUELING THE FIRE WITHIN

Hennesy first surprised Tractor Supply employees when he determined to save rather than sell the company. Then he surprised them again with something that proved to be a powerful move in terms of building loyalty within the beleaguered company.

He promoted from within.

Unlike his immediate predecessor, Hennesy didn't bring along with him people he'd worked with other places or from elsewhere in the Fuqua organization. Given the performance of Tractor Supply at this point, he would have been more than justified in cleaning house. But he didn't.

And, again, it caught folks off guard.

"After Tom had made his strategy proposal to Fuqua, he called me in," said Joe Scarlett. "He said, 'OK, Joe, let's work out how we're going to reorganize the business to cut our costs.'

"I'm thinking to myself – I'm the personnel guy in a company that's going down the drain, and I'm one of the first persons out. So I'm just there wondering how much severance I'm going to get," said Joe with his characteristic frankness. "So I sit down with Tom and he starts laying out the plans. He pulls out this organizational chart and he has this empty box at the top and underneath it he had distribution and personnel and information technology and finance and administration. And then he writes my name in the box and tells me that I'm going to be his number two person, the senior vice president in charge of finance and administration.

JOE IS QUICK TO TELL ANYONE WHO ASKS HOW MUCH HE LEARNED FROM TOM HENNESY.

"It was an enormous surprise – a thrill for me and one of those great opportunities that comes once in a lifetime.

"I walked in figuring I'd get three or four month's severance pay and wound up being promoted to senior vice president of finance and administration," said Joe with a hint of incredulity.

"That began a partnership between Tom and me that lasted fifteen years or so."

Hennesy also promoted three other individuals to his executive team who would figure prominently in the history of Tractor Supply during

Good Vibrations Not many corporations' conference rooms are outfitted with a gong. But then, Tractor Supply isn't just any corporation. The gong that graces the conference room is another of Joe Scarlett's ways of whipping up passion among the team. It all began in 1988 on a San Francisco incentive trip for TSC district managers and their wives. Joe was trying to make sure everyone was having fun. So he rented a gong and interrupted cocktails and the normal chitchat with a booming crash to announce dinner. More than fifteen years later Tractor Supply starts every meeting with the sound of the gong – all to keep the company's good vibe going.

the '80s. Joe Scarlett would be joined by Gerry Newkirk, Joe Maxwell, and Tom Flood.

Gerry Newkirk had grown up in Schenectady, New York. A graduate of Gordon College, he earned a degree in political science. After college, Newkirk spent three years in the service before getting out and enlisting in a management training program at Grossman's. Newkirk would learn retailing at the building materials company that had already given TSC Ed Savage and Bill Van Note. Newkirk, who managed a couple of stores for Grossman's and would be promoted to district manager, stayed with the New England-based building supply and lumber company for nine years before he was recruited by Bill Van Note to come to Tractor Supply in 1979. As a district manager, Newkirk was brought in to help the company with its ill-fated attempt to integrate building materials with its traditional farm supply lines.

GERRY NEWKIRK OF THE GANG OF FIVE

Newkirk believes that Hennesy tapped him because "I listened and then was able to execute. And I didn't necessarily always agree with him and that was the kind of thing that Tom would like."

Joe Maxwell was an automotive specialist who had risen through the ranks at Goodyear. Originally from the Arkansas-Louisiana-Texas oil patch region, Maxwell had headed off to work early to help support the family when his father died. He would earn his GED later while in the service. In 1964, he went to work for a subsidiary of Goodyear Tire Company that leased and operated automotive centers in discount department stores. Over the next sixteen years with the tire company, he would be promoted several times, from store manager to district manager. Eventually he would spend a total of eight years in the company's Canadian division, where he would be promoted to vice president and general manager.

When he joined Tractor Supply in 1980 as automotive merchandising manager, Maxwell was looking to come home to the United States and work in a more entrepreneurial company.

"Goodyear was a mega company and there were a lot of restrictions," said Maxwell. "They lived and died by the operations manual. Even if a rule was written before I was born, the rule was God. There was no entrepreneurship."

A native of Chicago, Tom Flood had the longest tenure with the company. He was hired as a bookkeeper for Tractor Supply in 1969 while he was still going to a junior college. Flood was cautioned to take a look at the company's spartan offices in a rough section of Chicago before jumping at the offer. It's fortunate that Flood had worked in his father's welding supply factory. The dilapidated condition of Tractor Supply's early company offices in Chicago didn't even faze him.

He would, however, witness deterioration of another kind. Flood joined TSC just prior to the sale to National Industries and so experienced the long, painful decade of misdirection and decline under the mantle of a conglomerate that eventually overshadowed the company's early glory years. Flood, who moved with the company from Chicago, would be the last of the four promoted to a leadership position when his boss left the company in 1981 and recommended him for the job.

"Tom Hennesy called me in his office and said, 'Your boss thinks an awful lot of you,' " said Flood, " 'if he's willing to leave the company and put you in charge.'

"That was my first real introduction to Tom Hennesy – the day he promoted me to controller."

Scarlett, Newkirk, Maxwell, and Flood – Hennesy had assembled an unlikely group to be his turnaround team. Other than Flood, who had cut his teeth at Tractor Supply, none of the five had any previous background in the ag industry or farm store retailing. Only one boasted more than a year of experience with the company. None of the five had ever been involved in a successful turnaround of this magnitude. In fact, two of the players had joined Tractor Supply to escape troubled companies. So what did they have?

They believed in Tom Hennesy and in the fact that he had believed enough in them to elevate them to positions of leadership. They were five strong personalities, each with different viewpoints, individuals who often disagreed strategically, who'd argue with one another from time to time about what they thought should be done, what could be done. But it was the values that Tom Hennesy espoused and lived out and what they were learning and how they were developing that kept them there and together. It was the culture taking root again.

JOE MAXWELL OF THE GANG OF FIVE.

"No, question, Tom was a complete change," said Tom Flood. "It was a chance to see how a corporation should really be run. It was enlightening."

Tom Hennesy believed in listening, listening to the customer and the people closest to where the action is: the people at the store level. He believed in doing whatever it takes to make the customer happy. He believed in spending time in the field, visiting the stores and seeing what was happening there. He believed in loving what you do. And if you didn't love it, then you should be doing something else. He believed in bringing others along, developing and promoting from within, sharing the wealth as a later employee stock ownership plan would show. He believed in giving responsibility and then not meddling. He believed in an open door and being accessible to people. He believed in working hard and having fun – treating folks to picnics at the office, dressing up in a green bowler and singing on St. Patrick's day, getting on the office intercom on a sunny summer day in August and saying "it's snowing in Memphis so everybody go home." He believed in the power of culture, celebrating his own Irish culture, and seeking to create a culture for the floundering company. And, first and foremost, he believed in doing the right thing. He was very serious about reporting the numbers accurately and very high on ethics and moral standards in business.

"Even to this day, Tom Hennesy's beliefs permeate Tractor Supply," said Tom Flood. "I think that's why we all held the highest respect for him. Not only was that the way he ran his business, but it was also the way he lived his life."

"Our mission and values, at first they weren't written down," said Joe Scarlett. "They were lived and spoken by Tom Hennesy. Tom would talk about ethics. Tom would talk about being the most dependable supplier. Finally, a few of those words were in the original plan we presented to Fuqua – to be the most dependable supplier of basic maintenance needs to the American farmer.

"Tom would talk and I would take the words down. I'm the author of our mission and values only in that I cared enough to put them into writing. But it started with Tom."

Who wouldn't want to be inside and at the beginning of something like that? Apparently Tom's beliefs caught hold beyond the home office and rang true with people in the store. So much so that the company slowed its losses by more than $8 million in one year.

BOLTS, NUTS, WASHERS
★ BY THE ★
POUND

Top quality, all new Hex Head and Carriage bolts. U.S. national course threads, with black oiled finish. Shipped Freight Collect from store, net prepaid.

LOW AS
$0.99/LB.

1980 BLUE BOOK

There were still numerous challenges. Early in 1981, a directive from Kay Slayden, president of Fuqua Industries, reorganized Tractor Supply into "two separate and distinct retail operating companies." The company was divided geographically between East and West. The Western company, under the direction of Ron Dettman, managed stores in Illinois, Iowa, Kansas, Minnesota, Missouri, Montana, Nebraska, North Dakota, South Dakota, Texas, and Wisconsin, and was headquartered in Omaha. The Eastern company encompassed Alabama, Arkansas, Indiana, Kentucky, Maryland, Michigan, Mississippi, New York, Ohio, Pennsylvania, and Tennessee, and remained headquartered in Nashville with Tom Hennesy as the president. The official word from Fuqua Industries was the move was made to "enable the two companies to become stronger regional marketing forces. In the new organization, we will be able to react more quickly and effectively to the rapidly changing needs of our customers."

"Tom pitched his strategy for the business and they said yes...but then lopped off seventy-five stores when they split the company," said Joe, the memory of the move by Fuqua more than twenty years ago still fresh enough to make him shake his head in disbelief. "Their logic was that the business was too big and that doing this would give each business unit 'greater management intensity.'

"All they did was waste a lot of money – they spent $1 million on another office."

Maybe the move wasn't about better serving the customer at all. Perhaps it was Fuqua's attempt to parcel up the goods for an easier and more profitable sale? Because selling the company was definitely on his mind, as Hennesy and crew soon discovered.

JUST WHEN YOU THOUGHT EVERYTHING WAS GREAT…

"At the beginning of 1982, Fuqua came to us and said, 'Listen boys, we love you, but we're out of here – you're for sale,'" said Joe.

It wasn't that Tractor Supply wasn't moving in the right direction. Things were moving quickly. In 1982, the company would reach sales of $128 million and break even just two years after posting a loss that should have drawn a close to the Tractor Supply story. But Fuqua was working to strengthen Fuqua Industries' financial position. To that end, he'd decided to buy back a portion of his company's stock. Apparently, he never anticipated how eager "the Street" was to divest itself of the once high-flying conglomerate. Fuqua anticipated that three million of the company's twelve million outstanding shares would be tendered, but when the offer was made, nine million – or more than 75 percent – of the shares were tendered. The move cost Fuqua more than $190 million, leaving the company with a heavy debt load and a tight cash-flow situation.

For the company that had undergone so many high level changes – the takeover by Fuqua, the firing of Savage, the arrival of Hennesy, and the reorganization of the company into two separate operational entities – this latest announcement was one that could kill the enthusiasm and belief Hennesy was creating. To keep this from happening, he quickly participated in a straightforward question-and-answer session to address the employees' concerns and questions. The interview was conducted within a month of Fuqua's announcement that it was entertaining buyers for Tractor Supply.

To the question of how yet another change in ownership would affect TSC employees, Hennesy responded: "The change in ownership for TSC should have no effect on any employee in the company. We have demonstrated during the past fifteen months a dramatic turnaround in our business – a turnaround that is little short of miraculous in the business world. With our recent track record, a change in ownership would probably provide us additional capital for further growth and expansion of an already healthy company."

Fuqua hired a broker to sell the business but also asked Hennesy to help in the search for a buyer, too.

"I spent days and days in the library trying to identify companies that might have an interest in Tractor Supply and who had the finances to actually make the purchase," Joe said. "Tom drafted a letter and we sent it out to the list with a prospectus, and all we got were a few tire kickers."

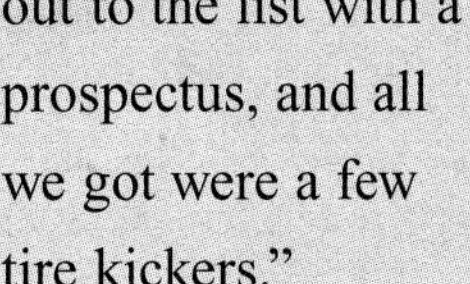

TOM HENNESY

THE GANG OF FIVE WOULD TAKE TSC FROM FARM, HOME AND AUTO BACK TO ITS FARM AND RANCH STORE ROOTS.

One of those tire kickers happened to come from a large tire company. But enthusiasm for the deal quickly seemed deflated when the official sent to have a look at the company arrived in Nashville intoxicated. Another deal was put on hold when the prospective buyer didn't like the phone system that Tractor Supply had installed.

"Though our performance was getting better, we had a checkered past," explained Joe. "The company was on the market for the better part of a year."

The bottom line: No one was interested in buying the company. And then, in walked Charlie Bradley. It may have just been dumb luck. Or it may have been the luck of the Irish.

Apparently, on the same day that Tom Hennesy and Tom Flood went to New York to take part in a seminar on leveraged buyouts, Charlie Bradley was in Atlanta approaching Fuqua on just such a proposition regarding Tractor Supply. It wasn't long after Hennesy had returned home that Bradley came to call and showed him how Tractor Supply could be bought by leveraging the assets of the company. Ironically, it was a means of acquiring a company for which J. B. Fuqua was well known.

"Charlie Bradley was a fascinating guy," remembered Joe Maxwell. "He was the youngest partner ever with Price Waterhouse and then he went out on his own and started a venture capital firm – Stanwich Investments Company of Greenwich, Connecticut.

"I think Bradley figured that Tom would be the only one doing the deal, but that wasn't Tom's personality. He was a great believer in bringing people along with him. He was that kind of a guy. He was a very generous man."

"How benevolent was Tom Hennesy?" asked Gerry Newkirk. "He included the four of us in the ownership of the business. He could have kept it all to himself. But he wasn't like that. After all, it was his relationship with Fuqua that made the deal possible."

In fact, part of the reason Hennesy enlisted Scarlett, Newkirk, Maxwell, and later Flood is that he wasn't sure about the deal himself.

"Tom was very reluctant at first," recalled Joe. "He'd been in a bakery business that had failed. He knew the problems that went with ownership. I thought it was a great opportunity, and I was excited about it."

And Joe Scarlett excited is a force to be reckoned with.

"But the rest of us were enthusiastic, so eventually we decided it was the thing to do."

According to Joe, Hennesy then approached Fuqua and convinced the company to guarantee the loans taken out by Tractor Supply's management on the equity.

"All five of us signed off on these loans, but the loans were guaranteed by Fuqua," Joe said. "So, if for any reason we wanted to walk away from it, we'd walk away.

"We really had nothing at risk."

As the deal was structured, Manufacturers Hanover provided $16 million of the purchase price, a venture capital firm by the name of Monmouth Capital contributed $1 million of equity and Hennesy, Scarlett, Newkirk, Maxwell, and Flood contributed a total of $200,000 in equity through a loan that was guaranteed by Fuqua.

Hennesy was instrumental in putting the financing together. His four new partners were relative newcomers to the world of venture capital.

"Hennesy kept talking about getting Manny Hanny to chip in on the deal," said Joe Scarlett. "The four of us just nodded and said, 'Oh, yeah, Manny Hanny.' But we had no idea who Manny Hanny was but didn't want to show our ignorance. We thought he was some big time money man Tom had a relationship with.

"Imagine our embarrassment when we realized that Manny Hanny was just financier slang for Manufacturers Hanover," said Joe with a laugh.

Other bits of intriguing information surrounded the Gang of Five's financial partners. Monmouth Capital was run by three men – Bill and John Roberts and Joel Rosenman. John Roberts and Joel Rosenman were famous for

Besides being the money men behind Woodstock, John Roberts and Joel Rosenman helped fund Tractor Supply's leveraged buyout by the Gang of Five.

WOODSTOCK MUSIC & ART FAIR

presents

AN AQUARIAN EXPOSITION

in

WHITE LAKE, N.Y.*

WITH

FRI., AUG. 15
Joan Baez
Arlo Guthrie
Tim Hardin
Richie Havens
Incredible String Band
Ravi Shankar
Sly And The Family Stone
Bert Sommer
Sweetwater

SAT., AUG. 16
Canned Heat
Creedence Clearwater
Grateful Dead
Keef Hartley
Janis Joplin
Jefferson Airplane
Mountain
Quill
Santana
The Who

SUN., AUG. 17
The Band
Jeff Beck Group
Blood, Sweat and Tears
Joe Cocker
Crosby, Stills and Nash
Jimi Hendrix
Iron Butterfly
Ten Years After
Johnny Winter

* check papers and radio for additional acts
All programs subject to change without notice

ART SHOW

Paintings and sculptures on trees, on grass, surrounded by the Hudson Valley, will be displayed. Would be artists, ghetto artists, and accomplished artists will be glad to discuss their work, or the unspoiled splendor of the surroundings, or anything else that might be on your mind. If you're an artist, and you want to display, write for information.

CRAFTS BAZAAR

If you like creative knickknacks and old junk you'll love roaming around our bazaar. You'll see imaginative leather, ceramic, bead, and silver creations, as well as Zodiac Charts, camp clothes, and worn out shoes.

If you like playing with beads, or improvising on a guitar, or writing poetry, or molding clay, stop by one of our work shops and see what you can give and take.

FOOD

There will be cokes and hotdogs and dozens of curious food and fruit combinations to experiment with.

HUNDREDS OF ACRES TO ROAM ON

Walk around for three days without seeing a skyscraper or a traffic light. Fly a kite, sun yourself. Cook your own food and breathe unspoiled air. Camp out: water and restrooms will be supplied. Tents and camping equipment will be available at the Camp Store.

MUSIC STARTS AT 4:00 P.M. ON FRIDAY, AND AT 1:00 P.M. ON SATURDAY AND SUNDAY.

It'll run for 12 continuous hours, except for a few short breaks to allow the performers to catch their breath.

AUGUST 15, 16, 17.

One day $7.00 Two days $13.00 Three days $18.00

For tickets and information write to:
WOODSTOCK MUSIC
BOX 996, RADIO CITY STATION
NEW YORK 10019

*White Lake, Town of Bethel, Sullivan County, N.Y.

3 DAYS of PEACE & MUSIC

Skolnick

Customers Eat Up Feed It may come as a surprise with feed and pet food now accounting for significant sales annually for Tractor Supply, but introducing the category was an uphill battle. Some didn't want the feed in their stores for fear of infestation and bugs. Few thought Tractor Supply could sell dog food. It just wasn't their customer. (This at a time when the stores were selling crock-pots and shotgun shells.) But the 25-lb. bag of Tractor Supply's own private label Retriever Dog Food for $3.99 was a major draw and kept people coming back to the store regularly. History repeated itself in 1997 when Tractor Supply tested super premium Hill's Science Diet pet food in the stores. Again there were concerns Tractor Supply didn't have customers who would part with $30 for a bag of dog food. The super premium pet food drew new customers and became another part of the company's appeal to affluent hobby farmers and city folks who had fled to rural addresses.

bankrolling the Woodstock concert, the defining concert of the '60s that took place in a farmer's field in upstate New York. Apparently, Roberts and Rosenman already understood the power of lifestyles connected to the land.

JOE MAXWELL

They invested $1 million in Tractor Supply and, in less than three years, they received $3.5 million back.

Everything was set. The negotiation was done, and the deal was struck. And so on December 28, 1982, Tom Hennesy and Tom Flood arrived in Atlanta to close the deal: A deal that, at the last minute, almost didn't happen.

"It turned out to be a very tough deal to close," said Flood. "Tom and I had done the forecast and all of the sudden, the deal got a little more expensive than we wanted and we said, 'We can't do it. We're going to have to call it off.'

"Charlie Bradley said, 'Wait a minute. What can we do to get this thing done? What will it take?'"

"'Another $2 million,' said Tom Hennesy."

Charlie Bradley went back to Manufacturers Hanover, but they said they weren't going more than the agreed to $16 million. And that's when Hennesy's relationship with Fuqua came into play again.

"Tom Hennesy goes in to speak to the CFO of Fuqua, who was sitting there working on the deal, and he ends up coming out of the deal with a $2 million loan from Fuqua," said Flood.

"As part of the arrangement Tom set up with Fuqua, we only had to pay interest on the first two years.

"I learned an awful lot from Tom Hennesy about negotiating a deal."

Of course, Hennesy had learned a lot from Fuqua. Enough that he and his four partners acquired Tractor Supply from Fuqua for $20 million under its book value. It was another case of the student outdoing the teacher. Suddenly, the man who had written the book on and boasted about buying companies with other people's money had just let someone buy one of his companies using his money.

Tom Hennesy now owned 40 percent of Tractor Supply. Joe Scarlett owned 20 percent. Gerry Newkirk and Joe Maxwell each owned 15 percent, and Tom Flood had 10 percent. Around the company, the partners became known as the Gang of Five.

It was an exhilarating moment. It was the first time in twenty-five years that Tractor Supply wasn't either a publicly held company or owned by a publicly traded company, the first time in a quarter of a century that control of Tractor Supply's future was again resting in the hands of its owners. And as it had done under its first private ownership, the company would again flourish.

Tractor Supply had been reborn. It would soon return to the track record of performance first established by Charles Schmidt and, for the next twenty-plus years, enjoy an unending string of profitable growth.

SLOW AND STEADY

The Gang of Five was now free to implement their ideas as long as they could come to some consensus on what to do. According to Joe, theirs wasn't just a partnership. It was a marriage. And like even the best of marriages, the union of these five independent-thinking individuals wasn't without its disagreements.

"We became a Gang of Five," said Joe. "In a marriage, you only have one spouse to deal with, and you have a disagreement from time to time. In a deal like ours, you had four spouses, and so naturally we had our disagreements.

EVEN AS A PRIVATELY HELD COMPANY, TRACTOR SUPPLY PUBLISHED ITS NUMBERS. AND, BY THEN, IT HAD NOTHING TO BE ASHAMED OF.

THE GANG OF FIVE FROM LEFT – TOM FLOOD, GERRY NEWKIRK, JOE MAXWELL, TOM HENNESY AND JOE SCARLETT – DON APRONS TO SERVE THEIR TEAM MEMBERS AT A COMPANY COOKOUT.

"We had some hard feelings over some issues, but we managed to get along because we all had a common interest. And I think that it's probably a credit to all five individuals that we all – every one of us, including Tom Hennesy – acquiesced to the group and managed to make things work.

"And, boy, did it."

Tractor Supply would make a profit in 1983 and never look back. By 1985, the venture capitalists were paid off and, by 1989, the man who had put the leveraged buyout together – Charlie Bradley – was himself bought out.

Tom Hennesy wrote in the company's 1985 annual report: "I believe our major strength in this organization to be the strong mutual respect and perfection which prevails among the Company's principals. Each of the other officer-shareholders, my friends Joe Scarlett, Gerry Newkirk, Joe Maxwell, and Tom Flood, were already part of TSC when I arrived, but not in their present responsibilities. These talented individuals are the secret of our success, and all they needed was the opportunity to show what they could do. Our daily relationship is that of a group of friends who share a common goal and who can function together smoothly and effectively. No senior management position in this company has been filled by bringing in someone from outside the company in the past five years."

Wait. Hennesy wrote that in the 1985 annual report? If Tractor Supply was privately held, why bother with an annual report? It was part of Hennesy's belief in running an open, straightforward company with nothing to hide. After the leveraged buyout, Hennesy felt strongly that the vendors were really carrying as much debt for the company as the bank was. So after the first year, he decided to issue an annual report.

1985 BLUE BOOK

"The people that are supporting us need to know how we're doing," said Hennesy. "I know the competition will see it, but I don't care. Long term, it's the right thing to do."

In addition to reporting the financial success of the company during its early years led by the Gang of Five, Hennesy's annual reports also provide a valuable look at the company's evolving mission and values statement.

In 1984, we see the first official statement of Tractor Supply's core beliefs. Inside the front cover of that annual report is the following statement, entitled The TSC Mission:

Our goal is to be the most predictably dependable supplier of basic maintenance needs to the American farmer. We also want to say to our customers, our customers-to-be, and to ourselves that TSC intends:

- ★ To be actively and positively involved in the future of farm life in America;
- ★ To dedicate ourselves to dependability in providing the goods and services our customers expect from us;
- ★ To charge fair and competitive prices;
- ★ To be cheerful, friendly, sympathetic, and interested as we deal with our customers;
- ★ To give the best of ourselves to our business, seeking always to excel;
- ★ To be an active and positive influence in the communities we serve;
- ★ To be fair and understanding in all our relationships;
- ★ To provide our associates with a secure, rewarding and prosperous future;
- ★ Finally, to be the very best we can be in all we do.

Although that early "mission" statement is a far cry from today's mission "to work hard, have fun, and make money by providing legendary service and great products at everyday low prices," it is the foundation for today's commitment "to be the most dependable supplier of basic maintenance products to farm, ranch, and rural customers."

The seeds of a great company had been sown. To grow and flourish, it would still require tending to.

KEEPING THINGS GROWING

During the 1980s, Tom Hennesy, with increasing help from others in the Gang of Five, would continue to develop his team, continue to establish the company's corporate culture and continue the company's slow, steady, and profitable growth that would ultimately provide the foundation of experience to support the rural revolution and incredible expansion of Tractor Supply at the dawn of the new millennium.

Through the course of the new Tractor Supply Company's first decade, a lot would happen. From 1980 to 1985, the company would grow from $100 million to $150 million. To underscore the importance of its people to its success, it would institute an employee stock ownership plan in 1985 and award more than $2.4 million in cash bonuses.

In 1986, the company would break ground on a new headquarters – more appropriately christened the Store Support Center – at 320 Plus Park Boulevard in Nashville, Tennessee. Joe Scarlett wouldn't see very much of his new office, that same year visiting 102 of the company's 140 stores, a practice he continues today. The same year, the company would experiment with Chick Days – a promotion in which chicks ordered by the customer arrive at the store for pickup. The experiment, which has since become a TSC tradition (much to the post office's chagrin – but it does ensure that on one day a year the mail is delivered early!) sold more than 135,000 birds and increased poultry feed sales by 255 percent.

In 1987, Joe Scarlett would be named president and chief operating officer of the company, while Tom Hennesy became chairman and CEO. Joe's first President's Message in the company's internal newsletter is on "guaranteed customer satisfaction," continuing a theme long championed by Tom Hennesy and core to the company's values. That same year, the company would offer the leadership of its Canadian store subsidiary the same opportunity it enjoyed in 1983, selling it to the newly formed company's executive management team.

By 1990, Tractor Supply had doubled its sales since the company's turnaround began with the coming of Tom Hennesy in 1980 and the development of his management team. Sales were now at $200 million and, more important, profits had grown from minus $13 million to an average of more than $2 million annually.

TRACTOR SUPPLY STORE SUPPORT CENTER IS UNDER CONSTRUCTION. IT WOULD CELEBRATE ITS GRAND OPENING IN 1987.

Equally as powerful an indicator of store performance as sales, customer letters were now

HIGH-KICK FOR A GROUP THAT CAN CAN.

The can-do attitude of the company's leadership – Joe Maxwell, Joe Scarlett, Tom Hennesy, Gerry Newkirk, and Tom Flood – kicked the company into high gear and up a notch. A happy moment during the 1986 groundbreaking for a new "home office" that would reflect the company's team-philosophy by being christened the "Store Support Center."

TOM
FLOOD

pouring in and the company regularly posted these success stories in the pages of *The Voice*.

Many of the letters focused on service, like this one from Owosso, Michigan.

"Recently my husband and I had reason to visit your store because my husband needed a $2 part for a fogger. The salesperson spent a lot of time searching for a supplier to provide the part. When the part came in, the fogger needed another part and Jerry ordered the needed part. The supplier sent the wrong part, so Jerry sold us the needed part from a floor model because he felt the customer satisfaction was most important. There is another farm supply store closer to us, but my husband and I will drive the extra 20 miles to TSC for the service. It is indeed a pleasure doing business with you."

GERRY NEWKIRK

GERRY NEWKIRK AND TOM HENNESY ENJOYED A CLOSE FRIENDSHIP.

Sometimes going the second mile in terms of service meant the customer would go the extra mile just to do business with you.

The Gang of Five had worked together for the last seven years. They had worked admirably well together, but tensions naturally existed among the five as they looked for new opportunity, a tension perhaps exacerbated by Hennesy's insistence on conservative growth.

"Tom believed in controlling your growth and controlling your financial situation so that you didn't have to borrow a lot of money," explained Tom Flood. "We added four or five stores a year.

"I think Tom's slow growth mode worked out real well during our early years of ownership because we were highly leveraged. It was a tough road that helped prepare us for the decisions we'd be making to grow the company more aggressively with Joe.

"You see, Joe was a lot more aggressive than Tom and wanted to do some things, wanted to see if the company couldn't grow a little faster and I think most of us internally supported him in his thoughts."

To his credit, Tom Hennesy recognized the need to provide opportunities and greater responsibility for the team of executives he had developed.

"Tom didn't necessarily want to retire," explained Gerry Newkirk. "I think Tom's view was, 'I need to provide opportunities for Joe and Gerry,' and if that meant retiring, so be it."

The challenge was providing Hennesy the liquidity he needed to step away from the business, to somehow come up with the funds to return his 40 percent share of the company. An IPO was one way of gaining liquidity for Hennesy, but he was strongly opposed to taking the company public. However, he would reluctantly agree to a merger with a public company. On three different occasions, they tried to sell the company. The closest they came was in 1990, when they attempted a merger with ConAgra.

"ConAgra owned a farm store chain called Country General," said Joe Scarlett. "So all five of us flew out to Omaha to meet with Mike Harper, the CEO of ConAgra at the time.

"I remember us all waiting for him in a conference room we still jokingly refer to as the 'seduction suite.' He thought his stock was pretty highly valued, but we thought we could work

IN THE WAKE OF 9-11 TRACTOR SUPPLY RESPONDED BY UNFURLING A MASSIVE AMERICAN FLAG.

something out, so we came to some semblance of an agreement.

"Then several of us went to Grand Island, Nebraska, to meet with Country General folks and we ended up learning a lot more about ConAgra than I think they wanted us to know," Joe said with a chuckle.

While talking to Tony Seitz, the president of Country General, Joe and his partners learned that Seitz was working on a request to ConAgra for a $2,500 check-signing machine.

"We couldn't believe the president of the company was asking for permission to spend $2,500," said Joe barely able to contain his incredulity.

"We just don't operate like that. Our culture and our values place a pretty high premium on trusting others to make the right decisions.

"We weren't about to take a big step backwards."

So Scarlett, Newkirk, Maxwell, and Flood went to Hennesy's house immediately after their trip and talked Hennesy out of the deal. They promised him they would help him find another way to get his money out of the business. Several weeks later, Joe led the group in putting together an offer for Hennesy's share in the company. They offered him the same share price that had been discussed with ConAgra. While the ConAgra deal had failed, it had successfully established a price for shares of Tractor Supply.

"So Tom put together a plan and converted his stock to preferred stock," explained Joe. "And we paid him off over a period of years according to the schedule he'd put together."

It was 1990, and Joe was growing into his role of president. He was developing a vision for the company. He was eager to keep things moving. Given the speed with which Joe regularly moves today – always on the run, visiting stores, quizzing customers, sitting on a bucket in the backroom of a store to talk values with a store's team members, or making a long road trip with his management team to get back in touch with each other and the store floors where business is done – it's hard to imagine Joe has the capacity to wait to move things along.

In the fast-paced, constantly changing world view of Joe Scarlett, in retail as in life, not moving is a pretty good indication that you're already dead.

WHATEV

Bacon CHEESEBURGER

ERE ARE THOSE WH

COMPROMISE

SCENE

ED TO THE LAND

THE TWO IS A LITTLE INITIATIVE

TSC

WITH THAT IN MIND AT TRA

WE EMPOWER ALL TEAM MEMBERS

PROD. CARMIC

DIR MANNING

DAY NITE DA

TO MAK

CHAPTER ★9★

IF IT AIN'T BROKE, BREAK IT

TRACTOR SUPPLY — ENTERS THE — SCARLETT AGE

"I'M GONNA LIVE WHERE THE GREEN GRASS GROWS,
WATCH MY CORN POP UP IN ROWS,
EVERY NIGHT BE TUCKED IN CLOSE TO YOU.
RAISE OUR KIDS WHERE THE GOOD LORD'S BLESSED,
POINT OUR ROCKIN' CHAIRS TOWARDS THE WEST AND
PLANT OUR DREAMS WHERE THE PEACEFUL RIVER FLOWS
WHERE THE GREEN GRASS GROWS."

- TIM MCGRAW, "WHERE THE GREEN GRASS GROWS"

A MAN ON A MISSION

Tom Hennesy's team turned Tractor Supply around in the '80s. Joe Scarlett's team took it to new heights. Joe stands before the annual managers meeting in Nashville, poised almost as a conductor ready to lead the assembled players. The accompanying din of air horns is music to his ears. It's the sound of people having fun, working hard, and making money.

THE SOUND OF BREAKING A BILLION DOLLARS Tractor Supply is a company that's used to making a lot of noise. In fact, before you go to its annual managers meeting you're issued a small package with two small foam earplugs you're supposed to jam into your ears. You know, the kind used by crews on road construction, factory floors, sawmills, and backstage at a heavy metal concert.

★

Some folks, such as Blake Fohl, Tractor Supply's vice president of marketing, upgrade their protection, covering the foam ear plugs with the sort of industrial earmuffs used by airport runway workers and cops on a gun range.

There's nothing like it in corporate America.

It's one part political convention, complete with its throng of placard-carrying, slogan-chanting crazies. It's one part a Mr. Wizard, do-it-yourself-at-home experiment gone bad with all manner of blinking chaser lights and air compressors, tied to two-wheelers and wired to batteries and truck horns and maybe your occasional odd barge or train horn. It's one part Indy 500 infield, with all of the teams circling. Here come Grif's Gorillas, No. 822. Erick's Executioners are No. 853. How about No. 842, McClain's Diehards, and 827, Haskell's Henchmen.

"This is the way you feel when you work for a company that believes in its people and respects them and shares the rewards of success," said one of the participants.

What you've just stumbled into – and more than one guest staying at the convention hotel in Nashville where the event is held wondered this very thing – what you're witnessing may be the greatest single display of passion and energy in American business. It's certainly the loudest. This is the Tractor Supply annual store managers meeting, where proud equals loud and employee enthusiasm is measured in decibels. This highly motivated store management team wants to make sure everyone knows, loud and clear, they believe in what they're doing.

"It's part of our culture," explained Blake Fohl. "If you can't see the personal pride, the passion that goes on at those meetings, then you're not really looking.

"All I would say is look in their faces. Forget the noise. Forget the banners. Forget all of that. Just look in the eyes of the men and women who are there. There's something deeply felt going on here."

Which is why Joe Scarlett smiles as he stands amid the din of horns and hoarse team members yelling at the top of their lungs. Joe is beaming, rocking on his heels and smiling, taking it all in and letting it wash over him like champagne in the winners' locker room at the World Series.

"Every year we have our national store managers meeting in February or March," explained Joe. "We've been doing it now since the early nineties. Early on, one of the groups got into cheering a lot and then they started bringing air horns. And now every year, everybody tries to outdo everyone else. One year, a group rigged up an air horn off a Union Pacific diesel train.

"I suppose the company could have put the kibosh on it right away," Joe pondered. "But we decided to just laugh. This is a very competitive and enthusiastic group that has fun when it gets together."

What company in America wouldn't want to have those attributes exhibited in its people? The pride. The enthusiasm. The competitive nature. The fun. The freedom. The camaraderie that allows a group to go crazy like this in each other's presence. These people genuinely like each other and what they do. They are having fun. There is just no hiding it.

"Bring it on!" Joe exclaimed amid the sea of enthsiasm. He is clearly in his element.

Joe Scarlett just may be one of the few chairmen who are comfortable with this frenetic level of activity. That's because Joe, himself, is in constant motion. He's everywhere – visiting approximately 150 stores every year. He just never stops. He's always taking aside anyone he can find, wherever he can find them, to share the company's mission and vision.

THE CELEBRATORY CACOPHONY AND CHAOS THAT HAS BECOME A CENTERPIECE OF A CORPORATE CULTURE WHOSE HALLMARK IS PASSION AND A CAN-DO ATTITUDE.

THE CEO WHO NEVER SLEEPS

Although he grew up in New Jersey, it's fitting that Joe was born in New York, the city that never sleeps.

Nowadays, everyone who knows Joe points to his energy and work ethic as the source of much of Tractor Supply's upbeat character and continual drive for success. Hearing this, Joe will quickly say, "No, it's all a team effort." But then every winning team has to have a coach who knows how to win. In fact, his management team uses the title of "coach" more often when referring to Joe than the title printed on his business card.

Coach, cheerleader, "our smiley-faced CEO," or just good ol' Joe. Like Tom Hennesy before him, Joe Scarlett is a man of many nicknames. More terms of endearment than titles, they serve as a pretty good indication of just how beloved Joe is among the Tractor Supply team members and how little real titles mean to him.

Over the years, his titles and his team's success have been complemented with their fair share of accolades. Joe was elected chairman of the International Mass Retail Association in 2001. In 2003, on behalf of the company's management team, he accepted the Southeast Area Entrepreneur of the Year Award in the Master Category from Ernst & Young. But titles and awards mean little to Joe.

What means most to Joe is getting the job done, whatever it takes.

Joe readily attributes his enthusiasm, energy, and work ethic to another team effort – that of his parents, Joseph and Evelyn Scarlett. (Yes, Joe is technically Joseph Scarlett Jr. But we recommend you just call him Joe. Because that's what he likes to be called, and Joe has a thing about calling folks by their own name, the name they want to be called by, whether a customer or a new acquaintance.)

Joe's enthusiasm, work ethic and strict moral underpinning were instilled by his parents. Joseph Scarlett Sr. and Evelyn worked hard to put Joe's father through undergraduate and graduate school. And Joseph Sr. was always proud to point out the fact that he was never without a job during the Great Depression, even though he worked on Wall Street at a time when most Americans didn't have a thing to invest or had already lost everything in the stock market crash. And Joe's mother was extremely ethical.

"She wouldn't even tell a white lie," Joe said. "I remember one time, I thought I was real clever as a kid. I went back behind this drugstore and grabbed a bunch of returnable soda bottles and then went around front and turned them in.

"Somehow my mother found out and made me go over there, apologize and pay back the money.

"It's something I'll never forget."

Not only did he never forget this lesson, but also he readily tells the story. Honesty about one's shortcomings is a Tractor Supply hallmark. Admitting mistakes is the first step in fixing them. And it's part of what's kept the company thriving in a post-WorldCom-Enron business environment in which corporate ethics are constantly being questioned. Scarlett left little room for doubt and speculation about his view on the issue when he circulated the following letter among everyone at Tractor Supply.

June 27, 2002

Dear Team Member:

"America's Corporate Meltdown" is the headline in this morning's *USA Today*. The article covers the wrong doing at WorldCom, Enron, Rite Aid, and so on with the implication that American business leaders are unethical and dishonest. This, obviously, casts a black cloud over all of us in the business community.

I am firmly convinced that only a tiny fraction of American business leaders are not honest and ethical. It is truly a shame that a few greedy bums are casting such a dark shadow over all of us. I, for one, am mad! I hope these criminals are fairly tried and spend a long time behind bars. At Tractor Supply, we are a mission- and value-driven company. "We talk the talk and we walk the walk." Our number one value is Ethics – "Do the right thing and always encourage others to do the right, honest, and ethical things." It is our pledge to you that Tractor Supply will always "Walk the high road" – always strive to make the most ethical business decisions.

The stories about people losing their life savings in 401(k) plans that were not managed correctly are truly heart-wrenching. At Tractor Supply Company, you personally direct the investment of all of your 401(k) money, and the management of these plans is by a third party. Markets go up and markets go down, but in the long term, those of you who have Tractor Supply 401(k) programs should be building a solid base of retirement funds for your future.

Again, I reiterate that our number one value is Ethics. We teach the right thing, we do the right thing, and we will be forever committed to the highest ethical standards.

Regardless of the current headlines, American business leaders are the best in the world. I urge you not to let the misdeeds of a limited number of people at a limited number of companies erode your confidence in our business leaders.

Sincerely,

Joseph H. Scarlett

Joe Scarlett
Head Coach

JOSEPH AND EVELYN SCARLETT INSTILLED IN JOE JR. THE VALUES AND WORK ETHIC THAT HAVE BECOME THE DNA OF TSC.

Being up front and honest about mistakes and doing whatever it takes to make things better is part of the corporation's culture and leads it to do remarkable things in order to honor its commitment to legendary service.

Joe has admitted to mistakes made along the way to building a billion-dollar company. A computer system upgrade made during late 1999 proved a laborious and costly task. But unlike the difficulties with a new inventory management system during the National years that proved so devastating to the company, the difficult 1990s technology upgrade process eventually helped propel the company forward instead of holding it back. Perhaps this was because everyone readily identified and admitted to the challenges and then took care of them.

Looking back now, Joe also admits it was a mistake to take on the job of president of Tractor Supply while at the same time serving as chairman of the board and chief executive officer of the company. He made this mistake in 1997 when Gerry Newkirk stepped down. Joe was rebuilding his management team. One by one, the Gang of Five was stepping aside as the company entered a new phase in its history. Joe Maxwell had already retired in 1996, and Tom Flood would follow Newkirk and Maxwell, retiring in 1999.

"After Gerry left, I took on both the roles of president and chairman of the company," admitted Joe.

"In retrospect, I may have bitten off more than I could chew," he said plainly, not pulling any punches, even though he's directing them at himself.

"We had to rebuild the management team. In 2000, I realized I just couldn't do both jobs the way I wanted them done."

That's when Joe found Jim Wright, and they've been joined at the hip ever since.

"I had to admit I needed the help and then go out and get it," said Joe. "It wasn't an easy decision but it was the right one.

"I think the work of Jim Wright has proven that."

Along with his mother's highly developed sense of integrity, Joe was also blessed with a seemingly limitless supply of energy and good health. His vitality has served him well, fueling the sheer will it took to maintain his positive outlook when

JOE, RECLINING? NEVER. HE'S JUST POSING FOR A PHOTO THAT APPEARED IN SOUTHWEST AIRLINES *SPIRIT* MAGAZINE.

associated with so much failure in his early career – the demise of Two Guys followed by the near-demise of Tractor Supply during the '70s.

Of course, there have been those rare times when his energy almost got him in trouble.

"I probably enjoyed chasing the girls a little too much in high school," said Joe. "My parents, who were both college graduates, thought I was going to wind up in jail or something."

Joe opted for the "something," and instead of jail, went to a first-rate prep school by the name of Newark Academy. With high school out of the way, the-always-on-the-go Joe was too impatient to stick around for anything more than one semester at Rutgers.

"I wanted to get on with my life," he said. And "get on" he did, working briefly for a supermarket chain and a bank before working at Two Guys for fifteen years before coming to Tractor Supply in 1979. He left one struggling company to join another. In both cases, the fortunes of the companies did not dampen Joe's enthusiasm. Joe's approach has always been to just jump in and get busy. To this day, Joe believes that his willingness to jump in and do whatever it takes to get the job done is what saved his job at Two Guys and then kept him on board during Tractor Supply's move to Nashville and the regime change that ushered in Tom Hennesy.

THE WORDS OF CHAIRMAN JOE

Along with his amazing attitude, Joe's energy and enthusiasm also resonate in his language. This is a man who lives according to a series of short provocative statements, firing them out like the small powerful explosions in the cylinder of an engine, the bursts of energy that drive a tractor and propel Tractor Supply constantly forward:

- ★ "If it ain't broke, break it and make it better. Everything needs to be constantly improved."
- ★ "If you're not having fun, get out of here. If you're not doing what you love, then you won't be productive."
- ★ "We'll proudly borrow a good idea from any where. We don't think an idea has to be ours to be good."
- ★ "Take care of the customer NO MATTER WHAT. You can't get into trouble for taking care of a customer. Today we're getting about half as many customer complaints as we were five years ago, yet our company is twice the size as it was before. That's because we're making tremendous progress in empowering our people to take care of our customers."
- ★ "Surround yourself with stars, you'll be a star. Surround yourself with turkeys, you're going to get sliced up for Thanksgiving dinner."
- ★ "One of the prime causes of business failures in this country is CEOs with big fat heads who aren't listening to their people."
- ★ "I pride myself on not making decisions. To stay nimble as a retailer, you've got to trust your people to make the right decisions."
- ★ "I love it when a store manager ignores me… because he's taking time with a customer."

These aren't careless comments. Joe's words are meant to bring to life the company's mission and values. They're exclamatory sentences uttered in a world that's more comfortable with questions and ambiguity.

Joe is acutely aware of the power of words and of speaking a vision. The realization came to him in

1990, a little more than two years after being named president and chief operating officer of Tractor Supply. After being in the farm store business for more than fifty years, the company had just passed the $200 million mark. That was good, but Joe began saying that in just six more years – by 1996 – the company would double its sales. Joe was giving the company just six years to double a sales number that had already taken Tractor Supply more than half a century to reach.

CALF EZE

FETAL EXTRACTOR

The pulling points shift the pull from one leg of the calf to the other, thereby, creating a zigzag type motion. The Calf Eze™ jack has dual locks for a dual-action pull, includes a third hook for those that prefer a single-action pull and has a cam-spring traction system that prevents the jack from slipping on the rods. The jack also has a locking mechanism that allows the user to lock the jack in place when needed. Comes with a cast-aluminum breechen, steel rods that quickly disassemble for easy clean up and is 72" in length when completely assembled.

21-86014.................$219.99

2003 BLUE BOOK

"When I first started saying it, I didn't think anyone was listening," Joe said. "I was sort of disappointed. But I kept on.

"I shared this vision ad nauseum with store managers, district managers, and executives over and over again. At one point, I almost gave up because I didn't think I was getting anywhere.

"But then, all of the sudden, I began to hear people saying the same thing."

Joe's "visioning" isn't some corporate adaptation of name-it-claim-it theology. His prediction was more like the well planned first lunar shot than it was Babe Ruth's called shot. Joe is opposed to just throwing numbers out there. His vision was and is always carefully grounded and comes complete with strategic plans, targets, new product offerings and improvements, merchandising ideas and distribution channels – all the nuts and bolts of retailing and precisely how the company will arrive at the number that he's floating out there. This vision creates a heightened sense of urgency and mission required to do anything truly great.

A BLOWN PREDICTION

By the way, Joe was way off on his projection that the company would grow from $200 million to $400 million in six years. And one thing about Joe, he's always the first to admit when he is wrong.

"Yes, I was wrong," he said. "I underestimated. We ended up reaching something more like $450 million.

"And that's the power of vision. It's not hearing something once. It's hearing it over and over again that makes the vision, the values and our mission so powerful. People begin to believe in where they're going and what they're doing. Before you know it, they're just unstoppable."

According to the company's annual report, "Tractor Supply reached record sales, record net income, and opened more stores than ever in 1996." With a total of 208 stores in twenty-four states, Tractor Supply began calling itself the "largest retail farm store chain in America." Having just doubled its size in five years, it planned to double its size again in five more years.

Once again, the company met its ambitious vision, growing to $850 million in sales by 2001, with 323 stores in twenty-eight states. It would take only one more year for Tractor Supply to add another $360 million in sales to exceed $1.2 billion dollars. To give some perspective to the magnitude of growth the company was experiencing, it had taken Tractor Supply fifty-seven years to reach the half-billion dollars in sales mark. But just five years to double it. Along the way, while reaching a billion dollars, the company's stock split.

If you'd bought Tractor Supply when it went public in 1994, your investment would have grown nearly sevenfold in ten short years.

What does Joe think about that?

Absolutely nothing. What's done is done. He's already talking about tomorrow. And visioning all over again.

It took awhile for Tractor Supply to get to this point. It took the right people and infrastructure and, well, just the right vision and ability to communicate that vision to get here. So maybe we should backtrack a bit and begin where the last chapter left off, the ushering in of Tractor Supply's Scarlett period in 1990.

A DOOR SHUTS. A DOOR OPENS.

Tom Hennesy was never a big supporter of accelerating the company's growth. He preferred to maintain the slow, steady growth the company enjoyed under his watch. Although Tom Hennesy was the engineer of the company's resurgence, he was never a believer in taking the company public. That task would fall to Joe Scarlett and his team.

"Tom was opposed to going public," recalled Joe. "But it's not like you can pass your interest down to the next family member. You've got five separate personalities involved, and to keep flipping ownership means the company can't grow because it keeps gobbling up cash to pay off each generation of owners.

"So that's why we decided to go public."

"Tom Hennesy was very upset by the notion of going public," Joe Maxwell agreed. "But we all believed either you're growing or you're dying and we couldn't grow substantially privately. The only way to do it was to go public and generate the funds."

According to Tom Flood, the first attempt to take the new TSC public was shelved in 1992 when the company under-performed in the quarter just prior to when Tractor Supply wanted to go public.

"So the brokerage firm said, 'Just give us a call when you've got things turned around and in order,'" remembered Tom Flood. "Well, in six months we called them back and they said, 'Wait, you couldn't have turned things around that fast.'"

TOM HENNESY

The brokerage firm was amazed at what the company had done. That kind of reaction to Tractor Supply's turn-on-a-dime agility and can-do attitude have become an ongoing refrain to Wall Street's view of the unusual company. In late 1993, Tractor Supply ended up finalizing everything to go public.

FOR MORE THAN 20 YEARS, TRACTOR SUPPLY HAS BEEN USING ITS TRUCKS AS MOVING BILLBOARDS.

In early February 1994, Joe Scarlett, Gerry Newkirk, and Tom Flood went on a "road show," traveling nearly 20,000 miles to twelve cities including London, England. During the two-week trip, presentations were made to hundreds of investors and fund managers. In order to make the whirlwind deadline, Joe and company even traveled by limo during the road show. But lest anyone think success had changed Joe Scarlett, please note that Joe made sure that the limo driver pulled into McDonald's drive-through so that he could begin the day with his traditional cup of coffee.

The road show finally came to an end the afternoon of February 17. The very next day the company issued an initial public offering of 2,855,000 shares of common stock at a price of

$20 per share. The company was listed on the NASDAQ under the symbol TSCO.

Before going public, Tom Hennesy graciously turned the reins of chairman and CEO of Tractor Supply over to Joe in early 1993.

HEY, JOE, WHERE ARE YOU GOING NOW THAT YOU'RE COMPANY'S GONE PUBLIC? I'M GOING TO McDONALD'S!

"Tom was all about creating opportunities for others," Gerry Newkirk commented. "He knew it was time."

Hennesy said simply, "Joe has been running the company with me looking on and consulting for some time."

At the same time, Gerry Newkirk was promoted to president.

NASDAQ®

It marked the passing of an important chapter in the history of the company. For ten years, with Hennesy at the helm, Tractor Supply had enjoyed steady, albeit slow, growth and stability and a much-needed respite from the previous decade's revolving door through which four presidents had quickly passed, along with much of the company's viability and success and fun, family-oriented atmosphere. Hennesy and the rest of the Gang of Five – Scarlett, Newkirk, Maxwell, and Flood – had turned the company around from a $13 million loss on just under $100 million in sales in 1983 to a $6.9 million profit on $279.2 million in sales a decade later in 1993. It was a dramatic change in fortunes. In the process, Hennesy had also mentored the leadership that would inspire the next generation of TSC success stories. The stability, expertise, ethics, and humanity that Hennesy brought to the company's top spot created the foundation from which Joe would propel Tractor Supply.

Even though it would take Joe more than a decade to assemble and develop his own management team, the rate of change at Tractor Supply was beginning to accelerate to keep pace with the needs of a changing marketplace and the emergence of previously untargeted and unrecognized consumer segments. Tractor Supply's definition of its consumer was about to expand significantly, as did the company's marketing efforts and unique product lines designed to reach the consumer.

MARKETING ISN'T JUST WHAT YOU DO WHEN YOU BUY GROCERIES

For the first time in its history, Tractor Supply's marketing and advertising efforts would expand beyond the direct mail, the Blue Book and circulars that had been a company staple since its founding with the first catalog in 1939.

Since 1983, Joe Maxwell had been Tractor Supply's vice president of marketing, a job that was created for him after he had discontinued the company's passenger tire line.

"I essentially eliminated my job as vice president of merchandising with responsibility for automotive and farm tires," explained Maxwell with a chuckle. "Which I guess demonstrates my objectivity, although not my instinct for self-preservation."

Maxwell had come from Goodyear to manage Tractor Supply's automotive line. He analyzed the tire line and discovered there was little potential for the company in the passenger and truck tire segments. That was because Tractor Supply only offered its customers the tires and not the customary services that they expected, such as front-end alignment, brakes and balancing.

"The tire business is extremely competitive," said Maxwell. "Did we want to make an investment in the infrastructure and hire some real mechanics in an operation of our size just to get in the business?

"Offering labor out in the shop was the only way to make much margin in the business."

Maxwell's analysis was accurate, and Tractor Supply's passenger and truck tire lines were discontinued. Merchandising, which had been split between Maxwell and Newkirk, was now consolidated under Newkirk as the company's vice president of merchandising. Maxwell was offered the opportunity to found the company's first fledgling marketing department.

"I began overseeing the company's marketing, advertising, and public relations around 1983," Maxwell said. "My forte was operations and merchandising, but, hey, there's not anybody in the world that figures they can't run advertising.

"How hard can it be?"

Maxwell is, of course, speaking with his tongue firmly embedded in his cheek. He knew he was tackling a huge challenge. Despite his relative inexperience, several significant marketing moves were made during Maxwell's tenure. The single most important may have been going back to the company's original name – Tractor Supply Company.

During the '60s, the company had begun expanding its merchandise in order to appeal to customers beyond the traditional farmer. The name Tractor Supply was dropped because it had too much of a farm identity and so the initials TSC were substituted. The only problem was no one knew what a TSC was.

Unlike BVD, ABC, or IBM, the company didn't have enough money to create awareness of TSC.

"While no one knew what TSC stood for, they had an emotional attachment to the word 'tractor,'" said Joe. "It has a rich association with the land and the rural lifestyle, and so Tractor Supply is a name that still resonates with our customers. And it's far easier to remember than TSC."

Under Maxwell, Tractor Supply also did its first image advertising – a series of radio spots that featured a jingle and voiceover.

"I remember the last series of radio spots we did," said Maxwell. "Jeffrey Buntin, the president

TRAVELLER SPORT SPECIAL

Designed & Styled For Compacts & Import Cars

SPORT SPECIAL TIRE SIZE	SHIPWT.	STK. NO.	FEDERAL EXCISE TAX	OUR LOW PRICE
5.90/6.00-13	17	3-0025	1.57	13.95
6.40/6.50-13	18	3-0026	1.81	15.45
7.00-13	19	3-0028	1.92	15.98
5.50/5.90 6.00-15	20	3-0027	1.88	15.45
5.60-15	17	3-0029	1.74	14.98
Black Tubeless				
5.60-15	17	3-0015	1.74	13.75
Outright Sale—Plus Tax—No Trade-in Required				

SALE PRICE
LOW AS
12.37
Plus 1.57 Tax

- Rugged Full 4-Ply Nylon Cord for extra safety, longer wear.
- Smart, Narrow Whitewall
- Non-Skid 5 Row Tread Pattern
- Low-Profile design

27 month tread wear guarantee

SPORT SPECIAL

TRACTOR SUPPLY CO 30TH ANNIVERSARY Special

SPORT SPECIAL

CUT 10% (From Prices Shown, Sale Ends Mar. 31st)

HOW SERIOUS WAS THE GANG OF FIVE ABOUT HONESTLY BETTERING THE BUSINESS? JOE MAXWELL DISSOLVED HIS OWN POSITION WHEN HE DISCONTINUED TSC PASSENGER TIRES.

of the local Nashville advertising agency we were using at the time, called me one day and said, 'I've got a great guy for the jingle. He's going to be a superstar one day and we can get him for something like $300.'"

In a city like Nashville with its wealth of musical talent trying to make it in the music business, premature predictions of "superstar" status are common. But in this case, Jeffrey Buntin got it right.

OSTRICH FEED

FOR GROWTH AND MAINTENANCE OF OSTRICHES AND EMUS

Contains all the nutrients necessary for proper growth and maintenance of your birds. The pelleted diet is easy to feed and reduces waste. Pellets look and taste the same which discourages birds from separating the diet and only eating the parts they like. You can be sure they receive consistent levels of the nutrients they need for good health. Calcium in the diet is derived from oyster egg shells, and it contributes to stronger eggs, resulting in better survival. Vitamin E and selenium in the diet aids in preventing muscular dystrophy and vitamin E and selenium deficiencies.

50 LB. 50-85102

2003 BLUE BOOK

For $300, Tractor Supply's radio jingles featured the voice of a then-obscure talent named – Alan Jackson.

With the success of the company's IPO, Maxwell was able to retire comfortably in 1996. "It was time to bring in somebody else with a different point of view," Maxwell said. "I knew we needed to go in a different direction, and I didn't know how to take us there. It was the right decision for me and the company."

Once again, Maxwell exhibited a personal strength in his straightforward analysis of the situation, and he continues to serve on the company's board.

FOHL'S FOLLY LEADS TO TRACTOR SUPPLY'S SUCCESS

Maxwell's departure left the marketing position vacant. Blake Fohl would prove an interesting candidate for his replacement. Fohl came to Tractor Supply with a degree in ag business and farm store experience with one of America's largest cooperatives.

According to his own admission, Fohl's career at Tractor Supply proved that Joe is serious when he urges people to venture outside the box and take intelligent risks without fear of being fired.

"As a hardlines buyer for the company, I developed a line of stationary power tools and called them Ironsmith," remembered Fohl, who joined Tractor Supply in 1992. "I did the packaging, too, and we won some pretty impressive awards for them.

"There was only one problem – the product quality was absolutely horrendous and it was probably one of the biggest failures in my career."

Fohl's frank acknowledgment of his failure is refreshing in today's jaded corporate environment. It's also representative of the kind of character that comprises today's Tractor Supply management team. Instead of being fired for his blunder as a buyer, he was given the opportunity to exercise his creative and analytical talents as Tractor Supply's director of advertising after Maxwell retired.

Fohl made the most of this new opportunity, delving first into the identity of the customer. Much as Charles Schmidt had built his first mailing list based on rural route information the government supplied to him, Fohl pored through the wealth of statistical information provided by the USDA free of charge and began building a demographic model of the company's customers.

Next he brought in one of the world's leading research firms, Yankelovich Partners, Inc., to do segmentation studies of the Tractor Supply's customer base to determine how many of its customers were really full-time, part-time or hobby farmers. The research revealed that only 8 percent of the Tractor Supply customer base called themselves full-time farmers. The majority of its customers – 47 percent – were part-time or hobby farmers.

Today, the company understands and knows its customers better than it ever has before. To illustrate that, the company's marketing department has come up with a consumer narrative to bring to life all of the numbers that research has been able to uncover. The narrative serves to put a little real life flesh on the statistical bones. It's used in informal presentations. There's no official, written version of it. It just sort of wells up spur of the moment during a presentation and it goes something like this:

LIFE OUT HERE

There once was a farmer who lived with his family way out in the country, away from the city, on 200 acres left to him by his father. And he and his family were Tractor Supply customers going way back. Then one day, he looks up and his children are grown and gone, while he and his wife have retired. So they decide to sell half of their land – 100 acres – in four twenty-five-acre parcels.

Now where once lived a single Tractor Supply family, there are five.

Chances are, each of the people who've bought one of our original farmer's twenty-five acre parcels is about 45 years old, is likely to be married with children at home, and works a full-time job on the side to fund his dream of owning what he unabashedly calls "a little piece of heaven."

Now that each of our four new landowners has acquired a piece of paradise, each decides to build a home. Not too close to the road, tucked back a bit, perhaps hidden from view by a windbreak of pines. With such a big front yard, he can't mow any longer with the small lawnmower he'd depended on in the city. He needs a big, sturdy lawn tractor. That's easy, because his Tractor Supply Store sells more lawn tractors per capita than any other retailer in America.

He keeps his lawn tractor in a small shed. He keeps his power tools there, too. There's a justifiable need for a log splitter or band saw or compressor or generator. Things that allow him to take care of problems all by himself.

WHEN BLAKE FOHL ISN'T BEHIND THE DESK, HE'S BEHIND THE WHEEL OF HIS PICKUP WITH A TRAILER OF DOGS HEADED OUT THERE.

Once you've got a pretty piece of land like this, you need to go through the ritual of claiming it for your own, putting down roots, marking it as your land. Nothing is better for doing that than a fence. And, fortunately, our new landowners know right where to get everything they need to get the job done – which is why their Tractor Supply Store is the leading supplier of agricultural fencing and fence-building know-how in the nation.

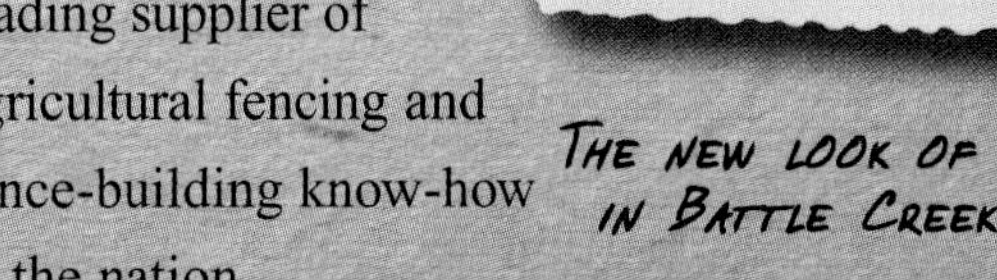
THE NEW LOOK OF TRACTOR SUPPLY IN BATTLE CREEK, MICHIGAN

Check behind the house, and you'll find his daughter has a horse. And that horse needs to eat, to be taken care of and have a block of salt, a trough for water, medicine for making it well when it comes down sick or for making sure it never comes down sick. Now he's discovered that Tractor Supply Store of his has an awfully wide selection of tack and equine supplies. It should, because it is the top equine and tack retailer in America.

Finally, you can't live this far from town with land, horses, dogs, tools, and all unless you drive a pickup truck to haul what you need. And should you need something for your pickup, that's right, you already know, Tractor Supply has it – from truck boxes to hitches and trailers.

Blake Fohl wrapped it all up saying, "Unique products. Seasoned advice. Supporting a lifestyle. Tractor Supply – It's where it all comes together. Good products, great customers and the very best store people you'll ever meet. Chances are someone there is going to know you by name."

Well, you get the point. But there are quicker ways of making the same point. And who better than speedy Joe Scarlett, the man always on the move, to come up with a quick way of painting the same picture?

According to Cal Massmann, Tractor Supply's chief financial officer and senior vice president, Joe has been known to simply point out that, "Last year we sold a half-million vaccinations for dogs and cats. That's a half-million times that one of our customers got a syringe, drew the medicine out of the vial and scooped up his dog or cat and gave him an injection. And it only costs him about $3 a shot. Most of you probably wouldn't do that, but that's our customer."

RETURNING TO ITS ROOTS

Just as Tractor Supply had welcomed the '90s by returning to its roots – reverting to its original name and re-staking its original claim as America's farm and ranch store – to newfound success, Americans, too, were returning to the land.

For the first time in decades, the number of rural routes was on the rise. A new hardworking breed of Americans was escaping the cities back to their rural roots. More and more baby boomers were finding refuge in the rural lifestyle as they retired. Having a little stock on the land was viewed by some as much a sign of success in life as taking stock in the market. Where the turn of the last century was greeted with the Industrial Revolution that drew America to the city, what some now called the Rural Revolution

was returning us to the land as the new millennium approached.

By 1999, farms generating less than $10,000 in annual income represented half of the farms in the United States. Hobby, recreational or part-time farmers – whatever you preferred to call them – were a significant force in the marketplace, spending more than $5.5 billion annually on farm supplies and representing the only farm income segment that is growing. New magazines designed to help these urban immigrants enjoy their newly discovered lifestyle emerged with titles like *Hobby Farmer*. No longer did Tractor Supply – as the company stated in its 1999 annual report – see a "For Sale" sign in front of a 1,500-acre spread as a lost customer. It viewed it, instead, as an opportunity to gain ten new customers, each with 150 acres to fence; each with a large lawn to mow; each with livestock, horses, dogs, and cats to feed; each with a need for the kinds of products Tractor Supply Company sells and the advice it dispenses free of charge.

Tractor Supply, with its renewed emphasis on mission, legendary service, seasoned advice, and quality products, stood uniquely poised to help customers not only select the right tools, but also provide the guidance on how to use them properly. They were moving beyond simple purveyors of product to becoming trusted advisors and the enablers of a lifestyle. They were cultivating new relationships with the people, becoming a lifestyle brand for the growing number of Americans who were embracing a life tied to a piece of land.

There's the letter carrier who moved out of the city to enroll his children in 4-H and raise chickens, rabbits, hogs, and quail on less than three acres. There's the man who just had to raise rabbits and was forced to flee the city to pursue his passion of raising hares and their heirs. There are family after family drawn to the country because of a child's love of horses. They could be a homeowner who only has a third of an acre in small-town America. It could be somebody who has five to 10,000 acres in production for corn or soybeans in Iowa. It could be a 500-acre cattle ranch in

Texas. Or it could be somebody in Tennessee or Kentucky with ten acres and a couple of horses in the backyard. In every case, these people have an emotional connection to the land. They also have a self-reliant and independent spirit. And there's no consumer more loyal than a self-reliant one once he learns he can rely on you through thick and thin, once you've developed a relationship and earned his trust.

Tractor Supply spent the better part of a decade putting its house in order – solidifying its mission, developing and empowering its team, cultivating its customer relationships by providing fair prices on the kinds of things people in the rural lifestyle need and count on day after day. Good people with passion and a vision, growing distribution, great vendor relationships – Tractor Supply was poised for something big.

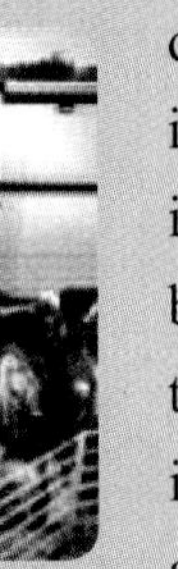

Tractor Supply and Carmichael Lynch partnered for television advertising that focused on storefronts and manager spokespersons rather than celebrities. Oh, yeah, and there's a few animals, too.

ONE OF AMERICA'S BEST-KEPT SECRETS GETS OUT

As Tractor Supply's customer and understanding of the customer have evolved, so have the advertising medium and message used to engage its customers.

All this solid research made Tractor Supply's marketing department a little too muscle-bound to be running the company's standard fare of print and radio, circulars, and annual Blue Book. They knew what could be done and what needed doing.

"Every time the company made a new hire, they're sent out to the field to work in a store for a week," explained Blake Fohl. "And most everybody who does will eventually go by the marketing department when they get back from their week and say, 'Blake, I worked in the store and the store where I worked has been in this town for ten years. Still, I bet ten times during the week, I was there when somebody came in and said, "I didn't know you guys were here. I didn't know what you had."'"

Tractor Supply was one of America's best-kept retail secrets. While it enjoyed amazing loyalty and trust, especially considering some of its lapses during the 1970s, it did not enjoy equally strong awareness. It was time the big secret got out.

"There was a great need for broader awareness of Tractor Supply," said Joe. "There were plenty of good customers out there not knowing that what they were looking for was right here waiting for them, just down the street in their hometown."

TRACTOR SUPPLY 'BRASES' ITSELF FOR THE BIG ASK

In order to get the Tractor Supply story out there to the growing number of people who lived and loved the rural lifestyle, Fohl built a total advertising program and initiated the marketing research and started looking for the people to build a marketing team. He developed the plan, but . . ."the funds just weren't available to actually do it," said Fohl.

Fohl had put everything together and was waiting, he thought, for the money. It turned out what he was actually waiting for was Jerry Brase.

A graduate of George Mason University, Brase moved to Tractor Supply after working for the Hechinger Company, a home improvement center chain based out of Landover, Maryland, and Builders Square in San Antonio, a warehouse home improvement retail concept and division of Kmart, where he was a divisional vice president in the merchandising department for four years. He came to Tractor Supply in 1997 as senior vice president of merchandising. Brase, along with Stan Ruta, formed the beginning of Joe's new

Tractor Supply Goes Hollywood When the props from the 1995 movie *The Bridges of Madison County* were being sold after it was filmed, Charlie Brendeland, vice president of sales and marketing for DeeZee, heard about the auction from the *Des Moines Register* and went. He traveled to Winterset, Iowa, where the movie was shot, and found a 1964 TSC catalog among the props. And what self-respecting Iowa farmer wouldn't have proudly displayed a TSC catalog at home in 1965, the year the movie took place?

management team. Beyond a considerable amount of merchandising expertise, Brase also brought to Tractor Supply a valuable knowledge of how to tap into the funds available for advertising.

Brase's approach to acquiring marketing dollars from the company's more than 1,200 vendors wasn't to simply ask for more advertising co-op dollars. Instead, he asked them to help fund a marketing program.

"In January 1998, we did our first-ever vendor conference here at Tractor Supply," said Brase. "We'd basically never talked to the supplier community with one voice. So Joe and Blake and I all got up there, and we talked about our vision for the business, where we are going, and what the challenges are.

"And then we told the vendors, we looked them in the eye and said, 'Guys, look, we're going to ask you for money. We're going to ask you for marketing support.'"

Behind the scenes at Tractor Supply, Brase's "Big Ask" was a little controversial, because the company was unfamiliar with the concept. Reaction ranged from Joe's mild questioning – "OK, Jerry, I'm going to have to trust you on this one because I just don't know where you're going with it" – to the buyer's abject horror at the idea.

At the very least, a good number of people were worried. But Brase wasn't one of them.

"Our vendors have the marketing dollars to support the business," explained Brase. "You just have to know how to go about getting to them. Our goal, certainly, is to make sure that our suppliers benefit from our growth over the next few years, so this is just a way for them to invest in our future together."

With Brase's guidance, Tractor Supply has forged what the company calls a true vendor partnership.

"'Vendor partnership' is an overused phrase," said Brase. "Everybody says it but at Tractor Supply we mean what we say."

SENIOR VICE PRESIDENT JERRY BRASE IS PART OF THE NEW GENERATION TRACTOR TEAM.

Tractor Supply's True Vendor Partnership seeks to make vendors more than suppliers of product – to make them partners in the Tractor Supply business by sharing in merchandising, managing inventory, cutting cost out of the supply chain, and testing new products in the stores. But it all begins with a relationship. Tractor Supply's vendor relationships begin at the very highest level of both organizations. With all of its top fifty suppliers, Tractor Supply's executive team maintains an ongoing top-to-top relationship.

Every year at the company's vendor partnership conference, Tractor Supply conducts a president/CEO luncheon.

"This past October, we had 105 presidents and CEOs attend our luncheon," said Brase, "making it one of the most distinguished gatherings of senior executives in the retail industry."

In addition, Tractor Supply provides its vendors with all the necessary sales data and inventory information so they can help improve the store's efficient replenishment. As part of this special relationship with its vendors, Tractor Supply also invites them to test new products and draw from the information gathered by the company.

JOHN LYONS ROUND PEN

15 panels with gate and drop pen kit combine to make a 60" diameter pen. Strength and Durability: Panels have 2" center support braces. The only panel made of strong, rust resistant aluminized steel. Drop pins are stronger than regular clamps. Efficiencies: Lightweight, easy to handle and move, easy to assemble and disassemble.

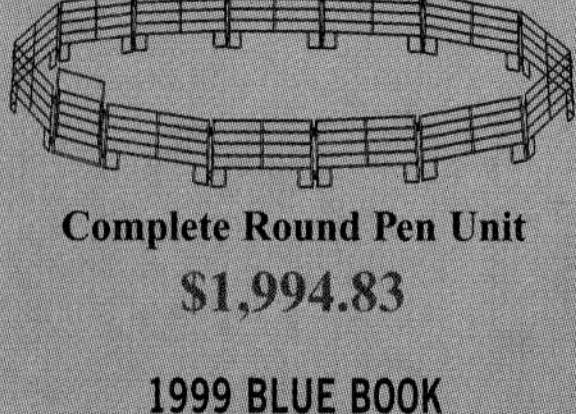

Complete Round Pen Unit
$1,994.83

1999 BLUE BOOK

"It all works to make Tractor Supply a more exciting place for our customer to shop," said Brase. "Often times they're seeing products at Tractor Supply first, before seeing them at a Wal-Mart, Home Depot, or Lowe's."

Recently Tractor Supply has experimented with extending its vendor relationships, testing a category management process in which select suppliers become category captains – an extension of the buyer – and work to maximize the return of an entire department.

"What I think excites our vendors most about this recent move is that they see Tractor Supply is not sitting still," explained Brase. "Tractor Supply is moving. We're not going to let any grass grow under our feet. We're growing as a company and inviting our vendors to join in, take part, and benefit in that growth."

Brase not only has a great mind for the business, he also has a great heart for it. That's because he is the customer.

"Let me tell you about Jerry Brase's lifestyle," said Joe with pride. "He lives about thirty miles south of Nashville. He has a lovely wife and two daughters who are all horse enthusiasts.

"And so he has a small barn, nine horses, a small tractor, a pickup truck, four dogs, . . . and he's not sure how many cats."

Brase's lifestyle mirrors that of the company's emerging equine customer so precisely that he's not only a regular subject in Joe's presentation to investors, but his daughter Ashley and her horse Dillon and cat Fiona were featured on the cover of the company's 1998 annual report.

THE TEACHER FROM COMFORT, TEXAS

Brase isn't the only key member of Joe's executive management team to embrace the rural lifestyle. Cal Massmann, Tractor Supply's senior vice president and chief financial officer, grew up in Northwestern Ohio in a small town of less than 2,000. He grew up baling hay, driving tractor, tending to animals.

"We talk about part-time farmers and hobby farmers. I talk about my cousins Kenny and Brian. My Cousin Kenny's father was a part-time farmer. He inherited enough land to live on the land but not enough land to make a living. Besides the farm, he works at a company that manufactures parts for the automotive industry. One of those small plants you see in the middle of an Ohio cornfield. My cousin Brian works for Dunn and Bradstreet and lives in Northern Indiana. His children

TSC TRACTOR SUPPLY Co

Where America's Farmers Shop

Record Financial Performance

Aggressive Growth Plans

Customer-Driven Merchandise Initiatives

Spreading the Word-New Marketing Initiatives

JERRY BRASE'S DAUGHTER ASHLEY AND HER HORSE DILLON GRACE THE COVER OF THE TRACTOR SUPPLY ANNUAL REPORT. OH, AND CAN YOU SPY HER CAT FIONA?

1998 Annual Report

raise sheep and went through 4-H and have decided to live the rural lifestyle."

This is not the kind of conversation you'd expect to have with the CFO of a billion dollar corporation. But, then, Cal Massmann is anything but your run-of-the-mill CFO. His name sounds more like that a ranch hand's casual moniker and his demeanor is more Main Street than Wall Street. His matter-of-fact way of making a point is casual and conversational and not the confrontational style favored by many who are bottom line focused. He prefers a short-sleeved cotton shirt to three-piece suit. He doesn't dress like a CFO. He dresses more like the grocer he grew up wanting to be or, maybe, a school teacher.

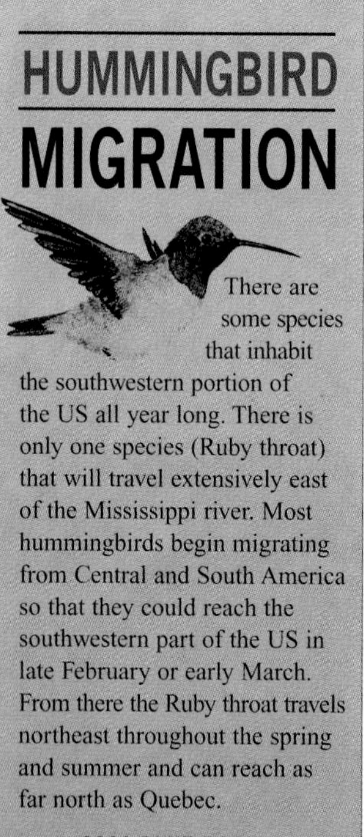

"Yes, I taught high school," said Massmann with a heartfelt laugh. "I thought teaching would be an opportunity to give back. I taught in a high school of around 300, a small town school in Comfort, Texas."

But Massmann wasn't your typical high school teacher. This most unusual teacher came to the classroom after a stint at the prestigious firm of Price Waterhouse where he worked in mergers and acquisitions for *Fortune* 500 companies; fifteen years in a variety of key financial management positions at W. R. Grace; and eighteen months at Builders Square as a senior vice president and the company's CFO.

He was a CPA and MBA with twenty years of experience, working with some major companies. Not your typical high school teacher's resume. In fact, this high school teacher was getting head hunter calls from the likes of Tractor Supply.

The call came while he was working his way through an alternative certification process to teach. And so, to the inquiries about possibly returning to the corporate world, Massmann said simply, "No, I'm onto something else."

Timing is everything. When the search consultant called again, Massmann had just been thwarted in an attempt to make a meaningful contribution to his students.

"There was a math teacher right across the hall from me who was also retired," remembered Massmann. "He had an engineering background and had his own construction company. The two of us saw that many of the Hispanic students at the school were never going to go to college and would probably choose to get into their family businesses. They didn't need the mainstream math course. What they needed was something more practical.

"We suggested this new course to the high school principal who thought it was 'a great idea.' He took it up with the superintendent and he said, 'That's great but those two guys can't legally do it because you don't have a vocational certificate.'

"I thought I'd left that kind of bureaucracy behind with the corporate world," said Massmann. "I knew I wasn't going to be able to tolerate this. There shouldn't be road blocks to getting things done. I knew I didn't live well in that kind of environment."

So in 2000, Massmann joined Tractor Supply as its senior vice president and chief financial officer, replacing Tom Flood. He brought to Tractor Supply firsthand knowledge of what it takes to be a *Fortune* 500 company and how to manage growth from a financial perspective. He also brought with him a rare ability to work with others and challenge the leadership.

"The CFO's role sometimes requires that you challenge the CEO," explained Massmann. "There needs to be mutual respect between the CFO and CEO so you can voice your differing objectives and ideas. There's definitely an environment of mutual respect at Tractor Supply that lets ideas be voiced and heard.

"I love the culture here. Joe communicated to me the values and the mission that Tom Hennesy and he had put in place. I was very interested in that, and a little bit of investigation showed me that this was the real deal.

"There are a lot of places with mission and value statements," he continued, "but very few that make those statements in the way they do business. Nobody says 'I'm a crook and I treat my employees terribly and I don't give a darn about my customer.' Nobody's going to say that.

"It was apparent to me that Tractor Supply stood for something," said Massmann. "That's why I'm here and not teaching school."

THE STRAIT TALK ON TRACTOR SUPPLY

Tractor Supply has a history of hiring its customers. Today more than half of the company's team members are farmers, horse owners, and welders. It was also true of the first national television spokesperson the company hired – George Strait.

"We knew through our research that 80 percent of our customers were die-hard country fans," recounted Fohl. "We wanted our spokesperson to be as attractive to and create as much an affinity with men as with women. We wanted that person to have a longevity that reflected our longevity as a company, and we wanted our spokesperson to live the lifestyle. He needed to have a family because our customers indexed higher than the national average for being family people."

Everything pointed to George Strait.

"He was perfect," said Fohl. "He was already a customer of our store. His family shops in our stores in Texas."

The Strait campaign ran for five years and featured the Texas singer around the campfire and on a lawn tractor. Strait reached out to women, a growing and important decision-making segment of the Tractor Supply customer base, assuring them, "There's a lot in those Tractor Supply stores for you, too. So just kick those guys aside and walk right in."

BEFORE GEORGE STRAIT WAS A TRACTOR SUPPLY SPOKSPERSON, HE WAS A CUSTOMER.

FORMER TEACHER CAL MASSMANN GOES TO SCHOOL ON THE NUMBERS AS TRACTOR SUPPLY'S CFO.

IN THE AGE OF MOBILE PHONES AND E-MAIL, CUSTOMERS STILL TAKE THE TIME TO WRITE A FRIEND.

LET'S GIVE THEM SOMETHING TO TALK ABOUT

Hennesy and his team planted the seeds of the company's culture in the '80s while Joe and his team accelerated the growth of the Tractor Supply's customer-oriented, service-based, fun-loving culture of the '90s. Learning customer's names and greeting them as soon as they came into the store. Taking them to the merchandise they were looking for, rather than simply pointing across the store. Turning any complaint into an opportunity to demonstrate the lengths to which Tractor Supply will go to satisfy its customers and personify the "legendary" in legendary service.

"We don't want to hear about a complaint in Nashville," said Joe. "If we hear about a complaint in Nashville, it means the store lost an opportunity.

"There's a statistic in the hotel business that says that if a guest complains because something isn't right and you fix it quickly, you get higher satisfaction ratings than if everything was fine to begin with. A person with a complaint tells ten friends while a person with a good experience only tells one."

Well, one by one, the good news has been pouring into Nashville and it's these stories, shared by customers, that give voice and substance to Tractor Supply's aim of "Legendary Service."

The folks at Tractor Supply love to share stories. The company's oral tradition is a natural given the fact that folks who live on the land welcome stories. And at Tractor Supply, sharing stories has become an important part of the company's culture – through e-mail, voice mail, speeches, annual reports, the company's intranet and Internet sites, the pages of the internal newsletter, *The Voice*, or simply swapped as coffee and hallway conversation. Sharing stories at Tractor Supply has become a multi-media art form. But the most powerful and meaningful voice is still that of the boss – and at Tractor Supply the boss is still the customer. Customer letters, reminiscent of the Charles Schmidt days, continue to pour into Tractor Supply.

"I farm and raise hogs near South Sioux City, Nebraska," wrote one such customer. "I have done business at your TSC store in Sioux City for 22 years. On June 11, I was in Sioux City coming home and as I was driving down Hamilton Blvd, my top radiator hose broke. Being a few blocks from TSC, I drove in to check it out. The broken hose was a disaster, but the people at TSC were a blessing.

"Lisa Dryer, a TSC employee, told me where I could get water and turned it on for me. Larry Knipplemeyer, store manager, drove me to a parts store so I could get a new hose. He not only did that, but also loaned me his tools so I could replace the hose.

"Mr. Scarlett, the story does not stop with this one occasion. Last month Jeannie Fisher, another TSC employee, was waiting on me at the checkout. I accidentally dropped a $20 bill on the floor when I pulled out my billfold. She called me up the same day and told me about it.

"I think you have a great bunch of people at the TSC Store in South Sioux City, Iowa. They are very friendly and very helpful. I wish more stores showed this high level of courtesy toward their customers."

The team's caring inspired the customer to mention everyone by name and write a letter of compliment in an age more given to complaint. The customer even recognized "the story does not stop with this one occasion."

NO ENVELOPE OR STAMP REQUIRED • MOISTEN HERE, FOLD, SEAL AND M…

At Tractor Supply Company, we are committed to giving you the best customer service and merchandise. What you have to say makes us better. We welcome all your comments and suggestions.

Stan Ruta *Stan Ruta*
Sr. Vice President Store Operations

Merchandise

	Yes	No		
In-stock on desired item(s)	●	○		
	Excellent	**Good**	**Fair**	**Poor**
Quality of merchandise	●	○	○	○

Team Members

	Yes	No
Were Team Members available to help?	●	○
Were the Team Members knowledgeable?	●	○

Checkout

	Yes	No
Was the checkout process fast enough?	●	○
Was the Cashier friendly?	*Very* ●	○

Shopping Experience

	Excellent	Good	Fair	Poor
How would you rate the overall shopping experience?	●	○	○	○

Customer Type

○ Full-Time Farmer or Rancher
○ Part-Time Farmer or Rancher
● Homeowner
○ Hobby Farmer or Rancher
○ Commercial Customer
○ Other

Additional Comments *My husband, son + I thought we would check out this "new" Store that opened up in Duncan, Okla. My husband's favorite Store to shop + browse was Orschelns. Drove me crazy! Now, it is Tractor Supply! I'm Okay with this because your Store was so clean, smelled good + had lots of Stuff I could use around the house. Thanks for opening up a store in the town where we shop the most. We live about 40 miles away but we shop at least once a week.*

OPTIONAL INFORMATION

Nam… *…Rd*

…3481

Store Location *Duncan, OK*

Time of Day *5-6 pm*

Date of Visit *6-18-04*

…NUMBER IS (615)366-4600

829/731

GREETINGS FROM Far Far Away

NO POSTAGE NECESSARY IF MAILED IN THE UNITED STATES

OKLAHOMA CITY OK 73 PM 19 JUN 2?04

MAIL

…SHVILLE, TN

"We have fantastic teams in our stores and there seems to be no end to the customer stories and no end to my thrill in sharing them," said Joe.

From something as simple as loading feed to taking their own time after hours to deliver a purchase too big for a customer's truck, staying open 24/7 or making sure generators and lights are available during an emergency. Tractor Supply stories are limited only by the imagination and ability of thousands of employees to come up with new ways to breathe new life into the company's culture and new meaning to the sign that hangs in every store announcing to everyone, team members and customers – "Satisfaction Guaranteed."

WHATEVER IT TAKES

"Don't pay attention to the 'Satisfaction Guaranteed' part – everyone says that," said Joe, referring to a sign that hangs prominently for all to see – customer and store team members – in every Tractor Supply Store across the country.

"It's what that sign goes on to say that gives the 'Satisfaction Guaranteed' real meaning."

What the sign goes on to say is: "Every team member has the authority to do whatever it takes." And that means a lot. It means the employee feels the trust of executives that they'll do the right thing. It means customers have the confidence that Tractor Supply will stand behind everything it offers. It means everything from keeping traffic moving through the checkout lines to having a good attitude. "Whatever" is really a totally encompassing thing. Still, there are some customers who don't believe "whatever" means "whatever it takes."

"They seem to come around and discover we mean exactly what we say when they come in with a return on merchandise because it's the wrong color and size, maybe without a receipt, maybe even something they don't honestly really remember if they purchased from us and they're braced for some resistance and ready for argument and primed for a fight," said Joe with his knowing smile. "Only to find we're ready to take it back and make them happy.

"'Yes' may be the most powerful word in the English language. I love to watch how their face changes when we say simply say, 'Yes.'

"Sometimes we have to say it twice because they don't hear us the first time."

Pivotal to the company's mission of working hard, having fun, and making money are team members in the store. People are the driving force behind Tractor Supply and the people in the stores are the backbone of the company. Over the last twenty-plus years, Tom Hennesy and then Joe worked hard to flip the company's organizational chart. To put at the very top, in the chief role, the people closest to the customer – the team members in the stores.

The importance of the store team is highlighted in the company's culture in numerous ways, like the company's language. Tractor

Supply began calling them associates and that has since evolved into the designation of "team member." It's more than words; Tractor Supply puts its money where its mouth is. When the company was privately held by the Gang of Five, they offered an employee stock ownership plan to team members. Since 1981, Tractor Supply has had bonus plans in place for everyone in the company. At the store, if you make your store's sales plan, you get a check. It could amount to an extra day or two of pay every month.

GUARANTEED

HAS THE AUTHORITY TO

R IT TAKES"

"The more bonuses people make, the better the company is doing," said Joe. "We love that. The more money we pay out in bonuses, the better everyone is doing. It's just that simple."

Words, money, professional development. The most important thing the people in the Tractor Supply Store Support Center give their team members is…their ear.

"Those closest to the work are the people who know the most about it," explained Joe. "Therefore, we're in the field a lot. We can't manage from the Store Support Center. I'll visit 150 every year.

"We strive to be the world's best listeners," he continued. "We try to create an environment where everybody can speak up. We encourage our people to be entrepreneurs, from the management to team members in the store.

"The most important ears in our company are the store managers and their crews."

Doing whatever it takes at Tractor Supply also means hiring the kind of store people who know what it takes, which in many cases has meant hiring the company's customers.

"One of the greatest compliments we receive from our customers is they want to work here," said Joe with obvious pride. "Customers make the very best team members and every one of our stores has farmers, ranchers, welders, and horse owners on staff. In fact, more than half of our team members throughout the company are farmers, ranchers, welders, and horse owners."

Having the right people and the right, can-do attitude in the store has helped return to Tractor Supply a bit of the environment that was part of its initial success in the early years of the company: the company's family feel.

According to whom? The boss, of course – Tractor Supply's customers.

"It's just a hometown store," said Luther Lenning, a customer in Lebanon, Tennessee. "The customer is always first with the people here, and a lot of us are on a first-name basis.

"I know most of the folks who work here – they're hometown people."

Another customer, this time in the Lapeer, Michigan, store, provided a poignant insight. Said Tom Courneya, "I can buy the things I'm buying at TSC anywhere. But because of the relationship and camaraderie I have with the people there, it makes it a fun place to shop. I walk in the door and hear someone from the back of the store yelling 'Here comes trouble again.' That's just the way it is.

"They're more than helpful, and we have a good time."

Not only are the company's people fun, knowledgeable and helpful, but today's Tractor Supply Store has a fun, inviting feel that complements the attitude of the people. Through the work of Jerry Brase's merchandising team, Tractor Supply has created a store experience that's as much about building relationships and hospitality as it is about selling stuff. You notice it the minute you hit the gate.

That's right – the gate at the entrance immediately suggests you've entered a farm store if there were ever any doubt. And there's something about driving up to that gate that makes you smile.

Maybe you've come because you're putting in a fence and need some advice about pulling it tight. You've got a mower that needs a part. An animal that needs feed or medicine. Whatever it was, you said to yourself, "I'll just go to Tractor Supply." You said it because it feels good. Something about just going there.

Sure, sure, you know the price will be right. That seems like a given. But there's something more about the store. The people. Friendly. Like a small-town kind of friendly where they know your name.

And there's something about the place. The way you go through a corral gate opening up into the parking lot. You pull in and there's the Tractor Supply sign with its familiar logo with the heavy block almost western type. And there's the red, you know, the sort of tractor or barn red. And that shape. What is it? The shape of a plow? A tractor grill? A barn door emblazoned with TSC and swinging in? Whatever it is – It's

warm and familiar. Like the store. Like the people inside.

And then there's the stuff. Spilling out along the front of the stores – lawnmowers and log splitters, go-carts and stacks of doghouses, trailers and cattle pens. You linger and look. It makes you curious. It draws you in.

Even the entryway is packed – a watering trough, a windmill, and a stack of grass seed. And the smell, you may not consciously notice it, but the faint smell of seed and feed and fertilizer and hardware and oil – that wholesome, do-it-yourself smell – permeates the place, washes over you and makes you feel good and ready to do something, make something, fix something.

Then you hear your name from the cashier. You exchange a nod or maybe ask where something is. And even though the store is relatively small, as stores nowadays tend to go, someone actually takes you to the thing you're looking for rather than leaving you to wander.

It's a clean, well-lit place. Wide aisles. Simple, straightforward signs announcing the various departments all in neat rows, traveling down the aisles like rows of crops in a garden each with a little sign letting you know what's been planted there – tools, hardware, pet food, equine, apparel.

The Tractor Supply shopping experience has been carefully mapped out, step by step. From the width of the aisles to the personality and setting of the various departments. The aisles are wider now because Tractor Supply learned that its female shoppers – women account for nearly half of the company's sales each year – are more comfortable in aisles they can wander without bumping into other shoppers. Departments are

SHELBYVILLE, TENNESSEE, STORE IN 2004

more clearly defined. And then there are the hundreds of little touches, the things that make it unique, the things that make Tractor Supply just a little bit unusual and fun. But still they're things that make sense. The toy animals. Live chicks delivered to the store on one wonderful and wild day every year. Paint in colors that are so very familiar even though you won't necessarily find them anywhere else – John Deere green and International Harvester red. The nuts and bolts by the pound – meant to be reminiscent of the old downtown hardware store that was once a fixture of every small town in America.

STAN RUTA AT THE 2004 MANAGERS MEETING

GINA ROBERTS USES HER EQUINE EXPERTISE TO ASSIST A CUSTOMER.

A great deal of the store's success today has been driven by the teamwork of Jerry Brase and Stan Ruta, senior vice president of store operations. According to Scarlett and Wright, the teamwork of merchandising and store operations at Tractor Supply is unusual. Brase and Ruta have taken what often is an adversarial relationship in retailing and made it a synergistic benefit for Tractor Supply. Instead of playing the blame game when an item fails in the stores, they work together to ensure success, sharing time, ideas, even employees. Whatever it takes is exactly what it takes.

"We just had a buyer position open in the ag product side of the business, and we filled it with a district manager," Brase said. "One of the great things about this team is that Stan supports that. If I go to Stan and say, 'Stan, I've got an opening for a buyer and I need a talented individual. Who do you have for me?' As my partner in store operations, he'll post that position out in the field. There are organizations where operations would try to hand its problems to merchandising.

"Stan's mindset, which I absolutely respect, is if this person can impact one store or can go to merchandising and impact hundreds of stores, he or she is much better off in Nashville making the greatest impact on the business.

"My working relationship with Stan is one of the strongest I've ever enjoyed with a senior operator and may be one of the strongest I've ever seen in the business."

Like Brase, Ruta has a real connection with the customer, the products and the lifestyle enabled by Tractor Supply. Growing up in upstate New York, Ruta learned a deep love for agriculture working on his grandfather's farm.

"That's where I spent all my time in high school," remembered Ruta. "I missed some football games and some basketball games, but I learned a great deal about life, about working hard, about what it took to get a job done."

Ruta went on to agriculture school and after graduating from college, took a job with Central Tractor in 1976. There, he rose rather quickly through the ranks from assistant store manager to store manager, to district sales manager, to regional sales manager. Then he left the company in 1994.

"I grew up with Central Tractor and it gave me a wonderful education and tremendous opportunity," said Ruta. "But I saw things change there. A group of investment bankers from New York bought the company and suddenly everything was about the short term. I was committed to the farm store business and to the long term. Their approach was all about making dollars instead of building a business.

"So, obviously, there was a gap between my vision of what a farm store chain should be and their vision."

Stan interviewed with Tractor Supply and was taken with Joe's passion for the business and his commitment to the company's mission and values.

"That was what I grew up with," said Ruta. "It held a strong attraction for me.

"Joe is a very inspirational leader. You know, a lot of CEOs of billion-dollar companies fly in private airplanes, go into a store in a suit and tie, and give the store a white glove finger test and intimidate people who work in the store. Not Joe. I mean, Joe comes in a Ford rental car, and he wants to speak with every team member who's in the store. He asks them their background, he talks to them, he takes notes, and he remembers people.

"And it's all genuine."

Drawn by the company's mission and values, Ruta joined Tractor Supply in January 1994 as a regional manager. In July 2000, he was promoted to senior vice president in charge of all store operations. The job wasn't handed to Ruta. It was earned.

"We had four people inside the company who expressed an interest when the job came open," remarked Joe Scarlett. "I asked them each to put together a plan on what they'd do short-term and long-term. I then spent half a day with each of the four, walking the store and discussing their plans and understanding their thinking and their approach.

"It was clear that Stan was the man. He was focused on the right things."

Since 2000, Ruta and Brase have been focused on greater standardization and consistency of excellence, incorporating plan-o-gramming and creating the unique Tractor Supply shopping experience, making the store the single touch point for the culture – the place where customer, unique products, and seasoned advice all come together.

EVERYTHING FALLS INTO PLACE

How far Tractor Supply has come since the decade of the '70s and its meandering direction, lack of vision, and its very near demise. It was a hard row to hoe. Its success and growth since seem fantastic by comparison. As a matter of fact, from the vantage point of the last twenty-plus years of success and growth, it's hard to imagine things were ever as bad as they were back then.

But there was a time when Tractor Supply sold jewelry, hair dryers, and blenders. Until everything just fell back into place. Or, maybe, was put into place is a better way to describe what happened.

First Fuqua Industries buys the company in 1978 and then puts Tom Hennesy in charge in 1981, and eventually sells the company to Hennesy and the Gang of Five. Within three years the company returns to profitability. Then follows a decade of slow growth, a reduction in the company's debt and strengthening of its financial position. Then Hennesy hands the reins to Joe and Joe and the leadership team take the company public in 1994. Going public makes additional capital available that is plowed back into store growth. Although fraught with difficulty, the SAP technology upgrade creates an infrastructure that is extremely scalable should the company take off. Should the company take off? In preparation for future growth, Tractor Supply closed its Indianapolis distribution center in 2000 – a facility that had been on line for more than thirty years – and opened a new 500,000-square-foot distribution center forty miles away in Pendleton, Indiana.

The right people and management team; the right mission, values, and vision; the right store support in terms of distribution and technological infrastructure – Tractor Supply was poised for growth. So when the right opportunity came along, Tractor Supply was prepared to take full advantage of it. One thing building on another.

It's said you make your own luck. While no one can determine where lightning strikes, carrying a lightning rod certainly ups the odds you'll be standing in the right place when it does.

In 2000, the first in a series of dominoes began to fall for Tractor Supply Company with a break in Florida that would ultimately result in a "once in a lifetime opportunity," according to Joe.

HUSKEE®
LOG SPLITTERS

All Huskee Log Splitters feature wedge and channel beam design. Removable ground stand and cutting wedge. Stripper plates to prevent jamming of wood on wedge. Replaceable filter. Unique channel beam for added strength. Cradle beam design to hold log in place. 26" log capacity. Auto-return valve. Available in most stores or can be special ordered.

21-53508..............$1,399.99

2000 BLUE BOOK

ONE SMALL STEP FOR TRACTOR SUPPLY

Over the years, Tractor Supply had been cultivating a relationship with Wal-Mart. Wal-Mart and Southwest Airlines are the two companies that Joe most admires. Their cultures and business approaches struck a chord with him early on.

"We're real students of Wal-Mart," Joe said. "I first became familiar with Wal-Mart in 1980 when they acquired Kuhn's Big K Stores. They had five-and-dime stores and discount stores and Wal-Mart was interested in the discount stores.

"Big K was here in Nashville. That's when I first really began paying attention to what they were doing. I went to a seminar at Santa Clara University – Jack Shewmaker, their vice chairman, was presenting – and it was just fascinating. I became immersed in what they do.

"Despite being the biggest corporation in the world and the world's largest employer, the people at Wal-Mart are very humble and down to earth.

"They know who they are," Joe said. "In spite of the numbers, they're very hospitable. They're now the largest grocer in the world with a significant retail price advantage over their competitors."

Tractor Supply's admiration of Wal-Mart has led to an association. Beginning in 1993, Tractor Supply began leasing space from Wal-Mart when the discounting giant would vacate one of its standard-sized stores to build a Super Center.

"They were great locations in towns and in the parts of towns where we wanted to be," said Joe Scarlett. "It was one of those wonderful win-win situations for Wal-Mart and Tractor Supply.

"Over the years we developed a pretty good relationship with their real estate department."

WAL★MART®

So good that in 2000, Tractor Supply snatched up ten Wal-Mart locations all at once in central Florida. Tractor Supply knew the buildings were available in the wake of a revamp of Florida that the discount retailing giant had undergone earlier.

It was a pivotal move, taking place at a time when Tractor Supply's major competitor, Quality Stores, was looking to expand with a major presence in Florida. Tractor Supply was poised with the financial resources, the people, training, distribution, store support systems, and, most important, the vision and the passion to succeed.

It performed a classic blocking move, opting to open ten new stores simultaneously. At the time, it was an ambitious and unprecedented move for Tractor Supply. The farm store chain had never opened that many stores simultaneously. Several important lessons were learned that would serve it later.

Rather than expanding the territory of an existing district manager, the Florida project was given its own district manager: Larry Means. This served to keep the rest of the company's focus on the performance of its existing locations rather than being distracted by the Florida project. The company recruited the ten managers to open the Florida stores from throughout the company. And, finally, Tractor Supply also developed a new, larger prototype with new assortments of merchandise specifically geared to the Florida market.

"In many respects the Florida store would become the forerunner of what we're doing throughout the company today," said Gary Magoni, regional operations vice president. "We changed the mix of merchandise in the store and how each of the individual departments was set.

"For example, we put in the largest ever horse and tack department and expanded the feed department. We carved out a special place in the store for seasonal products, like lawn and garden. The clothing department was made larger because the store itself was expanded to a bigger floor plan than we'd ever done before," explained Magoni.

"We'd always been careful to stay within a 12,000- and 15,000-square-foot floor plan. All of the sudden in Florida, we're doing 18,000- and 20,000-square-feet – that was space age for us." And like many of the products pioneered in outer space that find their way into everyday life, the planning, merchandising, training, and opening strategies pioneered by Tractor Supply in Florida would find their way into everyday applications throughout the company.

"We didn't know it at the time," said Magoni, "but Florida was a stepping stone. It was the most aggressive, most concentrated expansion we had ever undertaken at the time.

"It prepared us for something even much larger."

A special marketing plan was developed for the Florida store openings using the synergy of the concentrated geographical expansion. Tractor Supply experimented and supported the mass ten-store grand opening with billboards along Florida State Route 27 as well as grand opening TV spots, something it had never done before.

BEFORE 2002, QUALITY FARM & FLEET WAS TRACTOR SUPPLY'S LARGEST COMPETITOR.

WHEN IT COMES TO OCCUPYING SPACE ONCE HOME TO AMERICA'S NO. 1 RETAILER, TRACTOR SUPPLY IS WAL-MART'S BEST CUSTOMER.

Tractor Supply's Florida stores were an immediate success and have continued to thrive. By 2003, Tractor Supply had more than thirty stores in the Sunshine State.

"In fact, I think the whole darn peninsula is going to sink under the weight of Tractor Supply," said Magoni with a smile. "We certainly got ahead of Quality and that surprised them.

"We heard rumors that their management at the time was simply incensed by the fact that we were in there and did such a complete job so quickly."

Quality was beaten to the punch in Florida by Tractor Supply's ability to move decisively.

Let's Get Kicking Every hardworking, fun-loving team has a mascot. Tractor Supply is no exception. Its team mascot is a super hero, muscle-flexing, trash-talking red mule. During a funk the company was going through in 1997, an assistant buyer pulled out a drawing of a self-assured mule and started passing it around. It became known as the "Mule with an Attitude." Or as Blake Fohl likes to say, "It's a symbol of kicking ass and taking names." Tractor Supply was stubbornly determined then and now to do whatever it takes to get the job done.

MAKING ALL THE WRIGHT MOVES

"It can't be done."

"It goes against conventional wisdom."

"They're biting off more than they can chew. Just wait and see."

Those were the ominous whispers that circulated about Tractor Supply's purchase of many of the assets of its largest competitor – Quality Stores, Inc. – in January 2002. They were whispers heard around the retail world and maybe even in the backs of the minds of Tractor Supply team members when they first heard the news.

At the time, Quality Stores was larger than Tractor Supply, with more than 300 stores in thirty states and sales in excess of a billion dollars. Having the financial and management resources to successfully merchandise and manage a purchase of this magnitude seemed a pretty tall order. Especially for a company whose greatest accomplishment to this point in its modern history was to open ten stores in Florida.

But what Tractor Supply lacked in size, it more than made up for in fiscal strength – a fact that would ultimately prove disastrous for its competitor. Tractor Supply came to the bargaining table incredibly prepared to purchase Quality.

The seeds of Tractor Supply's acquisition of Quality Stores were sown with Joe's original vision to double the size of the company by 1996. With this, the company and its people realized the power of vision and set its sights higher. The theme of its 1998 managers meeting in Nashville was "Building to a Billion." It would take tremendous growth for the company to reach the billion-dollar benchmark. And so the vision was set and the work began.

Another key component to the Quality acquisition, interestingly enough, was Joe's realization in 1999 that he couldn't perform the duties of both president and chief executive officer, that it was just too big a job. Joe began the search that would ultimately give the company the talent it needed to successfully acquire its largest competitor. It's no accident that having the right people in place played a pivotal role in the Quality story.

In June 2000, Jim Wright was looking for a job. He was, as he described it, "successfully unemployed."

Wright had just completed the successful turnaround and sale of Tire Kingdom as the company's president and CEO. At the time Wright came to Tire Kingdom in 1997, it was a 150-store chain of tire stores facing significant financial and operational issues. Wright worked fast and within three years, the company was sold, and Wright was again looking for the right opportunity.

Wright had enjoyed a successful retail career and could now afford to wait for the right opportunity to come along. Growing up in Oshkosh, Wisconsin, Wright's first foray into retailing came at an early age when he worked in a gas station as a teenager.

He had a passion for automobiles. He restored several cars when he was in his twenties. He also had a passion for retailing.

"I doubt that anyone at age twelve, when asked by a parent or grandparent 'What do you want to be when you grow up?' would say, 'I want to be a retailer,'" said Wright with his straightforward, decided manner of speaking. He speaks with a comfortable air of experience.

"Somehow we start in retailing and it becomes so compelling because in retailing, at any level, the feedback to your decisions comes very, very quickly. In the store, the feedback is instantaneous. You make a decision to satisfy a customer and their faces light up and they pat you on the back and shake your hand and say 'thank you.' That's immediate feedback.

"I believe there's a certain level of people who are wired to be feedback junkies, and they find their way into retail," explained Wright. "I enjoy the pace of retailing, the change, the constant challenge, the people, both the customers and the team members. They're just invigorating."

Wright followed his heart for both automobiles and retailing and started working for Kmart in the automotive department while he was in college. He quickly became a full-time assistant manager and then served as auto center manager in several different Wisconsin cities.

Wright eventually found his way to the company's headquarters in Troy, Michigan, in 1982, after successful stints as district manager of both automotive and sporting goods. In Troy, he was given responsibility for the national operations of the discount giant's auto service centers. He moved from there into several positions as a buyer for the company. Wright was interested in being part of a winning team. By the mid-1980s, he realized that Kmart was "unlikely to be a long-term winner." And so he began seeking new challenges.

JIM WRIGHT IN HIS WESTERN AUTO DAYS.

In 1988, Wright joined Western Auto Supply Company as vice president of store operations. He continued to round out his retail experience serving in four different capacities during his eight-year tenure at Western Auto. Wright moved from store operations to vice president of merchandising, then executive vice president of wholesale and franchise stores and finally to EVP of U.S. and Caribbean stores, with about half of the company reporting to him and responsibility for about $1.2 billion in sales.

But then, Western Auto took a left turn, strategically speaking. Wright left and took on the new challenge of leading a turnaround at Tire Kingdom.

"What impressed me most were the people," said Wright. "After just spending three years of my life in Florida trying to hire great, highly motivated, drug-free, ethical, honest, and passionate retailers, I was struck by the fact that Tractor Supply – which had only been in the market four months – had managed in that time to find some really tremendous people.

"I asked Joe to explain how he was so fortunate. His response was, 'Our employees, our team members, are a lot like our customers and this is just who we are. Our customers tend to value the family, they value the land, they value the things they do, and they value their time. A square deal is a square deal. And as a company, we have historically continued to hire our customers.'

"I was very impressed," said Wright with a big smile, "and even more convinced that this was where I wanted to come."

Wright joined Tractor Supply in October 2000. He was the final piece to the management team Joe had worked so painstakingly to assemble, the team of Joe Scarlett, Jerry Brase, Stan Ruta, Cal Massmann, and, now, Jim Wright.

Joe had his team. Now all they needed was a challenge worthy of their talent. The challenge was not long in coming.

COMING HOME TO A COMPANY WITH HEART

Jim Wright's reasons for coming to Tractor Supply are revealing and at the heart of what ultimately gave the company the advantage in its dealings with Quality Stores.

First of all, Wright liked the niche and Tractor Supply's place within that niche.

"I felt like the customers were underserved and there was plenty of space in the market," said Wright. "The two largest players were Tractor Supply, at the time, with about three quarters of a billion dollars in sales, and Quality Stores in Muskegon, Michigan, at $1.1 billion.

"Now Quality was a private company, but they had some public debt. Their debt structure wasn't very good. In fact, it appeared they had some loan covenants coming up that it might be difficult for them to meet," Wright continued.

"So our position within the industry was intriguing."

After assessing the opportunity, Wright examined the resources in place at Tractor Supply to take advantage of the opportunity.

"We had a great balance sheet," said Wright. "You want to join a company that has an infrastructure that can be leveraged. We had that, too. And, we had opportunity in almost every area.

"We had the opportunity to improve the speed of marketing and merchandising. We had the opportunity to take time and costs out of distribution. We turned our inventory 2.1 times a year. We had the opportunity then, and still do, to get that well north of three turns a year."

And then, Wright identified the element that combined with a great balance sheet, space in the industry, a solid infrastructure and immediate opportunity to perform even better — made for an unbeatable combination in his estimation.

"The company had a heart," 'he stated simply.

"It had vision and it had a great, great cheerleader in Joe Scarlett. Just the passion of the founding entrepreneur was impressive. Joe was building this fabulous culture and an outstanding team over the past twenty years.

"The Tractor Supply culture is something that I have always aspired to. I've experienced it for brief moments in other companies, maybe for a year or two. But Tractor Supply has a great sustainable culture that has been that way for a long time. It was a very easy culture to fit into.

"It was like coming home."

There it is again, that family feel – one of the elements identified as key to the culture of Tractor Supply in its infancy in the late '30s and early '40s had returned to the company in its Scarlett Period.

Surrounded by Tractor Supply's pervasive and passionate culture, Joe and Jim seemed perfectly aligned. Their skill sets were complementary.

"Jim has exceeded my expectations in virtually every area," said Joe. "Although our work experiences differ, we share the same values and vision. So now Tractor Supply has two points of view shaping the company with a common mission guiding us.

"The greatest personal compliment our leadership has received took place in 2003 at one of our management training sessions," said Joe. "We always have a reception on the last night. There were a group of people who had worked for Home Depot, Lowe's, and Wal-Mart. They came up to me during the reception and said, 'Joe, we've listened to you and your whole leadership team. And you're all saying the same thing.'

"That's a real testament to how unified we are as a leadership team. It's all about the senior leadership being aligned in thoughts and actions. Today, we absolutely have the best leadership team since I've been with the company."

Given the history of the company, that's quite a statement.

By the close of 2000, everything was in place at Tractor Supply and there seemed to be an air about the place that there wasn't anything that this team couldn't accomplish.

This feeling was about to be put to the test.

QUALITY TIME

Big things don't always start out that way. They grow.

That's how it happened with Tractor Supply's acquisition of Quality Stores. It began almost imperceptibly. A phone call here. A phone call there. A bit of news. Throughout 2001, there were whispers that Quality had some outstanding loans that were coming due in the fall and would be difficult for the privately held company to meet.

ONCE A PROUD COMPETITOR, FARM & COUNTRY IS NOW A PROUD PART OF TRACTOR SUPPLY.

There are some interesting similarities between the history of Tractor Supply and the forerunner to Quality Stores – Central Tractor of Des Moines, Iowa. Both companies started in the tractor parts business in the '30s. Central Tractor began in Boone, Iowa, as a tractor salvage company in 1935 and opened a mail-order parts business similar to Tractor Supply's a year later.

The founders of Central Tractor, Jack Brody and his wife, Rea, were slower to make the move to retail than Charles Schmidt was. They opened their first retail store – Central Tractor Farm & Family Center – in Des Moines, Iowa, during the 1950s. In 1994, with nearly sixty stores, the company went public and changed its corporate name to Central Tractor Farm & Country and its store name to CT Farm & Country.

In 1996, Central Tractor was purchased by J. W. Childs Associates, a Boston investment firm. Like Tractor Supply during the National and Fuqua years, Central Tractor was viewed more as an investment than a business and would be pressed to grow by the company that controlled it. This absent form of leadership ultimately would not serve the fortunes or future of the company well.

During the late '90s, Central Tractor grew largely through acquisitions, doubling its size in 1997 with the purchase of ConAgra's Country General Store chain based in Grand Island, Nebraska, and its 114 locations mostly in the Midwest. The purchase of Country General would also usher in another private investment firm into the already fragmented ownership mix.

In 1999, Central Tractor merged with Quality Stores, based in Muskegon, Michigan, adding another 112 stores and $525 million dollars. The 360-store chain would operate in thirty states under a variety of names – CT Farm & Country, Country General, Quality Farm & Fleet, County Post, Central Farm and Fleet, and FISCO. The resulting hodge-podge left it with cultures, stores, people, inventory, and a computer infrastructure as varied as the names it operated under.

Although the merger between Central Tractor and Quality made it the largest farm store chain in America, it would also saddle the company with a huge debt that ultimately led to its demise.

In the summer of 2001, Tractor Supply was contacted and asked if it would be interested in buying a few Quality stores in the Southeast and a distribution center in Macon, Georgia. Tractor Supply and Quality could never come to terms on the deal, even though Quality eventually agreed to an offer from Tractor Supply they had previously rejected. But it was too late.

Quality ended up closing the twenty-seven stores they had tried to sell. At this point, Tractor Supply wasn't even interested in picking up the leases from Quality because the markets were now open. Tractor Supply no longer had a competitive reason to accept their real estate.

"At the time, we didn't realize that Quality was now saddled with twenty-seven empty stores they were paying rent on, at a time when they were under some real financial pressure," said Wright.

A few weeks later, Quality was again trying to sell locations. This time, a total of approximately 150 to 200 stores west of the Mississippi River. Tractor Supply's interest level went up.

"We were interested in many of those stores but were blocked at every point in the negotiation process," explained Wright.

"They wanted to sell but didn't want us to grow our chain at their expense when they exited those markets. Every time we got to the auction, it turned out that four of the stores we were interested in were part of someone else's packet of twelve and the packages had kind of been gerrymandered around what they knew we were interested in.

"And so we never were able to acquire any of the stores west of the Mississippi River."

Had Quality's organization not successfully thwarted Tractor Supply's attempts to buy a few stores early on, Tractor Supply's financial reserves might have been depleted to the point it could have never won the acquisition bid later on.

Tractor Supply may have lost the proverbial battle, but it was on its way to winning the war.

In November 2001, the weight of Quality's debts was finally too great and the company filed for bankruptcy. Approximately 150 Quality Stores were now on the chopping block. It appeared the bankruptcy was an attempt by Quality's management to reorganize the debt and buy back the company at auction. Theoretically, the company was for sale, but the Quality management team was only looking for an outside bidder as a way of validating the price they hoped to pay at auction.

"It became a real struggle just to get information," Wright recalled. "We felt like we had very little chance of success and the most critical thing was not to take the company off task while we were sorting out the details of a possible deal.

"We were a chain of 320 stores at the time and we needed to run those 320 stores. To their credit, our team wasn't distracted."

Initially, Tractor Supply was only interested in acquiring about forty stores in North Carolina, South Carolina, and Georgia. Getting the necessary information to make an intelligent bid on the stores at auction proved cumbersome. Tractor Supply would have to get the information on its own, in its own way, with its own people. And so team members traveled to the markets to literally walk the floor of all the stores the company was considering.

"This is the Tractor Supply culture, this is our brand – you don't sit around and wait for somebody to tell you to go do something, you just do it. You do whatever it takes," said Fohl.

And what it would take was more than Tractor Supply had ever imagined.

Wright learned from the investment banker putting the deal together for the creditor's committee that forty stores wasn't enough and that Tractor Supply wouldn't even get to the auction unless they were thinking more in terms of 150 stores.

"I called Stan Ruta and said, 'Stan, we have a dilemma,'" remembered Wright. "We're going to have to make this a bigger deal than we thought. I'm not sure the board is going to approve it. But I know that we have no chance of that approval unless we know a whole lot more about the stores in Michigan, Indiana, and Ohio.

FFA and TSC – Growing Together Tractor Supply and Future Farmers of America have enjoyed a 20-year partnership forged under Tom Hennesy. What began as a fund-raising campaign has grown to include job interview skills development; tractor, diversified livestock, ag sales, and equine programs; special awards at the national convention; and an endowment that funds two or three college scholarships a year. Why the deeply rooted commitment? "It's the right thing to do," said Tractor Supply's Jerry Brase, the 2003 FFA Sponsors Board Chairman.

"This is Sunday at 7:30 in the morning. Two o'clock that afternoon, I was on my way to catch a plane when my cell phone rang.

"It was Stan. Stan, Blake Fohl, and Mark Gilman were at the airport in Nashville, each of them with an airplane ticket. By Thursday night, they were back with measurements and photos and traffic counts on another sixty stores. I never asked them to do it.

"They just said, 'Gee, what do we need to make this thing work?" And on a Sunday they just said, 'OK, let's get on an airplane.'

"That's the kind of story you're going to find surrounding this organization, time and time again."

You can still hear the pride in Wright's voice. Pride not in the company's successful bid but in the team that rallied around the deal as it was unfolding.

Tractor Supply had the information it needed not just to make the deal but also to make it successful. What they learned told them they did not want to acquire the business. Not, at least, in the traditional sense.

The landscape of corporate America is littered by companies who've tried to merge and failed. Quality itself had been built by one merger after another. The result was dissimilar cultures, dissimilar formats, dissimilar products, and different computer systems in its stores. Tractor Supply decided it wouldn't follow the path Quality had taken. This wouldn't be a merger. Tractor Supply would keep only the stores that made financial and strategic sense. It also wouldn't saddle itself with closing out the existing inventory. Instead it put together a joint venture with three partners – Great American Group, Gordon Brothers Retail Partners LLC, and DJM Asset Management LLC, – that would liquidate all of the Quality inventory in the stores so that the stores would open without all of the baggage typically part of a merger.

"When they flip the switch to Tractor Supply, they are going to be clean," John R. Lawrence, analyst at Morgan Keegan & Co., was quoted in a newspaper story. "They won't have to take over old inventory and they have to sell it."

The switch had yet to be flipped. The drama was far from over.

HAPPY NEW YEAR

"Quality had come to believe we were modestly interested and that we would be very opportunistic in what we would pay for the company," Wright said. "They were confident they'd be able to buy the company at a very reasonable price. They also felt that as a large, publicly held company, we'd be very conservative when it came to responding to them."

To further complicate the process, and to Tractor Supply's supposed detriment, about three days out, they set the conference call auction for December 27, and the deal would close December 31.

"That is very, very quick," said Wright. "It's unusually quick and again was structured to be to their advantage and our disadvantage. We recognized that strategically and got to the auction, which began at 8 a.m.

"Our lawyers and teams were in New York when the auction began. Joe, Cal Massmann, and I were in my office as the auction began via conference call."

Tractor Supply opened with a bid of $75 million while the Quality management was at $73.5 million. The creditor's committee said that because of other considerations, such as severance costs, Tractor Supply would have to come in substantially higher to beat Quality's bid. It would take $79 million to match their $73.5. And so Tractor Supply raised its bid to $79 million. Quality countered with a bid of $75 million that would require $89 million from Tractor. Puzzled by the math, Tractor Supply took some time to respond.

To this point, Tractor Supply was only paying twenty cents on the dollar. Its partners in the acquisition had agreed to cover the other eighty cents to procure the inventory for liquidation. Once the bid reached $89 million, Tractor Supply was on its own.

Tractor Supply went back in and said yes to $89 million. The bids continued to rise until it was at $100 million from Tractor Supply.

"At this point, it was now eight or ten hours since the auction began and we had all gone home," remembered Wright. "I was working from my office at home and calling Joe and Cal every time it got more expensive. We said yes to $100 million.

"An hour later they came back to us at $101 million and without even blinking I said 102. Then I called Joe and Cal asked how much higher do we go and we talked strategy. If they came back at 103, I wouldn't hang up. I wouldn't blink. I would go right to 104."

That's exactly what happened. The bid came back to Tractor Supply and they went to $104 million immediately.

"We answered in a nanosecond, like we had truckloads of money," said Wright with a big million-dollar smile on his face. "Well, they folded at $104 million."

JIM, JOE AND CAL SMILE WITH THE WINNING BID ON THE QUALITY DEAL.

"So at the end of the day, after all the posturing and positioning, Quality simply did not bring enough money to the auction. And by beginning this on Thursday, now almost Friday morning before we finished, the Friday before the New Year's weekend with New Year's Eve on Monday, and the deal having to close on a holiday, they had eliminated their chance of going back and finding another $2 or $3 million."

According to Wright, Tractor Supply had gone into the auction estimating a 5 percent chance of winning. Friday night at 11:30 p.m. he was on the phone to every vice president in the company informing them that "unless the bankruptcy judge disagrees, we just bought a company."

The fun was about to begin.

110 DAYS THAT CHANGED TRACTOR SUPPLY FOREVER

The campaign to integrate the Quality stores into Tractor Supply was quickly christened Project 110. The company would open a total of 110 stores in 2002 – the stores that it had acquired plus those that were already in the works. According to the plan, the eighty-seven stores that had been acquired would be opened within 110 days after the company had taken possession of the first store.

"Yeah, the 110-day timetable was huge," said Wright. "I almost had to resuscitate Stan Ruta after the announcement."

The final platform in the Project 110 campaign enlisted the efforts of existing stores. The 323 stores and teams who enabled Tractor Supply to make the acquisition were challenged to perform at 110 percent of their operating profit plans. That was the definition of Project 110. It would forever change the company.

"We felt like the little kid that's sitting on the bench saying, 'Play me, coach. Play me, coach,'" said Jim Wright. "Suddenly the ball is in your hands and you're saying, 'What do we do now?'"

The first thing they did was assemble the team. The company's top eighteen leaders came in the Saturday morning after the Friday the deal was struck, the Saturday morning of New Year's Eve weekend. They all came in. They may have expected marching orders since Jim Wright had taken Western Auto through two similar sized acquisitions. Instead they were faced with this question – how do we do this? Jim and Joe recognized that only the ones actually making things happen would know how to get the job done. So they simply asked instead of ordered.

"We said to them, 'Here's what's about to happen,'" Wright said. "'We are a chain of 323 stores today. We're going to open eighty-seven stores in the first half of next year – eighty-seven new stores plus twelve or fourteen other new stores that were already in the works. At the same time, we're not going to falter on the 323. Given that as our guiding principle, we want everyone to think through what needs to be done. What work is involved. Think through who needs to do it. Think through how it will be measured. Think through what's the worst thing that could happen. And let's meet this afternoon, and we did."

By New Year's Eve, Tractor Supply had put together a plan. The team had identified hundreds, and in some cases, thousands of things that needed to be done and who needed to do them. It knew the worst things that could happen and what would be done first.

The first thing that needed to be done was take care of people.

So on New Year's Day, a team of people left Nashville for Quality Store's headquarters in Muskegon, Michigan, and on the first work day of 2002, they beat Quality's employees to work and delivered the news that Tractor Supply had bought their company. The news came from Tractor Supply and not from the prior management.

"While we were putting together the entire plan over that weekend, the prior management team had not even phoned some of their people yet," said Jim Wright. "We had our people on the ground, but the guiding principle was that we would not arrive as the conquering victors."

Blake Fohl, vice president of marketing; Kim Vella, vice president of human resources; and

Susan Divine, a human resources manager, made the trip to Muskegon.

"They had a great company before the Central Tractor deal happened," said Fohl. "When they merged with Central Tractor it destroyed their culture. Then their big dreams of going public one day and everybody making big piles of money were replaced by a trip to bankruptcy court. They left for Christmas break thinking they're going to come back and everything is going to be fine, only to discover on the day they arrive back to work that they're out of a job and there are two people from Tractor Supply in their nerve center.

"I couldn't help but imagine what if the shoe was on the other foot?"

Empathy was the order of the day.

"We wanted to be considerate of their feelings," said Vella. "What we had to do was make a connection with the store managers. The best way to do that was through the district managers. So we asked all the district managers to come in to interview with us."

The district managers were happy to fly in to interview, but what Tractor Supply didn't know was that all of their travel credit cards had been cut off with the sale of the company. Quality's district managers were wondering how they could cover the cost of an airplane ticket if they were about to be unemployed?

"When we found this out, we quickly mobilized and arranged for all of their travel," said Vella. "We just don't let things stand in our way. We'll make it happen. We're all empowered to make things happen, and we did. I think thirteen DMs got into Muskegon within two or three days. And of those thirteen, we hired ten. Then we went out through the district managers to talk to the store managers."

In all, Tractor Supply hired 100 of Quality's best store managers. The hiring of good people was even more important to the success of the project than the acquisition of the right locations.

"These were good people," said Vella. "We knew that if we could get a Quality store manager to come along with us, that was more than half the battle. All we had to do was teach them how we handle processes and procedures and begin to immerse them in the Tractor Supply culture.

"They already knew the farm store business. They knew their community. They knew their team."

KIM VELLA, BLAKE FOHL, AND SUSAN DIVINE (NOT PICTURED) GREETED THE QUALITY EMPLOYEES IN MUSKEGON BEFORE THEY GOT THE NEWS FROM THEIR OWN EXECUTIVES.

At the same time Fohl, Vella, and Divine were meeting with the Quality folks, Jim and Joe were meeting with the Tractor Supply team. They gathered the store support team together and set the tone for what would be as successful an acquisition of people and talent as it was of stores and locations.

"We told our team that there is a company 600 miles north of here, in our business, with folks just like you, who care as deeply about their careers and their customers and families as we do," said Wright. "Except for the grace of God, there go we.

"So as you talk to these people, recognize they are just like you.

"When we step back and ask why Project 110 was so successful in retaining all of the great people that we wanted to retain, that was it. Because the culture of this company made a statement. We went up there and said, 'We respect you. No, it didn't turn out like you planned but we know you're smart, we know you work hard, and we want to give you a chance to live your dreams.

"'The stores won't say Quality. They'll say Tractor Supply. But the business will principally stay the same. We have strong core values at Tractor Supply and that we think you'll appreciate.'"

Tractor Supply was successful in hiring ten of Quality's best district managers as well as 100 of its best store managers.

"I have a philosophy that companies – good companies – are filling a bank account with good will with their employees all the time," said Wright. "What happened with the Quality acquisition is that for many years Joe and his team had done that, kept continually filling the accounts with good will so that we could make a huge withdrawal when we needed to.

"Project 110 was a success because the foundation was in place long before the opportunity came along. And that's significant. Most companies fail to build that foundation of good will to create reserves of energy and intellect that can be tapped. Too many companies whip their people all of the time only to whip them harder when they have a challenge."

And there were many, many other challenges. After securing the talent, there were training needs. And so two groups of store managers were brought into Nashville, fifty people at a time, for intense two-week training sessions. While in Nashville, they lived together in an apartment complex near the store support center – sort of a TSC frat house that built an amazing camaraderie and allowed store managers to compare notes over casual conversation around the dinner table.

Vendors were given thirty days' notice that their volume was going to increase 35 percent in the next eleven months – most of it in the next three to four months. Instead of shipping products in case lot quantities to Tractor Supply distribution centers, vendors were asked to send smaller packs of four directly to the new stores. They were asked and they did it.

Tractor Supply's real estate team had to repair, move entrances, and paint eighty-seven stores. Ten to twelve team members with farming, ranching, welding, and horse-owning backgrounds had to be hired for eighty-seven stores. Those eighty-seven stores had to be merchandised with 14,000 SKUs. Advertising distribution in eighty-seven new markets had to be analyzed. The distribution center in Pendleton, Indiana, increased its workforce by 50 percent and had to increase the number of stores it served by nearly 50 percent.

During a three-month period, all eighty-seven stores were visited by Jim Wright, Joe Scarlett, or Stan Ruta. They took the time to sit down with the team members of each store and talk about the value and vision and mission of the company. Three of the company's top executives went out of their way to talk to the former Quality Store employees to give them a lasting impression of the people they were now working with and what Tractor Supply stood for as a company.

"To a person, the company just stepped up and did everything it was asked and with the highest degree of accuracy I've ever seen," said Wright. "It was an amazing thing to watch. Simply tremendous."

At the Store Support Center, team members were issued bags of different colored jellybeans from Jim Wright and Joe Scarlett. The candy was dubbed the Project 110 Survival Kit.

"The red was the 'My Boss Is Driving Me Crazy' bean," explained Kim Vella. "Pink was something about being stressed out. The yellow was 'Get Happy.' Green was the 'Chill Pill.'"

Through all of the hard work there was always an element of fun. All that was left was to make money. The Project 110 team met every Monday night at 5:30. Wright promised them pizza as they worked on trouble areas or things that were running late.

"We met for seventeen weeks," said Wright. "I only bought pizza three times because after that the meetings only lasted a half an hour or forty-five minutes. Nobody wanted to be the only person around that table of eighteen with something that hadn't been done."

Conventional wisdom says that acquisitions rarely work. They typically fail to achieve their anticipated sales, profit, and synergy. They frequently divert time and attention from the core business.

"None of that happened," said Jim Wright. "Existing stores achieved nearly 110 percent of their original target for the year. The new stores came out of the box ahead of schedule, beating our 110 day deadline and performing above our pro forma estimates."

After their training was completed, store managers were setting between eight and ten Project 110 stores a week. Project 110 team members who weren't opening their stores immediately went to help at other stores in the immediate area. Suddenly, stores started opening faster and faster. Teams had four weeks to set their fixtures, receive merchandise, train their teams, and open their stores. It was incredibly fast. As the project passed the midpoint, stores were opening in three weeks instead of four, and it created a great sense of pride.

What's the aftermath of such a flurry of training and openings in such a concentrated timetable?

"Once the stores opened, we went back and did audits on the new stores," explained Gary Magoni. "They were educational audits to follow up on any questions.

"In our second year now, the Project 110 stores – with two weeks of training for their managers – are scoring the highest audit scores in our history."

A lot of trust and good will was created, too, between Tractor Supply and its newest store managers, who were once a part of the company's biggest competitor. They simply couldn't believe it when Tractor Supply applied their seniority at Quality to Tractor Supply in terms of retirement and vacation. They didn't lose any ground with the change of ownership. In fact, they gained far more than they lost.

GARY MAGONI, REGION 5 VICE PRESIDENT

"I don't think they totally trusted that we would deliver on a lot of our promises," explained Magoni. "For example, when they came on board, we gave every store manager who opened a store a guaranteed $3,000 bonus just for opening up on time and on budget. I don't think they believed we'd pay off on our promise. They had questions in their minds because Quality had pulled back their bonuses many times. So when we paid them after that first year, there were monstrous bonuses. I think we galvanized the team and took a major step in their embracing the culture of this company."

"We are forever changed as a company," Wright said. "As a result, our people know that they can leap tall buildings and out run speeding trains. They're changed. Our biggest challenge as a company is now how do we keep that fervor alive.

"We've created a culture of giants."

A CULTURE OF GIANTS

With its rich history, its solid growth, its strong culture, and the distinctive niche it has fenced off in the minds and hearts of its customers, today Tractor Supply has moved beyond the realm of simple retail concept and into the arena of emerging lifestyle brand.

Today, the distinctive red, white, and black logo, with its western style block type and its quaint barn-red trapezium, dots small towns and medium-size cities across the American heartland. Tractor Supply is deeply tied to American culture. Its recent growth has mirrored a cultural phenomenon in the country – the return to traditional values and the land and a renewed interest in the things that live on the land. For farmers, ranchers, hobby farmers, rural folks, and horse people, Tractor Supply seems to have become the unofficial home office for the self-reliant lifestyle.

Tractor Supply is a part of popular culture, too. It's a brand that harmonizes with an America whose popular country artists top the charts with songs like, "She Thinks My Tractor's Sexy" and lyrics that echo the sentiments of a growing number of big city transplants with words like, "I'm gonna live where the green grass grows. Watch my corn pop up in rows. Every night be tucked in close to you."

Its catalog has decorated a Hollywood set to help create an authentic American farm background. Its "unique" products – in this case, a Band Castrator – have shown up on the *The Tonight Show* starring Jay Leno. Even the President of the United States has borrowed on Tractor Supply's reputation as a symbol of the rural lifestyle to his advantage.

When President George W. Bush wanted to meet privately with a handful of representatives

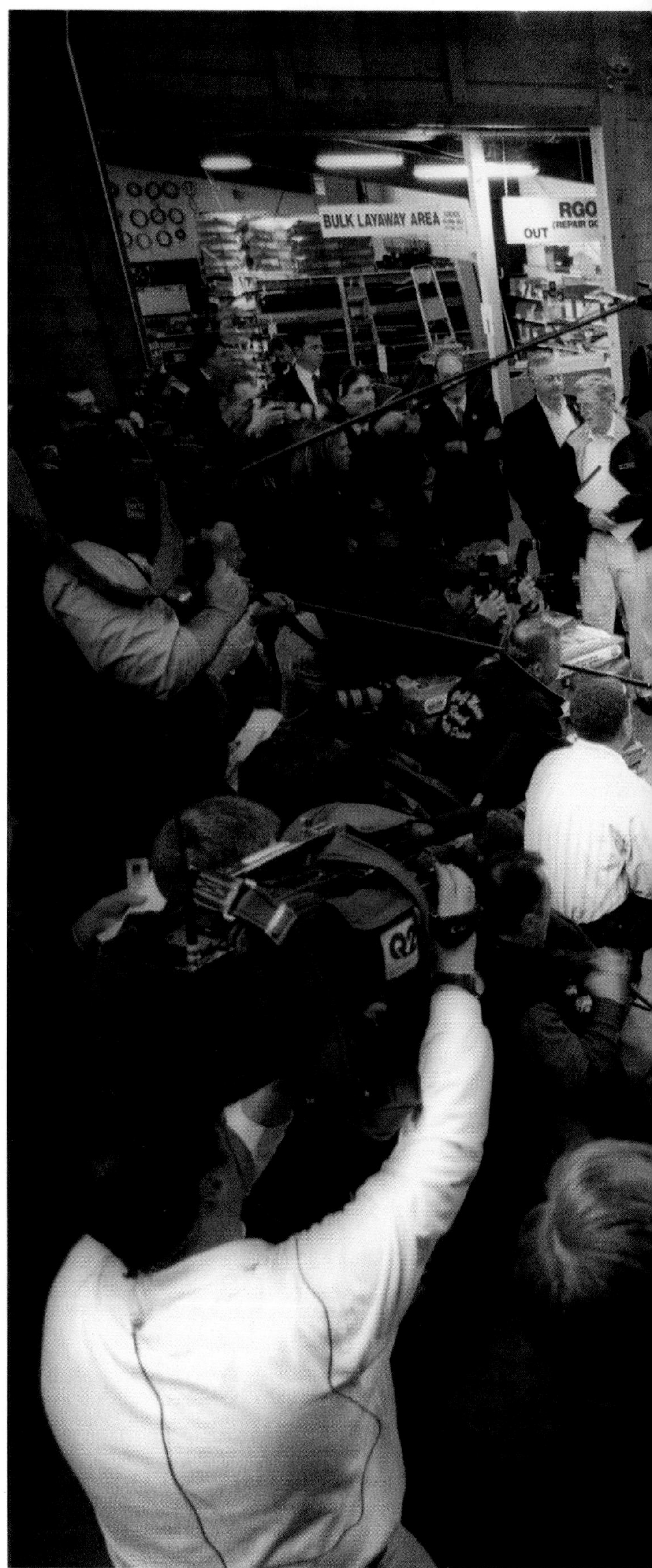

The press gathers and plops down on a feed sack during President George W. Bush's town meeting at the Tractor Supply Store on Main Street in Billings, Montana.

from Montana's farm and ranching industry on their own turf, he dropped by the local Tractor Supply Store on Main Street in Billings, Montana. The audience sat for this informal meeting on folding chairs and fertilizer bags. Bush had come looking for "hardworking, God-fearing, family-loving people" with a promise to make Americans proud of the White House again. He couldn't have picked a better place as a backdrop to his message and its sentiment.

It's a brand whose mindset mirrors what has been recognized as the American character for centuries. In its work with a new advertising partner named in 2002, Carmichael Lynch, the agency that helped build Harley-Davidson into the great American icon brand, Tractor Supply discovered that although its customers are both male and female, traditional farmers and hobby farmers, small town citizens and exurbanites – although its customers vary, they all have one thing in common: They are "self-reliant."

★ UDDER CREAM ★
Antiseptic and bactericidal.
Contains lanolin.
28 OZ. JAR
KENDALL UDDER CREAM
22-12491........................$7.99
1996 BLUE BOOK

In other words, the people who pull into a Tractor Supply – whether it's in a Mercedes SUV or a Ford pickup – all consider themselves fiercely independent folks who enjoy "being their own boss." Down-to-earth people moved by actions and not words. Strong individuals who like to be challenged and find greater fulfillment in seeing a job done by themselves. They find comfort and challenge and life in the land, what they call their "little piece of heaven." Is there an American who doesn't feel proud, who doesn't hear strains of "America the Beautiful," who wouldn't want to be identified as a "self-reliant"?

As described by Carmichael Lynch and as lived by Tractor Supply's customers – "Out Here" is a place where: "There are fences to mend. There is grass to cut. There are dogs to feed. There are horses to groom. There are busted things to fix. There is hay to bale. There are trailers to tow. There are tools to sharpen. There is wood to split. There is a supply store that helps get it all done." Tractor Supply is the place that "provides the tools, supplies the advice that enables people to thrive out there, provides the means to pursue a lifestyle that others only dream of. One based on an honesty and integrity that comes from being rooted in the land, that provides 'the stuff you need out here.' "

Wow, pretty heady stuff for such humble beginnings. All of this, from a simple twenty-four-page tractor parts catalog that became popular in money-conscious Post-Depression America. All of this from a once-confused retail chain that appeared to be on the way out in the 1970s and a lifestyle we generally considered had been supplanted by life in the city.

The Tractor Supply story is such a remarkable and compelling one because it is the story of a brand and a culture and a business that has proven itself by being successful…twice.

Beyond the obvious differences of size and scope and sophistication between the store as it began back in 1938 and as it is today, there are some powerful similarities in the principles at work, then and now. Principles and a culture that appear to have been abandoned when the company collapsed as a part of the conglomerate culture of the 1970s.

OUT HERE

YOU'LL FIND

CALLUSED HANDS

AND

UNCALLUSED MINDS

THE RURAL LIFESTYLE. SURE IT'S A LOT OF WORK, BUT THE PAYOFF IS A CLEAR CONSCIENCE, GOING TO BED THE GOOD KIND OF TIRED, AND THE SATISFACTION THAT COMES FROM GETTING THE JOB DONE YOURSELF.

★ YOU LIVE IT ★

AND AS A TSC TEAM MEMBER, IT'S UP TO YOU TO ROLL UP YOUR SLEEVES AND HELP OTHERS LIVE IT TOO

TSC TRACTOR SUPPLY Co | THE STUFF YOU NEED OUT HERE

Tractor Supply has always been a place where the individual mattered but teamwork was lauded. Strong individuals working as a team – Charles Schmidt, Bill Cleary, Gard Abbott, Wes Walker and Max DeForest – made this company what it was at its successful start. What it has become today has been largely shaped by the work of new generations of strong individuals with a knack for working as a team – Tom Hennesy and the Gang of Five, Joe Scarlett and his new team of Jim Wright, Jerry Brase, Stan Ruta, and Cal Massmann.

DOROTHY AND JOE SCARLETT READY TO GREET TEAM MEMBERS AT A RECENT MANAGERS MEETING.

Tractor Supply has never taken itself too seriously and has always known how to have fun. There were the famous manager all-night poker games in the early days of the managers meeting, in which President Wes Walker was known to take the time to sweeten the pot. Today's annual managers meeting is a case study in not being too stuffy to get loud and get proud. Fun filters its way throughout the company. Whether it's the ringing of a Chinese gong that brings meetings to order or a bright red mule flexing its muscles and baring its teeth as a symbol of the company's winning attitude.

Tractor Supply, at its best both in the beginning and today, has been successful because it's hitched its star to a niche. It did what it did better than anyone else. It's stayed "out of the headlights of the big box retailers," as Joe likes to say. Tractor Supply was making money in its first months of operation because Charles Schmidt had discovered a niche. It continues to be successful today because Joe and team continue to develop, explore, re-invent, tinker, test, but always within an understood and defined niche. In fact, the company lost its way when it tried to be everything to all people instead of being more and more what people had come to rely on from its farm and ranch store friend.

Tractor Supply values people. Customers and team members. It listens to its customers and, because customers just have a way of knowing they're being listened to, those customers keep calling, writing, e-mailing, and coming back. It empowers its team members to listen to the customers as well and to "do whatever it takes" to make things right. Then and now, Tractor Supply has shared its success with the folks who make the register ring on the store floor, whether with stock or bonuses made available to everyone in the company. Today, the company sees bringing aboard good people as the heart of what will ensure its success for the future.

Tractor Supply was and is successful because it hires its customers. Early on, Charles Schmidt appreciated the wisdom of hiring all of the farm boys when they came back from the war. Today, the company requires farmers, ranchers, horse owners, and welders as part of each store's team. And the customer has responded, showing trust, by not only shopping but also hiring on at Tractor Supply.

Tractor Supply has thrived because of its open door policy when it came to ideas and the exchange of ideas. Charlie Schmidt had his morning coffee with his brain trust and Joe Scarlett has his coffee on the road with management team in tow as they pick the brains of everyone from team members and customers to competitors as they drive across the country.

Tractor Supply has been successful – at its onset and today – because it understood its mission, the place of importance it held in the lives of its customers. It has been an enabler of a self-reliant lifestyle. Whether it was the farmer with a broken-down tractor in the field and in need of a part before the harvest was lost or today's hobby farmer in need of a little advice from a friend who's a bit more seasoned when it comes to stretching a fence tight.

Tractor Supply has been successful because it kept things exceedingly simple. From the simple name Charles Schmidt gave the company to its straightforward customer service policy – "do whatever it takes" – everything is plainly stated. Sure, it's employed a lot of complex technology and research, analysis, and brainpower along the way, but it's all been in an effort to keep things as simple as sunshine.

There are others, so many other striking similarities and comparisons that could be drawn, but in the end none as important as this one – people. Simply stated, the character of Tractor Supply at its best and its very worst is and has been determined by the character of its people. Ethics beyond reproach and doing the right thing have not always been the given at Tractor Supply. But the company has done its best when its character was the very best.

NUMBER
TSC 0769

TSC TRACTOR SUPPLY Co

SHARES

COMMON STOCK

TRACTOR SUPPLY COMPANY

INCORPORATED UNDER THE LAWS OF THE STATE OF DELAWARE

SEE REVERSE FOR CERTAIN DEFINITIONS

CUSIP 892356 10 6

THIS CERTIFIES that

is the owner of

FULLY PAID AND NON-ASSESSABLE SHARES OF COMMON STOCK, PAR VALUE $.008 PER SHARE, OF

TRACTOR SUPPLY COMPANY

transferable on the books of the Corporation by the holder hereof in person or by his duly authorized Attorney upon surrender of this Certificate properly endorsed. This Certificate and the shares represented hereby are issued and shall be held subject to all of the provisions of the Restated Certificate of Incorporation, as amended, and Amended and Restated By-laws, as amended, of the Corporation (copies thereof being on file with the Secretary of the Corporation) and the holder hereof, by accepting this Certificate, expressly assents thereto. This Certificate is not valid unless countersigned and registered by the Transfer Agent and Registrar.

Witness the facsimile seal of the Corporation and the facsimile signatures of its duly authorized officers.

Dated:

COUNTERSIGNED AND REGISTERED:
EquiServe Trust Company, N.A.
TRANSFER AGENT AND REGISTRAR

BY

AUTHORIZED OFFICER

TRACTOR SUPPLY COMPANY CORPORATE SEAL 1982 DELAWARE

SECRETARY

CHAIRMAN

TRACTOR SUPPLY ISSUES STOCK AGAIN IN 1994.

C.E.
SCHMIDT
WORKWEAR
DURABLE GOODS
TSC TRACTOR SUPPLY Co
THE STUFF YOU NEED OUT HERE
TOOLS
HOME IMPROVEMENT
VEHICLE MAINTENANCE
YOUR PRIZE BELT BUCKLE
DESERVES NOTHING LESS
WEEKLY
SEE THE IN-STO SPECIA AT YOU LOCAL
Brush-On Bed Liner Kit
TSC # 1033006
Register/log in for local price
© 2004 Tractor Supply Compa
Santa Rosa
Petaluma

CHAPTER ★10★

LOOKING AT THE LAY OF THE LAND

OPPORTUNITY FOR MILES

"I'D RATHER WAKE UP IN THE MIDDLE OF NOWHERE THAN IN ANY CITY ON EARTH"

- STEVE MCQUEEN

WHERE THE GREEN GRASS GROWS

The new millennium in America dawned bright for Tractor Supply with more and more Americans abandoning the city for the wide-open spaces. The people who live out here live life on their own terms. They do it themselves. And look to Tractor Supply for the expertise and the stuff they need for life out here.

OPPORTUNITY FOR MILES What do you see when you look at a piece of land extending out to the horizon? Our customers see opportunity. They see something that needs doing, growing, fixing, hauling, tending to or tinkering with. There's always some kind of improvement to be made. In America, the land has always represented opportunity and freedom, stretching as far as the eye can see and the heart is willing to go. Whether you have forty acres or 400 acres, it's all the same. We have the freedom to make of it anything we wish. And in the process, we also make something of ourselves.

★

Through most of the twentieth century, Tractor Supply has been there, helping America fulfill the promise of the land and the people who work the land, enabling them to pursue their dreams and the simple pleasures of the rural lifestyle. Today, Tractor Supply looks to the landscape of the new millennium and sees plenty of promise and opportunity of its own. Its management team has studied the lay of the land, the social climate, attitudes toward leisure and work, and the search for things that give meaning along with pleasure, the migration back to the land and rural roots, the steady rise in addresses along rural postal routes, the transplanted baby boomers, the business executives and blue collar workers who divide their time between their work and their labor of love on the land.

"We're in the early phase of a cultural trend – America's return to its roots," explains Jim Wright. "There is a time-distance equation at work today that makes living out, away from the city, away from the traditional workplace, more attractive. Transportation and technology have advanced to the point where we can have both the work we want and the life we want and the means to commute or telecommute between the two.

"The return to rural America is not a fad or a trend. It's a lifestyle. At Tractor Supply, we enable that lifestyle. We give people the tools and seasoned advice they need for life out here. So given this emerging cultural trend, this lifestyle and the places around the country we have yet to venture, there is an incredible opportunity for the future of Tractor Supply.

"We've identified 1,300 viable locations for Tractor Supply stores around the country. There's plenty of opportunity for the future. Opportunity is not the challenge. Ensuring that all of the new team members we will hire stay true to our mission and values as we go about seizing that opportunity is the challenge."

JIM AND JOE

When you talk with Jim Wright, he alternates between looking you square in the eye and looking at a point three inches over your head. You get the feeling that's exactly where his sights are set – some distant point that at the moment is beyond you, above your head. Even so, Jim has a way of making you feel incredibly at ease with the unknown. It's the inexplicable sort of ease you feel when you're in the presence of someone who knows precisely where he's going, how he's going to get there and that you're invited to come along. This sense of ease and confidence is what made Wright's role so critical to the success of Project 110 and important as the company moves to the future.

JOE AND JIM – ONE GREAT TEAM

In 2004, Jim was named CEO of the company.Part of Jim Wright's role as president and CEO of Tractor Supply is to look ahead, continually check the lay of the land. It's not that Joe Scarlett lacks a vision for Tractor Supply's future. He has one. It's just his vision for the future places Jim at the forefront.

JIM SPEAKING AT 2004 MANAGERS MEETING

His cheerleader's heart is comfortable in stepping back, entrusting others and supporting their vision for the company he's worked so hard and long to help nurture. And that's part of the reason the future of Tractor Supply appears so bright – the level of cooperation and teamwork at the highest levels of the company.

Jim Wright and Joe Scarlett are a team. Jim calls it "great alignment." Joe calls it "being joined at the hip." Whichever term is used to describe it, the result is the same – a singleness of purpose and consistency of direction that serve the company well.

"The best retail ideas are never born behind a desk," says Wright. "They're born on the road, on the store floor, where the customers are and the real action is in retailing."

Like Joe, Jim's passion is palatable, but it's not the fun, frenetic energy and cheerleader enthusiasm that is Joe Scarlett's signature. Jim's passion burns beneath an eternally at ease exterior. It glows in the eyes that seem forever fixed on some point in the distant future.

"At sixty-five years, we're really just an adolescent in terms of our development," Wright explains. "We were a very small, conservative company for a long, long time. It gave us time to build a company and forge a culture."

In fact, it gave the company time to forge that culture not once, but twice. Only in losing hold of it once was its value realized. Sustaining that culture, holding onto that one precious link to the past, is the critical first step in the future of Tractor Supply.

"I don't think people realize how fragile a culture is and how important it is to sustain a successful culture once it is in place," Wright says. "Ours has been a springboard to our recent success and will only grow more important as the number of stores and team members increases and our speed to market accelerates.

"We're now a *Fortune* 1000 company. But history is littered with the names of companies who reached the *Fortune* 1000 only to fail miserably. In most cases, they failed because they lost sight of what got them there in the first place. They lost sight of their mission and values. They lost sight of the culture that made them successful.

"At Tractor Supply, we know where we came from. We will remain humble, frugal, and passionate. We'll stay true to who we are and tightly focused on what we do."

From City to Suburb – The Story of the Home Office Tractor Supply's first home office was literally that. It was in Charles Schmidt's home where he started the company at his kitchen table. He next rented a vacant floor at 1217 West Washington Boulevard and tried to make the dismal location more acceptable by advertising, "Tractor Supply Company. WLS is directly across the street from us." During the boom times following World War II, Tractor Supply moved to its second headquarters at 2700 North Halsted Street. The space was larger but not any more luxurious. After going public in the spring of 1959, the company bought a rickety forty-year-old brick building located at 4747 North Ravenswood Avenue. It would be Tractor Supply's last Chicago address. In 1979, on the heels of being sold to a larger conglomerate for the second time in ten years, Tractor Supply moved to 915 Murfreesboro Road in Nashville, Tennessee. Tractor Supply's fifth home opened its doors in 1987 at 320 Plus Park. It was the first headquarters the company would build and marked the success under the new private ownership of Hennesy, Scarlett, Newkirk, Maxwell, and Flood. Scarlett would christen it the "Store Support Center." In July 2004, Tractor Supply moved to its new Store Support Center at 200 Powell Place in Brentwood, Tennessee. As part of the Maryland Farms complex, the new office appropriately stands on a field that was once farmland.

THE FAST EAT THE SLOW

While the company's mission, values and core business will remain consistent, other things will continue to change at an increasingly accelerated rate, according to Wright.

"Bigger doesn't necessarily mean better," says Wright. "We're more interested in getting faster in the future. We believe 'the fast eat the slow' and not 'the big eat the small.' We're going to become faster to market. More aggressive. Speed to market is a state of mind. At Tractor Supply, we embrace the Intel practice stated by Andy Grove – 'Fail often, early, and cheaply.'

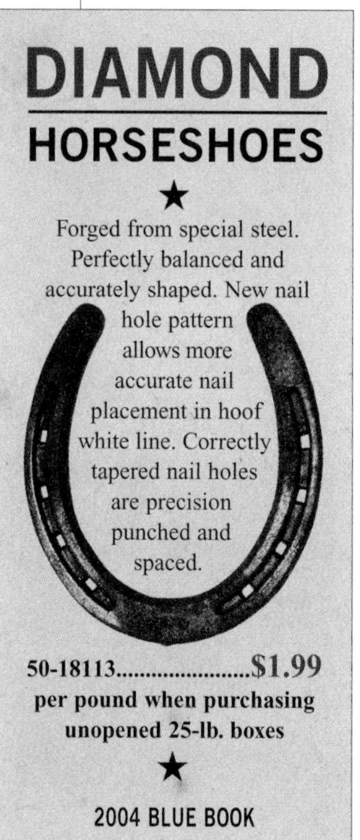

"To that end, we constantly test new items or lines. Hundreds of products are in perpetual testing. Some tests may be in five, ten, or fifty stores. The success of those products will be determined by our customers. We are always in the market, shopping competitors, looking for new products. In addition to hundreds of current vendors, we hold open buying days when hundreds of vendors present their products.

"Speed to market and change are just a part of life in retailing and they will become even more critical in the future.

"To increase our speed and efficiency, we've added distribution capacity in recent years in Texas, Georgia, and Maryland. We continue to look ahead with plans to add more distribution space in other parts of the country."

Tractor Supply's store size will remain the same as it is now – a relatively small store, a fraction of the size of big box retailers. But that's the only number associated with the store that will remain unchanged in the future.

"We plan on accelerating the rate of growth within our ability to provide infrastructure and top quality people," says Wright. "Long term, we will continue to improve our sales average per store. We'll improve our space utilization and display footage, increase the product density, freeing up room to add new categories."

The numbers multiply and Wright's smile deepens.

"We're a billion-dollar company. We'll soon be a $2 billion company and, before the close of the first decade of the twenty-first century, we'll nearly double that number again.

"Yes, there are certain risks associated with getting bigger. But the risks are even greater if we were simply trying to maintain the status quo." Or as Joe would say, 'If it ain't broke, break it. Break it and make it better.'

"What got us to $1 billion is the same thing that will get us to $2 billion and beyond – our values, our culture and our passion," continues Wright. "That's our foundation, and it's strong enough to support a far bigger company than we are today."

IT ALL BEGINS WITH PEOPLE

Culture, mission, values, and passion – they begin with people.

"Yes, there are a whole lot of new skills we'll need to develop. It's different when you get bigger," Wright acknowledges. "The whole people engine – recruiting and rewarding team members – is very critical to our future.

"We've already identified some of the members of our next generation of leadership and we monitor their development quarterly. We must recruit and reward team members at all levels. Good and passionate people who embrace the culture and our core values."

Once again, company culture is the standard against which Tractor Supply will grow its people.

"There's a 20/60/20 rule at work here," says Wright. "Twenty percent will readily get it and adopt the culture. Sixty percent will eventually get it. And twenty percent will resist it and may, in fact, sabotage it.

"Many companies make the mistake of trying to win over resistors. But the resistors need to be ferreted out and sent packing. The time that would have been devoted to them is far better spent praising the early adopters.

"If a manager doesn't fit our culture, we talk, coach, and provide a chance for change. If there's no change, then we release the individual to be successful somewhere else. We do this regardless of how strong the individual's performance.

"Culture is fragile and the team is always looking to its leaders to see if they blink."

Hiring to culture also puts team members in a better position to live up to their shared mission of working hard, having fun, and making money.

"We want to make Tractor Supply a great place to work and a great place to shop."

Wright pauses, smiles and then continues. "Note the order – a great place to work first," he says. "If it's a great place to work, then our team members will create the environment, uncover the products, and provide the legendary service that will ultimately make it a great place to shop.

"And if it's a great place to work and shop, then, naturally, it will be a great place to invest."

Wright sees his role and the role of other executives at Tractor Supply as simply looking ahead – what he and Joe call visioning – communicating that vision and just plain getting out of the way.

"At Tractor Supply, we turn the organizational chart upside down," says Wright. "I work for all the people in the stores and distribution centers. They pay my salary; in fact, if those in the aggregate do not earn a bonus, neither do I. Management's job is to build the culture, set the strategy and policy, allocate capital and resources, hire and develop great people, encourage them, recognize success publicly, deal with failure privately, and get out of the way."

SHELBYVILLE, TENNESSEE, ASSISTANT MANAGER DAWN WILSON READIES THE STORE FOR CUSTOMERS.

The future success of Tractor Supply might best be summed up in that single phrase – get out of the way. Tractor Supply's success in the future will be based on the speed with which its leadership can get out of the way to let the team serve a growing number of customers who, themselves, long to return to out-of-the-way places.

Everything is just a matter of "getting out of the way," "doing the right thing," and "working hard, having fun, and making money." It's that simple. Though, often it's the simplest of things that are the most difficult to do...and the most worthwhile in the end.

Just ask the tractor parts catalog company that grew up to become America's No. 1 Farm and Ranch Store Chain.

On February 18, 2004, Jim Wright, Joe Scarlett, Cal Massmann and friends celebrate TSC's opening event at the New York Stock Exchange.

★ ACKNOWLEDGEMENTS ★

Like Tractor Supply, this book was a team effort. Tractor Supply team members offered up information, searched their files for photos and in some cases answered last-minute pleas for help.

Thanks for working hard without the promise of fun or the prospect of money – Gary Bowers, Jerry Brase, Ed Clark, Mike Dillon, Kenny Erickson, Blake Fohl, Jay Gratzek, Mike Graham, Dana Hanson, Debbie Johnson, Irvin Kupper, David Lewis, Cal Massmann, Gary Magoni, Sue Maxwell, Steve Parks, Tom Parrish, Stan Ruta, Joe Scarlett, Jonathan Swiskow, Kim Vance, Kim Vella, and Jim Wright. Of course, the rest of the Tractor Supply team of more than 7,000 has to be thanked. Your success funded this project as you continued to write the latest chapter in our history. May it be the best one yet.

This project also drew on a number of former Tractor Supply family members who responded faithfully to the call. Thank you, Ray Branson; Tom Burenga; Don Butzen; Canadians Murray Cummings and John Kropp; Chuck Dickerson; Bill Doering; Max DeForest, who showed a special devotion to this project; Norm Gallagher; Gang of Five members Tom Flood, Joseph Maxwell, and Gerry Newkirk; Gwen Herald; Bart Masterson; Jack McCracken; Past TSC Presidents Larry French, Edwin M. Savage, Richard "Dick" H. Schaefer, and Larry Schweik – thanks for answering the tough questions; and to John Pugsley; John Reinhart; and Kay Gorecki Walker, the thoughtful fly on the wall for forty years.

Though removed from the business of the company, there were those with personal ties who proved invaluable. Richard "Dick" Schmidt, the son of Tractor Supply founder Charles Schmidt, devoted countless hours to the project as well as flying the author to the distant places Tractor Supply calls home. Dick, you're a wonderful son. Thanks for helping us honor your father's legacy. Others outside the company who helped were Wes Walker's two sons, Baird and Mark Walker – your collection of early customer letters was a real gem and provided more than a few grins.

Speaking of customers, they lent a hand, too. Thanks go to Don Clark, Dave Bouchard, Ed Dobrinski, Roger Evans, Dale Hagen, G.G. Henny, Clarence Lester, Delmar Nelson, Scott Stoffel, and Jessy Guzman. Then there are our ever-willing-to-lend-a-hand vendors, such as Everett Mealman and Krystal Cartwright of PBI/Gordon Corporation and Charlie Brendeland of DeeZee. Thanks, too, to Dr. Dwight Warren at the Charles E. Schmidt Biomedical Center on the campus of Florida Atlantic University.

Pulling several all-nighters to keep this project on schedule were the good people at Dye, Van Mol & Lawrence. They included Lindsey Allmon, Ann Ewing, Courtney Gover, Beth Jones, Elizabeth Lewis, Jan Mattix, Beth Poe, Jeff Porter, Susan Morgenstern, Dawn Scott, and Amy Smith. Julia Robinson also took a turn at the daunting job of keeping Nelson's office organized.

Finally, a whole host of organizations and people pitched in to provide many of the hundreds of photographs that illustrate this book. They are: AP/Wide World Photos – Bill Fitzgerald; *Atlanta Journal-Constitution* – Pam Prouty; David Bailey; Kirk and Lorene Bell; The Buntin Group; Carmichael Lynch; Cott Corporation – Gregory Kerr; Charles Cowdery; Bobbye Manning; Dave Hilbert; Wolf Hoffman; J P Morgan Chase – Shelley Diamond; Greg and Jennifer Lewis; Library of Congress; *Louisville Courier-Journal;* Mt. Carmel High School; NASDAQ – Katchen Stonehouse; National Future Farmers of America Organization – Mickie Miller; North Dakota Heritage Center – Sharon A. Silengo; Southwest Airlines *Spirit* magazine and Debbie Chessor, University of Chicago; Chicago Historical Society; U. S. Department of Agriculture; Ward County Historical Society – Mark "Tim" Timbrook; Warioto Farms, Inc., WLS (Chicago); Buddy and Belenda Woodson, and Lili Ann Mages Zisook.

Undoubtedly because of the sheer number of people who jumped in to help, we've left someone out. To those unsung heroes, we also give a heartfelt thanks.

THE PEOPLE YOU NEED OUT HERE

TSC TRACTOR SUPPLY CO

BIBLIOGRAPHY OF SOURCES 

Abbott, Gardner. "Tractor Supply Company – Chronological Facts." (unpublished note), circa 1941.

Alford, Carlin J. "The History of Tractor Supply." *The Voice* 19, no. 3 (June 1998): 8-9.

Battle, Bob. "Ground Broken for TSC Complex." *Nashville (TN) Banner*, October 9, 1986, C4.

Baxter, Emme Nelson. "TSC Chief Took Magical Career Road: From Disc Jockey to Farm Supplies." Executive Spotlight. *The Tennessean*, October 23, 1988, D2.

"Bernard Barnett, Lawyer, Industrialist, Dies at 1971." *Louisville (KY) Times*, December 12, 1987.

Bird, Pete. "Ex-Leader of TSC Sues in Job Loss." *Nashville (TN) Banner*, June 12, 1981, C4.

Black, Sam. "Format of the Future." *Farm Supply Retailing* (August 1998): 15-18.

Bloom, Jonah. "Lessons from a Tractor Company's Marketing Coup." *Ad Age.Com*, May 24, 2004. http://www.aday.com/new.cms?newsid=40596

Brooks, Candice. "Tractor Supply Hopes Stock Split Lures More Investors." *The Tennessean*, July 22, 2003.

Brooks, John. *The Go-Go Years: The Drama and Crashing Finale of Wall Street's Bullish 60s*. Hoboken, NJ: John Wiley & Sons, 1999.

Calloway, Joe. *Becoming a Category of One: How Extraordinary Companies Transcend Commodity and Defy Comparison*. Hoboken, NJ: John Wiley & Sons, Inc., 2003.

"Candid Interview with Tom Hennesy." *The Voice* 4, no. 2 (April 1982): 6.

Caulfield, John. "Central Tractor Joins Quality Stores." *National Home Center News*, April 19, 1999.

Cartwright, Krystal. "PBI Gordon 1954." (unpublished memorandum), 2002.

"Central Tractor Farm & Country to Combine with Quality Stores in a Cash and Stock Merger." Business Wire, March 29, 1999.

Chakravarty, Subrata N. "Ransom." *Forbes* 152, no. 1, July 5, 1993, 40.

"Charles E. Schmidt." The Schmidt Companies, http://schmidtcompanies.com/biomed.html.

Childers, Scott. "The History of WLS Radio." *Chicago Radio Time Capsule*. http://www.wlshistory.com.

Clark, William. "Young, Vigorous Tractor Supply Sees Its Biggest Growth Ahead." *Chicago (IL) Sunday Tribune*, August 21, 1960.

"Community Discount and Tractor Supply Change Merger Plan." *Wall Street Journal*, November 8, 1967, 2.

"Company Here Gets Control of Food Firm." *Louisville (KY) Times*, July 6, 1968.

Conger, Rand D., and Glen H. Elder, Jr. *Families in Troubled Times: Adapting to Change in Rural America*. New York: Aldine de Gruyter Press, 1994.

"Conglomerate Ponders Hard Lessons of '69." *Louisville (KY) Times*, April 20, 1970.

Croft, Tara. "The Dealmaker's Resume: Joe Scarlett of Tractor Supply Co." TheDeal.com, Autust 30, 2002. http://www.thedeal.com/NASApp/cs/CS?pagename=TheDeal/TDDArticle/TDStandardArticle&bn=NULL&c=TDArticle&cid=1030493826338.

Crouch, Lori, Neil Santaniello and Edna Negron. "Financier Charles Schmidt Dies at 83." *Sun Sentinel (Fort Lauderdale, FL)*, May 3, 1996.

Daverman, Richard. "Supply in Demand." *Business Nashville,* March 2002, 16-21.

Dempsey-Tegeler & Co. *Tractor Supply Co. Prospectus*, January 14, 1959.

Derdak, Thomas. "Fuqua Industries, Inc." *International Directory of Company Histories* 1. Chicago: St. James Press, (1988): 445-47.

Donaldson, Lufkin & Jenrette Securities Corporation. *Tractor Supply Co. Prospectus*, February 17, 1994.

"Dorothy F. Schmidt." *The Schmidt Companies*. http://schmidtcompanies.com/dorothy_schmidt.html.

"Executive Changes." *New York Times*, May 21, 1971.

Fasig, Lisa Biank. "Store Not Just for Farmers." *Cincinnati (OH) Enquirer*, January 3, 2001.

"Fighting for the Wheel." *Time*, June 6, 1977, 57.

Flood, Tom. "Tractor Supply Company Goes Public." *The Voice* 16, no. 2 (Store Managers Meeting Issue 1994): 35.

Fohl, Blake. "Marketers Should Get Emotional about Their Products." *The Tennessean*, July 19, 2003.

___. "TSC Is No Longer America's Best Kept Retail Secret." *The Voice* 19, no. 5 (November 1998): 8.

Forrester, Brian. "Tractor Supply Plows Quality Row to Growth." *Nashville (TN) Business Journal*, May 13, 2002.

"Forum Q & A: Joe Scarlett – Tractor Supply an Active Senior." *The Tennessean*, June 9, 2002, 2E.

Fuqua, J. B. Fuqua, *How I Made My Fortune Using Other People's Money*. Atlanta: Longstreet Press, 2001.

"Fuqua Modifies Terms for National Industries." Corporation Affairs. *New York Times*, September 28, 1977.

Gallagher, Leigh. "Best Managed Companies in America." *Forbes*, January 12, 2004, 173.

Gentry, Connie Robbins. "Chain Cultivates Farming Niche." (Tractor Supply Co. reprint of story appearing in *Chain Store Age*), March 2000.

Gersema, Emily. "Nearly Half of All Farmers Have Internet, USDA Says." Associated Press, July 29, 2003.

Gosselin, Peter G. "Enron Latest in Line of Financial Fiascoes." *Los Angeles Times*, February 24, 2002.

Gransbery, Jim. "Bush Has Private Meeting with Farmers, Ranchers." *Billings (MT) Gazette*, May 27, 2001.

Hanson, Dana. "In Memory of Thomas J. Hennesy." *The Voice* 22, no. 3 (Special Edition 2001): 1.

___. "What's in a Name?" *The Voice* 17, no. 3 (Spring 1993): 1.

Hartmann, Stacey. "Tractor Supply Co. Efforts Paying Off." *The Tennessean*, January 22, 1999.

___. "Tractor Loads Goods onto Web." *The Tennessean*, May 1, 1999.

Henderson, Jason R. "Will the Rural Economy Rebound with the Rest of the Nation?" *Economic Review*, published by Center for the Study of Rural America and Federal Reserve Bank of Kansas City, January 2002.

Hennesy, Tom. "Gone…but Not Forgotten." *The Voice* 13, no. 4 (July-August 1991): 2.

Hennesy, Tom. "My Christmas Message." *The Voice* 12, no. 6 (November-December 1990): 1.

Hershberg, Ben Z. "Fuqua Industries Delays Purchase of National." *Louisville (KY) Courier-Journal*, December 21, 1977.

Herzog, James. "IRS Alleges Yarmuth, Woman Shared Firm's Funds." *Louisville (KY) Courier-Journal*, August 3, 1976.

"History of Tractor Supply." (unpublished memorandum), June 30, 1996.

Holt, Donald D. "J. B. Fuqua's Grand Design." *Fortune*, June 18, 1979, 123.

Houghton, Donald M. "Yarmuth Is Tough but also Sensitive to Public Opinion." *Louisville (KY) Times*, April 20, 1970.

Howell, Debbie. "Tractor Supply to Buy 85 Quality Stores." *DSN Retailing Today*, January 21, 2002.

"Important Bulletin: Reorganization of TSC Industries." *The Voice* 3, no. 2 (May 1981): 1.

"Joe Scarlett Named President of TSC." *The Voice* 9, no. 2 (April 1997): 1.

"John Schack Celebrates 40 Years with TSC!" *The Voice* 5, no. 1 (March 1983): 6.

Kallay, Mike. "Fuqua Holders OK National Acquisition." *Louisville (KY) Times*, January 3, 1978, E5.

___. "Lover of the 'Big Deal'...Yarmuth's Hobby Is National Industries." *Louisville (KY) Times*, March 1969.

___. "National Closing Office Here." *Louisville (KY) Times*, October 6, 1978, E4.

___. "National Industries Finds Itself in an Unexpected Position." *Louisville (KY) Times*, September 21, 1977, B-16.

___. "The Wedding's on, but National Reluctantly Accepted Fuqua as Suitor." *Louisville (KY) Times*, November 29, 1977.

Kruger, Renée M. "Cultivating a Farmer's Market." *Discount Merchandiser* (August 1998): 18-22.

"Louisville Conglomerate Checks Firms Carefully." *Louisville (KY) Courier-Journal*, May 15, 1969.

Macauley, Irene. "Corporate Governance: Crown Charters to Dotcoms." *Museum of American Financial History* (2002) http://www.financialhistory.org/fh/2003/77-1.htm.

"Mages Holders Approve Merger with Goodman, A Discount House Chain." *Wall Street Journal*, December 11, 1961, 7.

"Mages Holders Approve Plan to Issue Common Rights; Shares Increased." *Wall Street Journal*, April 24, 1961, 6.

"Mages Sporting Goods Control Is Purchased by Law Student, 23." *Wall Street Journal*, March 2, 1961, 24.

McCampbell, Candy. "Tractor Supply Will Add More than 100 Stores." *The Tennessean*, January 2, 2002.

Miller, Karen Lowry. "Megacompanies: The Giants Stumble." *Newsweek* 120, no. 28, July 3, 2002.

Miller, Karen. "Tractor Supply Thrives Happily in the Shadows." Associated Press, July, 2003.

"Minority Ventures Held Peril." People and Business. *New York Times*, September 25, 1975.

Murphy, Maxwell. "Tractor Supply Has Been Riding High." *Wall Street Journal*, August 21, 2002, B1.

Murphy, Pat. "Bearings Turned into a Bonanza: The Tractor Supply Co. Plows a Straight Furrow to Success." *Chicago (IL) Daily News*, February 12, 1964.

"Nashville Office Opens." *The Voice* 1, no. 4 (Fall 1979):1.

"Nashville Office Ribbon Cutting Held." *The Voice* 1, no. 5 (Winter 1979): 1, 3.

"National Industries, 2 Firms It Controls Are Planning to Merge Holders, Boards of All 3 Concerns Must Approve; National Bidding to Acquire 2 Other Companies." *Wall Street Journal*, January 26, 1968.

"National Industries Reports: Conglomerate Ponders Hard Lessons of '69." *Louisville (KY) Times*, April 20, 1970.

"National Industries Set to Buy 33% Interest in TSC Industries Inc." *Wall Street Journal*, February 3, 1969.

"Outline of American History, An." U.S. Department of State's Bureau of International Information Programs, http://usinfo.state.gov/products/pubs/history/toc.htm.

Pripps, Robert. *The Big Book of Farm Tractors*. Stillwater, MN: Voyageur Press, 2001.

Rice, Valerie. "Everything Old Is Blue Again." *The Voice* 16, no. 1 (January 1994): 1, 16.

Russell, Keith. "Strong First Quarter Boosts Tractor Supply." *The Tennessean*, April 17, 2003.

___. "Tractor Supply's Grass Is Greener." *The Tennessean*, July 12, 2002.

Rutter, Richard. "Farm Equipment Makes Gains; Sales Up for 2nd Year in a Row." *New York Times*, August 11, 1963; 1, 10.

Searcey, Dionne. "U of C Benefactor Charles E. Schmidt, 83." *Chicago (IL) Tribune*, May 6, 1996.

"Scarlett Is New Chairman, Newkirk Becomes President." *The Voice* 15, no. 1 (January-February 1993): 1, 5.

Scarlett, Joe. "At TSC, We Guarantee Customer Satisfaction." *The Voice* 9, no. 2 (April 1997): 2.

___. "State of the Company Report." *The Voice* 10, no. 1 (February 1988): 1, 2.

___. "The Legacy of a Leprechaun." *The Voice* 22, no. 3 (Special Edition 2001): 2.

___. "Tractor Supply CEO Urges Employees to Have Faith, Uphold Ethics." *The Tennessean*, July 14, 2002.

___. "TSC History." *The Voice* 14, no. 3 (May-June 1992): 21.

Scarlett, Joe, Gerry Newkirk and Tom Flood. "Tom Hennesy – Our Mentor, Our Friend." *The Voice* 17, no. 3 (Early Summer 1994): 1, 14.

Schulman, Sol. "Simonelli Is President of National Industries." *Louisville (KY) Courier-Journal*, 1975.

Schmidt Family Foundation. *Charles Schmidt* (unpublished biography), 1997.

Segal, Harvey H. "The Time of the Conglomerates: The Urge to Merge." New York *Times Magazine*, October 27, 1968. http://www.mindfully.org/Industry/Conglomerates-Time.htm.

Smith, William. "A Sporty New Look but Still Colored Red." *Georgia Trend* 9, no. 9 (May 1994): 47.

Snyder, Naomi. "President Will Be Tractor Supply CEO; Scarlett to Stay Chairman." *The Tennessean*, July 13, 2004.

___. "Tractor Supply Exploring Sites." *The Tennessean, December* 7, 2003.

Sobel, Robert. *The Rise and Fall of the Conglomerate Kings*. Beard Books, 1999.

"Stanley Yarmuth Dies; Built National Industries." *Louisville (KY) Times*, September 15, 1975.

"Stanley R. Yarmuth, 50, Founder of National Industries, Dies." *Louisville (KY) Courier-Journal*, September 16, 1975, B11.

"Stanley Yarmuth Led Conglomerate," *New York Times*, September 16, 1975.

Teeple, Charles. "Assets Growing Fast at National Industries." *Louisville (KY) Times*, September 28, 1964.

___. "How National Industries Fits Diverse Operations." *Louisville (KY) Times*, April 12, 1965.

___. "Louisville Firm Buys Control of Katy Line," *Louisville (KY) Times*, October 19, 1964.

___. "National Industries Sells Its Stock in Katy Railroad for $2.25 Million." *Louisville (KY) Times*, March 9, 1967.
"The Schmidt Family Foundation." The Schmidt Companies. http://schmidtcompanies.com/foundation.html.

"The Wild Ride of Stanley Yarmuth: A Conglomerateur Who Rose with the Soaring Sixties now Fights to Hold His Gains." *BusinessWeek*, August 8, 1970, 41.

Thompson, Jim. "Financially Stronger NII in Acquisition Mood." *Louisville (KY) Courier-Journal*, May 19, 1972.

___. "National Industries Asks Return of $500,000." *Louisville (KY) Courier Journal*, March 30, 1979.

___. "National Industries Being Sold to Atlanta Company." *Louisville (KY) Courier-Journal*, September 20, 1977, C1.

"Tom Flood Promoted to Vice-President of Finance." *The Voice* 5, no. 5 (September 1983): 1.

"Tom Hennesy Biographical Summary." *The Voice* 17, no. 3 (Early Summer 1994): 10.

Tractor Supply Co. 1989. Service Mark Principal Register. Registration No. 884,786, registered January 20, 1970, renewal approved November 20, 1989.

___. 1994. Service Mark Principal Register. Registration No. 1,846,015, registered July 19, 1994.

___. "Company Profile." (unpublished memorandum), August 30, 2000.

___. "Fueling the Fire Within." (Powerpoint presentation), June 18, 2002.

___. "Initial Public Offering of Tractor Supply Company Common Stock at $20 per Share." News release, February 18, 1994.

___. "Key Management Profiles." (unpublished memorandum), August 30, 2000.

___. "Spring-Summer 2003." (Powerpoint presentation), 2003.

___. "Summary of Trademarks." (unpublished memorandum), September 2001.

___. "The Good Life Is Out Here." (Powerpoint presentation), Spring 2003.

___. "The Stuff You Need Out Here." (Internal company brand book) 2003.

___. "Tractor Supply Fact Sheet." (unpublished memorandum), August 30, 2000.

"Tractor Supply Co. Appoints General Counsel." *The Tennessean*, November 14, 2003.

"Tractor Supply Company Announces Retirement of Thomas O. Flood." Business Wire, April 5, 1999.

"Tractor Supply Co. Elects." *New York Times*, November 3, 1964, 44.

"Tractor Supply Co. Set to Acquire Community Discount Centers Inc." *Wall Street Journal*, September 26, 1967, 9.

"Tractor Supply Company Tills Rich Field as 1998 Sales Hit $600 Million." *Discount Store News*, July 12, 1999.

"Tractor Supply Picks Minnesota Advertising Firm." *The Tennessean*, August 22, 2002.

"Tractor Supply Says 1st Period Sales Rose 27% from '61; Net Up." *Wall Street Journal*, March 7, 1962, 6.

"Tractor Supply Says Sales Increase 48%." *The Tennessean*, October 15, 2002.

"Tractor Supply to Open 56 New Stores Saturday." *Nashville (TN) Business Journal*, May 7, 2002.

"TSC Has 'The Stuff You Need.' " *AgriMarketing*, April 2004, 58.

"TSC Industries Executive Realignment." *The NII Eye* (a publication of National Industries Inc., Louisville, KY, May 1973): 6-7.

TSC Industries, Inc. v. Northway, Inc., 426 U.S. 438 (1976).

"TSC to Relocate to Nashville, Tennessee," *The Voice* 1, no. 3 (Summer 1979):1.

Trumbore, Brian. "The ITT Story, Part II." *Buy and Hold: A Division of Freedom Investments*, 2002, http://www.buyandhold.com/bh/en/education/history/2002/itt_pt_2.html.

U.S. Department of Agriculture. *Agriculture Fact Book 2000*. Office of Communications, November 2000.

___. "A History of American Agriculture 1776-1990." http://www,usda.gov/history2/text4.htm.

___. *Power to Produce Handbook*, 1960.

Vivanco, Liz,."Gardner Abbott, 88; Started Tractor Supply Business." *Chicago (IL) Sun-Times*, October, 2000.

Walker, Wes. "Tractor Supply Company – The First 30 Years." (unpublished memorandum), 1968.

"Welcome to Minot." *Minot Area Chamber of Commerce*. http://www.minotchamber.org.

Wenz, Rod. "Louisville Conglomerate Checks Firms Carefully." *Louisville (KY) Courier Journal*, May 15, 1969.

"With New Stores Opening, Tractor Supply Earnings, Sales Jump." *Nashville (TN) Business Journal*, July 16, 2002.

Wright, Jim. "TSC – A Brand to Shout About." *The Voice* 23, no. 6 (Fall 2002): 1.

ANNUAL REPORTS

Tractor Supply Co. *1960 Annual Report*, 1960.

Tractor Supply Co. *1961 Annual Report*, 1961.

Tractor Supply Co. *1962 Annual Report*, 1962.

Tractor Supply Co. "25th Anniversary Year." *1963 Annual Report*, 1963.

Tractor Supply Co. "Our 100th Store Year." *1964 Annual Report*, 1964.

Tractor Supply Co. *1965 Annual Report*, 1965.

Tractor Supply Co. *1966 Annual Report*, 1966.

Tractor Supply Co. *1967 Annual Report*, 1967.

TSC Industries, Inc. *1968 Annual Report*, 1968.

TSC Industries, Inc. *1983 Annual Report*, 1983.

TSC Industries, Inc. *1984 Annual Report*, 1984.

TSC Industries, Inc. *1985 Annual Report*, 1985.

TSC Industries, Inc. *1986 Annual Report*, 1986.

TSC Industries, Inc. *1987 Annual Report*, 1987.

TSC Industries, Inc. *1988 Annual Report*, 1988.

TSC Industries, Inc. *1989 Annual Report*, 1989.

TSC Industries, Inc. *1990 Annual Report*, 1990.

TSC Industries, Inc. "Dedicated to the American Farmer." *1991 Annual Report*, 1991.

TSC Industries, Inc. "The Look of Things to Come." *1992 Annual Report*, 1992.

Tractor Supply Co. *1994 Annual Report,* 1994.

Tractor Supply Co. *1995 Annual Report*, 1995.

Tractor Supply Co. *1996 Annual Report*, 1996.

Tractor Supply Co. "Letter to Stockholders." *1997 Annual Report to Stockholders*, 1997.

Tractor Supply Co. "Where America's Farmers Shop." *1998 Annual Report*, 1998.

Tractor Supply Co. "Serving the Unique Lifestyle Needs of America's Farm, Ranch and Rural Customers." *1999 Annual Report*, 1999.

Tractor Supply Co. "Whether You've Got One Acre or 1,000: Tractor Supply and the Rural Revolution." *2000 Annual Report*, 2000.

Tractor Supply Co. "Our Sales Team: A Farmer, An Equine Enthusiast, and a Welder." *2001 Annual Report*, 2001.

Tractor Supply Co. "Out Here." *2002 Annual Report*, 2002.

★ CREDITS ★

PICTURE CREDITS

AP/Wide World Photo, pages: 10, 122-123. *The Associated Press*, page: 14. *Atlanta Journal-Constitution*, pages: 17 (Charlotte B. Teagle), 150 (Calvin Cruce). *Billings Gazette*, page: 221. *Chicago Historical Society*, (Hedrich Blessing), page: 110-111. *Cott Corporation*, page: 121. *David Bailey Photography*, page: 228. *Library of Congress, Prints & Photographs Division*, pages: 20, 25 (LC-USZ62-83392), 92 (LC-USZ62-113634), 167 (LC-USZC4-5198). *Library of Congress, Prints & Photographs Division, FSA/OWI Collection*, pages: 18-19 (LC-USF34-057893), 24 (LC-US36-D-007108), 31 (LC-USF33-T01-001562-M2), 36 (LC-USF33-012239-M5), 40 (LC-USF34-057928), 53 (LC-USW33-018433), 77 (LC-USF33-012101-M5). *Louisville Courier-Journal*, pages: 116, 118, 120, 136. *Metropolitan Government Archives*, page: 140. *Mt. Carmel High School*, page: 89. NASDAQ, pages: 21, 186, 234-235. *National FFA Organization*, page: 213. *Richland Industries*, page: 106. *Southwest Airlines, Debbie Chessor*, page: 182. *Special Research Collection Center, University of Chicago Library*, pages: 26, 27, 28-29, 30. *Wally McNamee/ CORBIS*, page: 92. *Wal-Mart*, page: 207. *WJBF*, page: 141. *WLS890 Chicago*, page: 45.

LYRIC CREDITS

Page: 23

"God Bless America: by Irving Berlin

Page: 139

Big Yellow Taxi

Joni Mitchell

Pages: 177

"Where the Green Grass Grows"

Words and Music by Jessica Leary and Craig Wiseman

Parts for IHC McCORMICK-DEERING All Models

GOVERNOR PARTS for ALL MODELS

Governor Shaft Assembly

Repl. IHC No. 4240DAX. Complete as pictured. Fits all models.

Stk. No. 13B24. 3 lbs. **$2.98**

Stk. No. 13B30. Gov. Spring Pin, repl. 7117T. Each **6c**

Stk. No. 13B31. Gov. Ball Pin, repl. 12214D. Each **4c**

Stk. No. 13B32. Gov. Conn. rod pin, repl. 12700D. Each **4c**

GOVERNOR BUSHINGS

Bronze bushing, for all models.

Stk. No. 13B28. Standard size **37c**

Stk. No. 13B29. .010 undersize **39c**

SPRINGS

9c Each

Stk. No. 13B25. For 10-20 to KC69612 and 15-30 to TG50130.

Stk. No. 13B26. For 10-20 KC69613 up, and 15-30 TG50131 up.

Stk. No. 13B27. For Farmall and F-20.

GOV. SLEEVE with BEARING

Fits short end of governor shaft shown above. Bronze casting, with double row bearing. Repl. 555DX.

Stk. No. 13B45. Each, complete **$2.98**

Governor rod cover for IHC

Stk. No. 13B46— IHC 1452D **89c**

OIL PUMP GAUGE

Fits all McCormick-Deering Models. Farmall, 10-20, 15-30, and 22-36. Replaces IHC No. 16924H. Sturdy accurate, and dependable.

Stk. No. 13B20. 1lb. **59c**

WATER TANK and HAND HOLE COVER SET

Four pieces, as pictured. Cover, cover gasket, radiator cap clamp bolt, and radiator cap clamp.

Stk. No. 13B9. 2 lbs. **55c**

Stk. No. 13B10. Cover only, 1 lb. 21c — Stk. No. 13B12. Bolt, 17c

Stk. No. 13B11. Gasket only, 9c — Stk. No. 13B13. Clamp, 15c

STEERING KNUCKLE PIN SETS

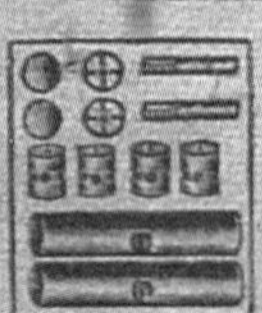

Complete sets of new parts to repair both steering knuckles. 2 Pins, 4 brass bushings, 2 lock pins, 2 thrust washers, and 2 expansion plugs, exactly as pictured.

Set for 15-30, 22-36 — Complete. Stk. No. 13B21 7 pounds **$2.45**

Set for 10-20, F-30 and Reg. Farmall — Stk. No. 13B22 6 pounds **$1.98**

FAN PARTS for Farmall, 10-20, 15-30

FAN BEARING

Fan Bearing, Roller and race. 2 used. Repl. 10392D. 6 oz.

Stk. No. 19102 .... **59c**

FAN FELT SET

Felt and Retainer. 3 pc. assembly, felt and retainers.

Stk. No. 10B3 .... **7c**

FAN SHAFT

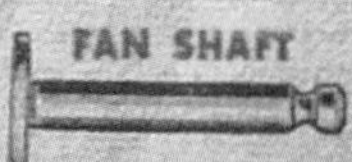

For 10-20 and Farmall. Repl. 10385D. 1½ lbs. Stk. No. 10B2 .... **69c**

Fan shaft for 15-30. Repl. 4291DA 2 lbs. Stk. No. 13A49 .... **79c**

Belts on page 16

OIL PUMP GEARS for FARMALL, F-20, 10-20

Stk. No. 13B5. Driver Gear, replaces 10344D. Ship. wt. 4 oz. Each **49c**

Stk. No. 13B6. Impeller Driven Gear, repl. 10336D. Ship. wt. 4 oz. Each ....

For 15-30, and 22-36

Stk. No. 13B7. Driver Gear, replaces 537DB. Ship. wt. 4 oz. Each **55c**

Stk. No. 13B8. Driven Gear, replaces 536DB. Ship. wt. 4 oz. Each ....

Make Your Tractor Look Like New, Too

Protect the finish and add to the appearance of your tractor with this quick drying enamel in just the right shades of red or gray. One can is plenty to do a first class job.

Stk. No. 13B33. Red, for late models.

Stk. No. 13B34. Gray, for older IHC. 4 lbs. ...... Quart Can **79c**

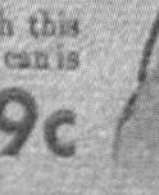

TRANSMISSION BEARINGS

Farmall Regular, 1924-32

1307 Single Row ball brg. for Spline Shaft Rear, Main Shaft Rear, Pwr. Takeoff Shaft Rear. 3 Required. Repl. 10691V. 1 lb. .... Each, **$1.49**

5307 Double Row ball brg. for Spline Shaft Front, Main Shaft Front, Pwr. Takeoff Shaft Front. 3 Required. Repl. 13927V. 2 lbs. .... Each, **$2.98**

Farmall F-20, 1932-39

1208 Single Row Ball brg. for Main Shaft Rear. Repl. 18575H. 1 lb. EACH, **$1.29**

1307 Single Row Ball brg. for Spline Shaft Front, Main Shaft Front, Pwr. Takeoff Shaft Fr. & Rear. 4 Required. Repl. 10691V. 1 lb. .... Each, **$1.49**

1309 Single Row Ball brg. for Spline Shaft Rear. Replaces 14225H. 1 Required. 2½ lbs. .... Each, **$2.75**

McCormick-Deering 10-20

C-3145 Roller Brg. with Race, for Spline Shaft Front and Rear, Bevel Pinion Shaft Front, and Pwr. Takeoff Shaft Rear. 4 Required. Repl. IHC 4738TC (12139DB & 4739TA). 2¼ lbs. .... Each, **$2.59**

C-3105 Roller Brg. with Race, Pulley Dr. Shaft Front. 1 Required. Repl. IHC 4592DC (11186DB & 4594DA). 3 lbs. .... Each, **$2.79**

C-3150 Roller Brg. with Race for Bevel Pinion Shaft Rear, 1923-27. Repl. IHC 4754DC. For early shaft with removable pinion. 4 lbs. .... Each, **$3.45**

C-3155 Roller Brg. with Race for Bevel Pinion Shaft Rear, 1927-34. Repl. 12323DA. For late models with one piece pinion & Shaft .... Each, **$3.15**

COMPLETE SET of Six Roller Bearings and Races, listed above, for 10-20, 1923-27, below KC60450. Priced Lower in Sets. Set No. BS12.

COMPLETE SET of Six Roller Bearings and Races, listed above, for 10-20, 1927-34, above KC60451. Check Serial Number. Set No. BS29 .... **$15.65** 17 lbs.

McCormick-Deering 15-30

C-3105 Roller Brg. with Race for Bevel Pinion Shaft Front, Pulley Drive Shaft Front and Rear, Spline Shaft Front and Rear. 5 Required. Repl. IHC 4592DC (11186DB & 3594DA). 3 lbs. .... Each, **$2.79**

C-3125 Roller Brg. with Race for Bevel Pinion Shaft Rear, 1921-26. 1 Required Repl. IHC 4419DC (11183DB & 4421DA) 7¼ lbs. .... Each, **$4.85**

C-3135 Roller Brg. with Race for Bevel Pinion Shaft Rear, 1927-28. 1 Required. Repl. IHC 11258DA (11255DA & 4421DA) 7 lbs. .... Each, **$4.85**

COMPLETE SET of Six Roller Bearings and Races, listed above, for 15-30, 1921-26, below TG42490. Save by buying a Set. Set No. BS1530.

COMPLETE SET of Six Roller Bearings and Races, listed above, for 15-30, 1927-28, after TG42491. Check Serial Number. Set No. BS2236 .... **$17.95** 23 lbs.

McCormick-Deering 22-36

447-432 Tapered Cone and Cup for Spline Shaft Front, Bevel Pinion Shaft Front, and Pulley Drive Shaft Rear. 3 Required. 2¼ lbs. .... Each, **$2.85**

526-552 Tapered Cone and Cup for Spline Shaft Rear. 1 Required. 3 lbs. Each, **$3.68**

6379-6320 Tapered Cone and Cup for Bevel Pinion Shaft Rear. 1 Required. 8 lbs. .... Each, **$8.09**

536-532A Tapered Cone and Cup for Pulley Drive Shaft Front 1929-30, below TG123021. 1 Required. 4 lbs. .... Each, **$4.08**

3982-3920 Tapered Cone and Cup for Pulley Drive Shaft Front, 1931 up, after TG123022. 1 Required. 3½ lbs. .... Each, **$3.27**

BULL PINION BEARINGS

For McCormick-Deering 10-20

C-3150 Roller Brg. with Race, Fits LEFT Side 1923-34, RIGHT side, 1923-26 (KC50280). Repl 4754DC. 4 lbs. .... Each, **$3.45**

C-3155 Roller Brg. with Race, Fits RIGHT Side only, 1926 and up, after KC50281. Repl. 12323DA. 4 lbs. .... Each, **$3.15**

For McCormick-Deering 15-30

C-3125 Roller Brg. with Race, Fits LEFT Side 1921-28, RIGHT Side 1921-26 (TG48155). Repl. 4419DC. 7¼ lbs. .... Each, **$4.85**

C-3135 Roller Brg. with Race, Fits RIGHT Side only, 1927-28, after TG48155. Rep. 11256DA. 7 lbs. .... Each, **$4.85**

For McCormick-Deering 22-36

6455-6420 Tapered Cone with Cup, used on both sides 22-36. 2 Required on Tractor. Repl. 13332D. 12 lbs. .... Each, **$11.17**

COUNTERSHAFT BRAKE PARTS for FARMALL, F-20, and F-12

LINING

Moulded Type—Holes Drilled to Fit.

Stk. No. 8B44. Inner 15101DA.

Stk. No. 8B45. Outer, 15102DA. **19c**

Ship. weight 8 oz. per pc.

SET OF 4 PIECES,

Stk. No. 8B46. Complete set. Ship. wt. 2 lbs. with rivets **75c**

BRAKE SHOES

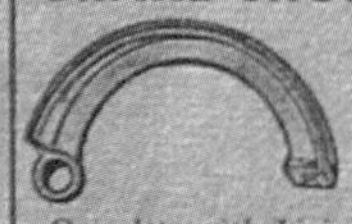

99c Each

Complete with Lining.

Stk. No. 8B47. Inner, repl. 1534DAX. 2 used.

Stk. No. 8B48. Outer, repl. 1535DAX. 2 used. Ship. wt. 2½ lbs. each.

CABLE, SPRING

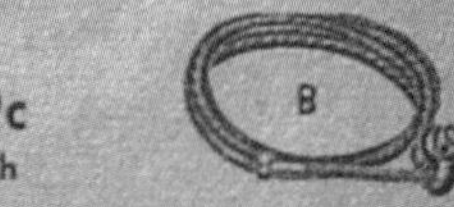

Stk. No. 8B49. Brake Cable Complete, repl. 15206DBX. with Shackle. 2 used. 1 lb. Each, **89c**

Stk. No. 8B50. Shoe Spring, 2 used, repl. 15200D. 6 oz. Each **9c**

STEERING PARTS for FARMALL

Repl. IHC	Picture	DESCRIPTION	Lbs. Oz.	Stk. No.	EACH
15111DB	A	Steering Sector, 22 teeth, T10716 up	4–	8B34	$4.75
15112DAX	B	Steering Gear, 23 teeth	5–	8B35	4.25
15113DB	C	Steering Shaft Pinion Gear, 8 teeth	1–	8B36	.60
15143D	G	Steering Bevel Pinion Shaft	1–	8B38	.55
15280D	D	Steering Bevel Pinion Bushing	6–	8B39	.23

WRITE FOR OUR COMPLETE 1940 TRACTOR PARTS CATALOG